WOMEN WRITING
IN THE
PERSON-CENTRED APPROACH

EDITED BY
IRENE FAIRHURST

PCCS BOOKS
Ross-on-Wye

First published in 1999

PCCS BOOKS
Llangarron
Ross-on-Wye
Herefordshire
HR9 6PT
UK
Tel +44 (0)1989 77 07 07

Women Writing in the Person-Centred Approach

ISBN 1 898059 26 8

Cover design by Denis Postle.
Printed by Redwood Books, Trowbridge, Wiltshire, UK

CONTENTS

Section III: Gender and Relational Issues

Cover design: Apple trees in fruit

Apples contain many health-promoting ingredients — 'An apple a day keeps the doctor away'— and are also recognised as significant in spiritual healing. The Bach Flower Remedies utilise crab-apple for many emotional problems, including self-dislike.

The Apple symbolises the giving of love and is significant in myths and legends dating back to the Greek Goddess Aphrodite, the supreme goddess of love and beauty, whose symbol was the apple. In druidic lore, three drops of liquid from the essence of sacred apples are the source of three streams corresponding to the three pillars of the druidic Tree of Life, which represented unity in male and female.

For the cover of this book, I have chosen the apple tree in fruit, symbolising fruition of female inspiration.

For more information about apples and other trees, I recommend, *Tree Wisdom — The definitive guidebook to the myth, folklore and healing power of trees* by Jacqueline M. Paterson, published in London by Thorsons, 1996.

Preface

The idea for this book evolved through a series of conversations between Pete Sanders, of PCCS Books, Tony Merry, series editor, and myself. Pete first surprised me by saying that he wanted me to edit a book for PCCS Books — that 'I was the person to do it'. I was moved by his trust in my capability. Later, Tony came up with the proposal of putting together a collection of papers written by women, and the project took off. I was excited at the outset. For years I have tried to encourage women to write about their experiences and have celebrated publishing successes with friends and colleagues. I identified with the concept of internalised sexism where we believe ourselves to be inferior to men in fields of academia and cognitive expression, and spend our lives holding back to facilitate male counterparts (be they husband, partner, boss, father, son or whomever) to achieve professional recognition in their chosen fields.

Although these days, the trend has moved away from Shirley 'life's-too-short-to-stuff-a-mushroom' Conran's concept of 'Superwoman', and despite the influence of the women's movement, many of us find ourselves running what feels like several lives at once in order to maintain a satisfying standard in the many aspects of a modern life-style. Most women in heterosexual relationships still happily bear the responsibility of child-raising, which — especially in the case of daughters — seems to last until they have children of their own, when they often, more than willingly, become supportive grandmothers as well.

According to Marilyn French, (1985) throughout the Middle Ages, the only education open to girls was in convents or at home by tutors paid for by wealthy fathers. Many of these women turned to literature as the only accessible way to practise their talents. The field of literature women first entered was 'courtly love', an activity confined to the aristocracy, taking the form of female 'troubadours' pouring out their love from an entirely male view point.

Education began to be extended to girls during the 15th century and more daughters studied alongside their brothers in homes which could afford private tutoring. Unfortunately education during the Renaissance was particularly male oriented, designed to develop the universal Renaissance *man* and instilled into women the attributes of submission and gentility, and above all, domesticity. Marilyn French relates the tale of Isabella Morra, whose brothers considered her learning improper and imprisoned her.

Some historians suggest that a certain Christine de Pisan was the forerunner of the women's movement when, during the late 14th century she began the counter-attack against the vicious debates in literature conducted by men against women. French quotes Ruth Kelso (1956) who writes in *Doctrine for the Lady of The Renaissance (1956)*, (reprint Urnaba, Ill: Univ.of Illinois Press, 1978);

> *Vituperation of women seems always, as far back as we have any record, to have been a manly sport. Nor was it ever confined to any one religion or class. Folk tales notoriously make women the butt of their satire, and Scheherazade's bedtime stories are one long penance for women's infidelity. But it took the Middle Ages to produce the phenomenon called the war of the sexes.*

Christine de Pisan was the first woman to enter the political literary arena and she opened the way for other women to join what was known as the *querelle des femmes*. The growing importance of science during the late 16th century excluded women even more and this situation continued into the 18th. This exclusion of women from learning has had a profound effect on our contribution to literature. During the Reformation in England, girls attended inferior schools to boys, who went to grammar schools to be taught the classic languages on which so much formal education was based.

This brief synopsis of some of the history of the early subjugation of women in learning and literature illustrates how patterns were set for our view of ourselves as inferior — St. Teresa of Avila writes in 1579:

> *If we can remember these two things, sisters, the time you have spent in reading all this, and the time I have spent in writing it, will not have been lost. Wise and learned men know them quite well, but we women are slow and need instruction in everything*
>
> *These interior matters are so obscure to the mind that anyone with as little learning as I will be sure to have to say many superfluous and even irrelevant things in order to say a single one that is to the point, The reader must have patience with me, as I have with myself when writing about things of which I know nothing; for really I sometimes take up my paper, like a perfect fool, with no idea of what to say or of how to begin.*

Today we might expect things to be different, but we find that in the field of counselling and psychotherapy, on person-centred training courses, women usually outnumber men by about 85%. In our literature, the opposite is the case. In the publication *Client-Centered and Experiential Psychotherapy in the Nineties*, the book of papers presented at the first conference on Client-Centred and Experiential Psychotherapy in 1988, of the 52 papers, 7 are by women. This situation is replicated in most editions of collected writings, so I hope this book will be both timely and welcome.

My intention is to offer a forum where renowned women in our field present their thoughts, feelings, ideas and findings alongside lesser known, and first-time authors. There was no thought that the book would be representative of a stereotyped genre — it was not written specifically *for* women or *about* women. It is intended to provide a forum for women with something to say to meet together and for some to find our voice.

The contributions speak for themselves, spanning a wide spectrum of styles and a variety of subjects including a slightly scary short story and two poems. I am particularly happy to include the chapter by Maria Villas-Boas Bowen — reading it re-connected me with her. She was a truly magical person and I am deeply indebted to Suzanne Spector for obtaining the paper for us. In Suzanne's words 'our intention was to honour her memory'. She is sorely missed.

I want to acknowledge the patience and gentle encouragement of Pete and Maggie from PCCS books and to say how much I appreciated their trust in me as a newborn editor. And, of course, I want to express my appreciation to Tony who has offered me advice, guidance, and as ever, much valued friendship and support.

I dedicate this book to my daughter, Rachel Williams.

Irene Fairhurst
June 1999

References

French M. (1985) *Beyond Power: On Women, Men and Morals,* GB: Johnathan Cape Ltd.
Teresa of Avila (1579) *Interior Castle,* New York: Image Books Doubleday, Trans. and Ed. Peers E. Allison (1961)

A Trainee's Journey into Unconditional Positive Regard

1

Jane Bingham

As a fledgling client-centred therapist just emerging from diploma training, I've studied many descriptions and definitions of unconditional positive regard several times over a period of years. It is only recently, however, that I've come to realise just how limited and selective my own understanding has been.

Prior to counselling training, my background as a teacher and lecturer supported what I saw as my generally benevolent and tolerant personal disposition. With hindsight, I now see that I'd developed a rather ghastly, lopsided and over-sentimental attitude towards Equal Opportunities issues.

I enthusiastically became part of an almost evangelical crusade to stamp out discriminatory practice in schools and colleges. Engaging in numerous training workshops and courses on disability, minority ethnic, cultural and religious issues, I seized every opportunity to provide children and students with situations which would challenge their stereotypical views. School libraries and reading schemes were subjected to zealous scrutiny and I consigned many books to the furnace, on the grounds that they did not meet the Equal Opportunities policies set out by national and local government.

It was from this background that my first limited understanding of the nature of unconditional positive regard was based.

As far as family influences were concerned, I grew up listening to my mother reading from the Little Black Sambo books and later was encouraged to read *Robinson Crusoe* for myself. (Cracking good reads all of them, as far as plot was concerned, but unfortunately heavily overweighted with racial stereotyping.) My mother would publicly point out and refer to the 'dear little piccaninnies', as though children with darker skins than mine were some delightfully rare and exotic breed of animal. Remorsefully, but steadfastly, my father refused to entertain the thought of taking in what he referred to as 'coloured people' as lodgers in our leafy suburb of middle-class Birmingham, since he believed they would undoubtedly 'lower the tone' and the market value of our house.

Yet, although I have been exposed to what might be considered some of the most pernicious of racist influences, I believe I have retained remarkably few of my parents' prejudicial views. So why could I trust myself as an adult to appreciate and differentiate, for instance, between the good literary style and illustrations in a book and its stereotypical content, but not trust others to use such books appropriately with young children? Why couldn't I trust others to make their own decisions and come to their own understandings without my intervention?

Perhaps toddling up one of the avenues to my past has helped me to examine the roots of my own conditionality a little. I recognise that at the outset of my counselling training, I was only paddling on the edge of a very deep ocean as far as understanding unconditional positive regard was concerned. I think I am presently somewhat deeper . . . maybe even as far as my knees!

Upon entering counselling training, I recognised that I carried many prejudiced and stereotypical views that could result in my relationships and understanding of others being limited and unrealistic. Like most of us, I could call upon past experiences of being judged and evaluated negatively. I knew how damaging the effects of this was and worked hard to become more aware of conditional evaluations operating in myself.

It's perhaps not surprising that it has only been through my actual experiences of struggling to communicate unconditional positive regard to clients (sometimes failing; sometimes succeeding) and in examining how and why this occurs, that I began to develop a much deeper and broader understanding of the challenging nature of unconditional positive regard.

Early on in my training, my original understanding came from what might be referred to as the philosophical foundation from which unconditional positive regard springs, i.e. my belief in the potential of every living organism for growth (the actualising tendency). I can experience this belief in a client's potential for growth and self-direction without even meeting them. It's a belief that I hold for all people and I don't have to be in psychological contact with them to do so. Once in psychological contact with a client, however, the reality and degree to which this belief has become part of my being, is subjected to many challenges.

I understand that there is an interesting background to Carl Rogers' own perceptions of unconditional positive regard. I'm aware of how he spoke of the 'necessity and sufficiency' of the core conditions to bring about successful therapy for a client and just how powerfully healing their experience is of their therapist's communication of unconditional positive regard. What I had not been aware of until recently, was that in an interview Rogers gave in Dublin, he indicated to his interviewer that perhaps there had been a misunderstanding about the necessary and sufficient nature of unconditional positive regard. He said that what he *actually meant* was, that we were very fortunate if unconditional positive regard existed between us.

So what is unconditional positive regard? In 1967 Rogers wrote:

When the therapist is experiencing a warm, positive and acceptant attitude toward what *is* in the client, this facilitates change. It involves the therapist's genuine willingness for the client to be whatever feeling is going on in him at that moment — fear, confusion, pain, pride, anger, hatred, love, courage or awe. It means that the therapist cares for the client, in a non-possessive way. It means that he prizes the client in a total rather than a conditional way. By this I mean that he does not simply accept the client when he is behaving in certain ways, and disapprove of him when he behaves in other ways. It means an outgoing positive feeling without reservations, without evaluations. The term we have come to use for this is unconditional positive regard. Again, research studies show that *the more this attitude is experienced by the therapist, the more likelihood there is that therapy will be successful* (p. 62, my italics).

This reference is for me one of the most moving (and almost lyrical) descriptions that I have come across thus far, in Rogers' work.

Did his Dublin interviewer miss the significance of the final sentence (which I have placed in italics)? Do trainers and trainees, myself included, have a tendency to interpret the 'necessary and sufficient' aspect of the core condition of unconditional positive regard, as what Rogers referred to as being mistaken for 'an absolute, an all-or-nothing dispositional concept' (Rogers, 1957, p. 225 in Kirschenbaum and Henderson, 1989)?

Does the mistake in understanding come from a cognitive struggle to understand the elusive nature of theory? So when we have only half understood, we set our limited understanding in tablets of stone , seeing only what we want to see or what is easy to see and go no further? Was Rogers' intellect, operating through his sometimes tortuous, written expressions, too lofty for many of us to grasp fully? Are we only too happy to seize upon a simplistic, limited set of rules? Is that in turn fed by our need to interpret two of the core conditions, empathy and unconditional positive regard, as a neat set of skills or techniques which we can learn cognitively and then subtly (or not) portray and 'apply' to our clients?

Rogers went on to make the following clear distinction between unconditional positive regard as an attitudinal ideal (which has been confirmed as being one of the necessary and sufficient conditions for therapy in his and others' research findings) and the degree to which even an *effective* counsellor may *actually* experience it:

It is probably evident from the description that *completely unconditional positive regard would never exist except in theory*. From a clinical and experiential point of view I believe the most accurate statement is that *the effective therapist experiences unconditional positive regard for the client during many moments of his contact with him, yet from time to time he experiences only a conditional positive regard* — and perhaps at times a negative regard, though this is not likely in effective therapy. It is in this sense that unconditional positive regard exists as a matter of degree in any relationship (ibid, my italics).

Are the sections where I have inserted italics further examples of the bits I, and others, (including Rogers' interviewer) missed and were unable to appreciate?

Mearns and Thorne (1988) focussing upon the same issue, suggest that the degree to which a counsellor achieves (and by this I assume they mean, both 'experiences' and 'communicates') unconditional positive regard for their client, is related to the degree to which the counsellor's particular personal boundaries operate:

> . . . it should be noted that in its literal sense it is impossible to achieve 'unconditional' positive regard. Every counsellor is human and fallible and therefore must have some 'personal limits' that might be exceeded by her client: the counsellor cannot therefore guarantee unconditionality. However the person-centred counsellor is likely to be 'less conditional' than most other people with whom the client will relate.

It seems to me that in the following extract, Rogers (1958 in Kirschenbaum and Henderson, 1989) suggests that when he experienced himself having offered less than unconditional positive regard towards his clients, it was because some part of the client's experiences and feelings were impacting upon him negatively. His statement here would seem to indicate that his self-concept and its associated conditions of worth were challenged in some way, causing his own defence mechanisms to protect him from the perceived threat.

> Still another issue is whether I can be acceptant of each facet of this other person which he presents to me. Can I receive him as he is? Can I communicate this attitude? Or can I only receive him conditionally, acceptant of some aspects of his feelings and silently or openly disapproving of other aspects? It has been my experience that when my attitude is conditional, then he cannot change or grow in those respects in which I cannot fully receive him. And when — afterward and sometimes too late — I try to discover why I have been unable to accept him in every respect, I usually discover that it is because I have been frightened or threatened in myself by some aspect of his feelings. If I am to be more helpful, then I must grow and accept myself in these respects (p. 122).

So can I, can we, be gentler with ourselves and openly admit our humanity? Looking at the words and terms which Rogers and others have used to describe unconditional positive regard, I acknowledge that I have neither received nor offered to another person *entirely* acceptant, prizing, warmly valuing, caring and respectful attitudes in which there was a *complete* absence of possessiveness or judgement. I have received and offered this attitude, however, *inconsistently*!

I consider myself fortunate to have experienced both giving and receiving positive regard and appreciate just how good this makes me and others feel. What I am also increasingly aware of is the depth of personal empowerment, liberation, autonomy and mutuality which also occurs, when the 'conditional' components of positive regard are decreased. (At this point, part of me is saying, 'But you knew this all along, this awareness has been inside of you all the time!' — of course I did, of course it has!)

My experiences both as a client and a counsellor confirm that the more frequently I and my clients receive positive regard in which the conditional components are minimalised, the more likely it is that we can achieve our potential for growth.

Rogers also identifies the fact that when we find ourselves only able to offer positive regard to the positive (as we perceive them) aspects of our clients it is just as unfacilitative and damaging to the clients' process, as it is to offer them negative regard. How many of our own unhealthy conditions of worth are formed and reinforced by the conditional *but positive* regard of our parents, teachers, friends or even college facilitators for instance? How many of us have experienced being evaluated positively as a threat, when we also yearned to have our mistakes, our weaknesses and our fallibilities, our entire human wholeness accepted? How many times have we heard statements along the lines of, 'You're so good at such and such'; 'You are such a good cook'; 'You're such a loyal friend'; 'You're a really good boy, you always shares your toys'; 'I'm really proud of you, you've got over your father's death so well'; 'You are so good-looking and attractive'; 'Seventy-five per cent for English! Great!'; 'You're always such a polite and obedient child'.

What happens to the parts of us that are less 'good'? What happens to the parts of us that are angry, sad, hostile, in pain etc. when those around us only seem to be able to focus positively and acceptantly on our peaceable, happy, 'healthy' bits? I don't have to *hear* someone's *negative* evaluation of my addiction to nicotine, when they tell me just how strong-willed and clever I am when I stop smoking. It is implied.

What happens to the parts of me, that are completely in the dark — say, understanding client-centred theory and putting it into practice — when someone tells me my understanding is superior to theirs and is of a consistently high standard? What happens is, that there is a tendency for my doubts and fears, my uncertainties and my lack of understanding to go into hiding in this relationship. I might feel a temporary 'ego-massaging' boost, but it is very temporary. If I am to grow in understanding, I need to feel that I can explore my lack of it safely, otherwise I too remain stuck in the evaluation of myself only in terms of what I positively *do* understand, and stagnation becomes the result. Rogers (1958 in Kirschenbaum and Henderson, 1989) made this very clear when he wrote the following:

> Curiously enough, a positive evaluation is as threatening in the long run as a negative one, since to inform someone that he is good implies that you also have the right to tell him he is bad.
>
> I have come to feel that the more I can keep a relationship free of judgment and evaluation, the more this will permit the other person to reach the point where he recognizes that the locus of evaluation, the center of responsibility, lies with himself. The meaning and value of his experiences is in the last analysis something which is up to

> him, and no amount of external judgment can alter this. So I should
> like to work toward a relationship in which I am not, even in my
> own feelings, evaluating him. This I believe can set him free to be a
> self-responsible person (p. 123).

Experiences of college supervision have suggested to me that when I find myself struggling to offer unconditional positive regard to a particular client, examination of this reveals that I may actually be more unconditional towards them, than I am towards a client with whom I feel in some way more connected. This has prompted me to ask myself questions along the following lines. When a client who has been consistently open to the process and has felt free to disclose some painful issues has received their counsellor's approval of this, what happens to their process when they get stuck and are no longer able to be open about their feelings?

What is happening to my process as a counsellor, when I only feel acceptance towards a client if, for example, they are in touch with their feelings? What is happening when I experience myself offering increased/decreased attentiveness when my client talks about their sadness, but not about their rage? What if I find myself smiling, nodding and otherwise conveying subtle approval towards a client when they talk about their sexual difficulties and I stop doing so when they talk about work? What is happening in me, when I find myself leaning towards and holding the hand of a weeping client, but seem to become a bit distant at other times?

For me as a trainee counsellor, committed to client-centred practice, it would seem just as important to focus upon (and by the way, remarkably difficult), and to examine the degree to which conditionality begins to operate in my relationship with my clients, when that conditionality is using positive evaluations of them as the criteria. (When I have experienced conditionality towards a client operating in me and it is based upon negative evaluations and negative regard of them, it seems relatively easy to admit that into my awareness.)

For example, I found myself increasingly irritated by the behaviour of a client, who continually sniffed throughout sessions. I found myself on one occasion, mildly dreading the arrival of someone who was rapidly assuming a label, 'The Sniffer' in my mind. The extent to which I was able to stay within this client's frame of reference was being contaminated by my own issues about sniffing. Acknowledging the source of my irritation and re-focussing my attention on trying to understand and accept them as whole person, actually resulted in my own feelings of irritation dissipating, as I brought myself back to my client's frame of reference. Curiously, the continual sniffing of another client who spent the same number of sessions weeping, did not have the same effect!

Conditionality was operating towards both clients, but my self-concepts were less challenged by admitting to my awareness that I found one client's sniffing irritating and distracting. Uncovering the fact that I appeared to find it easier to respect another client whose sniffing behaviour came from the affective aspect of her experiencing grief, was at first deeply uncomfortable. I was making a positive evaluation of the grieving client whose behaviour informed me that she was 'in touch with her feelings', maybe it made me feel good that this client had entered the therapeutic process, thereby feeding my conditions of worth. (I can only consider myself to be an effective counsellor if my client is openly self-disclosing and is in touch with their feelings.) If I ask myself the question, 'What if my client wasn't like this?' I begin to recognise that my regard for them is conditional upon their ability to continue to move through the process!

If, for instance in supervision, I describe my connection with one client and not another, my liking for one more than another, my experience tells me it is quite real and human to do so. Beating myself up doesn't lead me to explore or to be able to question the ways in which my entirely human conditionality works. I have come to see that self-flagellation can be a neat little defence mechanism in itself. (If I beat myself up before my supervisor or facilitator has a chance to do so, I'll probably avoid having my own conditions of worth challenged by them.) But maybe if I can keep a sense of balance and equilibrium here; if I can be more acceptant of myself and go beyond the guilty stuff, I discover that I genuinely do believe in my client's tendencies for actualisation.

Jerold Bozarth (1998) expresses this in the following way:

> The basic curative factor lies in the client's normal motivational drive of actualization. It is this tendency that is the fundamental curative factor lying within the person. The reference to unconditional positive regard as the curative factor assumes the thwarting of the natural tendency; hence, making it necessary that the client become more directly connected with the actualizing tendency through unconditional positive self-regard (p.83).

If I can be acceptant of the fact that my responses to clients are sometimes more conditional than at others and feel able to explore openly what is going on inside me; then when this occurs, I really begin to be able to understand how unconditional positive regard works and what it is inside of me that can prevent it from working. If I understand that, then there is a greater likelihood of my being able to offer *unconditional* positive regard more consistently to an individual client and to a wider range of clients.

My desire to do so comes from a healthy place. If I can get in touch with my human conditionality, if I can raise my awareness of how and when and under what circumstances it operates and increases, then maybe I stand a good chance of being able to minimise it and become even more facilitative to all my clients. If I find it easier to offer unconditional positive regard to one client than another, or to one client at specific times and not at others, there is a way that I can get in touch with that and improve my ability to offer it to them equally.

I'm also convinced of the interdependence of the core conditions. How can I communicate unconditional positive regard to a client and have any hope that they will receive this, unless I genuinely experience it? This attitude needs to come from a congruent position; it's no good feigning it. If I'm truthful about my relationships with clients then I realise that there are some I really look forward to being with more than others, which is conditional. I'm also deeply interested in the notion that there is perhaps only one core condition i.e., trusting the actualising tendency. It seems to me that it is the client's capacity for growth that is the engine, which drives the therapeutic relationship.

Conditionality also operates within my relationships with co-trainees. There are times when I've become really bored with what I have experienced as the sluggish nature of the group process and other times when I've felt excited and enthusiastic. My ability to offer positive regard to the group in my college training has frequently been conditional, as has been my ability to offer it to the individuals who make up the group. I definitely respect some of them more than others at different times. I definitely feel more warmth towards some, than others.

When my co-trainees have been concerning themselves with being open about their feelings, have appeared well-motivated and seemed to have been working hard, owning their own statements, I feel great and really connected with them. Is what I'm experiencing under these circumstances, empathy and unconditional positive regard? Or is it more to do with a 'comfort zone' of identification?

What I find surprising is, that the times when I have had to struggle hard to offer unconditional positive regard to the group are the times when I genuinely felt a positive shift occurring in my conditionality. For example, when I recognised that I was becoming bored and irritated because a co-trainee was rambling on anecdotally about the *content* of their experiences, then recognising and owning my feelings, deliberately putting them to one side and re-focussing my attention upon what my co-trainee might *actually be feeling*, usually resulted in a more powerful and meaningful experience for both of us.

It seems to me that my ability to offer empathy to someone is dependent upon the extent to which I experience and communicate unconditional positive regard *and* vice versa. I'm more likely to be able to get close to understanding what my client's experience is, if I feel genuinely warmly acceptant and respectful towards the whole of them. If I can understand what my client is experiencing then this has the effect of decreasing any conditional attitudes which belong to me and which might influence my communication towards them.

The beginnings of an internalisation process of linking the theory on unconditional positive regard with my practice came about around halfway through my diploma course. My course supervisor enabled me to examine my own understanding thus far and most importantly enabled me to bring the less comfortable aspects of my own experiences with unconditional positive regard into my awareness. He also offered to the group an experience of his in which his unconditional positive regard for a group member had been challenged, how this had resulted in his incongruent behaviour and how he had subsequently come to examine how conditionality operated within him. I had felt privileged at the time to have witnessed open self-scrutiny and honesty from a facilitator. I felt that his behaviour gave me encouragement to take similar risks with my self in the large group.

What I am sharply aware of are the 'troughs' and 'peaks' of my learning process and how the 'peaks' of deeper insightful awareness are always informed directly through my own experience and internal valuing system. Finding myself less defensive and more open to the flow of my experiencing has also resulted in feeling that many of the paths, previously seen as threatening and dangerous, are now just 'different' paths. I see 'peaks' in a different way too, reaching one is not so much a destination in itself as a position from which to view further possibilities on the journey. Although the views can be briefly exhilarating!

Sometimes a 'trough' phase has enabled me to explore my self both inside and out of my relationships with clients. (I have to say how much I have come to value a student-centred learning approach and how it has enabled me to let go of *some* of my rigidly held conditions of worth, accumulated in over half a century of being.)

I have discovered that I can really trust my self, my inner self, my actualising tendency, it's probably the only part of me that I can truly rely upon. The development of self-acceptance and self-awareness has enabled me to get in touch with some kind of distilled essence of my self. I have learned that nothing in, or out of, client work, informs me so richly or so deeply, as my own experiencing in action, in awareness. Increased self-awareness and self-acceptance have increased my positive self-regard. I feel somehow more solid and yet more fluid.

Increased unconditional positive self-regard and increased unconditional positive regard for others seem to be two sides of the same coin, each informing, enhancing and balancing the other. Can one have *increased* unconditional positive regard? If it is unconditional then how might it be increased or decreased in quality? I recognise that the quantity of unconditional positive regard that I communicate can be increased, as can my receptivity to it, or perhaps I can only experience positive regard on a continuum in which conditionality is increased or decreased? I value my desire or will to extend the core conditions to my self and others. This now comes from an almost tangible part of me and is no longer an abstract set of external concepts.

Experiencing unconditional positive regard for another person doesn't seem to depend on, or be related to, how well I *know* or am *known* by them, but it does seem to be informed by the extent to which I understand and am understood. Such *knowingness*, that is, the need to access certainty, used to be important to me and now seems to have been an illusion. I feel comfortable with not knowing, with uncertainty, with the ultimate mystery of my individuality and that of other people. The vestiges of my 'need to know' about the mechanism of the human psyche is being tempered by my humility in the face of its vastness. Understanding small portions of my self and offering my understanding of small portions of another's experience for this moment in time, seems like a rewarding enough and a hard enough task.

Confirming my humanity as a person, who also happens to be a client-centred counsellor, is good enough and what I may become through increasing self-awareness and personal development is likely to be experienced by my clients as more facilitative. So we are very fortunate, we are indeed blessed, if unconditional positive regard exists between us.

References

Bozarth, Jerold.(1998) *Person-Centered Therapy: A Revolutionary Paradigm*. Ross-on-Wye: PCCS Books.

Mearns, Dave & Thorne, Brian. (1988) *Person-Centred Counselling in Action*. London: Sage.

Rogers Carl R. (1957) The Necessary and Sufficient Conditions of Therapeutic Personality Change, in *Journal of Consulting Psychology,* Vol. 21. Reprinted in H. Kirschenbaum and V. Henderson, (Eds) (1989) *The Carl Rogers Reader*. London: Constable.

Rogers, Carl R. (1958) The Characteristics of a Helping Relationship, in *Personnel and Guidance Journal,* Vol.37. Reprinted in H. Kirschenbaum and V. Henderson, (Eds) (1989) *The Carl Rogers Reader*. London: Constable.

Rogers, Carl R. (1961) *On Becoming A Person*. London: Constable.

For once the camera has accurately captured the entirety of my experience — positive regard, love towards another, in which the 'conditional' component was almost non-existent.

PSYCHOTHERAPY: THE PROCESS, THE THERAPIST, THE LEARNING

2

MARIA VILLAS-BOAS BOWEN

The process

The Tibetans believe that hidden deep into the heart of the Himalayas, in a valley surrounded by high snow peaks, lies a mysterious kingdom of incredible richness and beauty. The ground is purified with scented water and strewn with flowers, and the palaces are covered with gems. Wish-fulfilling trees, which make any wish made under them come true, abound. The people are calm, happy, cooperative, and connected, and the king is a benign and compassionate ruler. In Shambala, as they call this kingdom, ancient power and knowledge are preserved. The pilgrim who braves the hardships and overcomes obstacles along the way reaches the sacred land and finds the learning necessary to master time and to be liberated from any bondage. Peace, harmony, freedom, wellness, and abundance reign. The happiness and joy there can compare only with that of the gods themselves.

Those who have studied the myth of Shambala find two ways of understanding the Tibetan texts. Are they describing an actual geographic location, or is the kingdom a metaphor for the hidden depths of the mind, a description of the journey of the human spirit, or our Inner Self on the path to self-realization and complete liberation?

While the Tibetans may journey through space to enter a higher state of consciousness, Carl Rogers has traveled through time to describe a similar higher level of human awareness. His 'Person of Tomorrow' (Rogers, 1981) is one who taps vast inner resources for self-understanding and for self-directed behavior. This person is free, harmonious, wise, and peaceful, and is able to deal creatively with whatever changes may come. Trusting inner guidance, instead of relying on science, technology or institutions, the Person of Tomorrow relies on personal authority, is caring, capable of intimacy, open to others as well as to inner experience. Life is whole, guided by an integration of the varied energies rather than being motivated solely toward material gains or status symbols. Furthermore, the Person of Tomorrow is guided by a spiritual search. Unlike Shambala, Rogers doesn't promise happiness and joy that will compete with the gods; a person with these characteristics cannot fail to have a rich and fulfilling life.

The underlying theme of both the myth of Shambala and the Person of Tomorrow seems to be that we have within ourselves resources that, if tapped, will make us more connected with ourselves, others, and our social and spiritual values. Joined with these sources, our lives are likely to express greater freedom and awareness.

The Tibetans have elaborate guidebooks on how to get to Shambala, some of them in the form of poems which have been preserved on ancient wooden block prints. They use imageries to describe the inner feelings and experiences of the pilgrims, and describe rituals for tapping the energy necessary for certain stages of the journey. They tell of ways of overcoming obstacles and describe the terrain which lies ahead. Rogers, in a different, more subtle way, describes how the process of psychotherapy can help one travel into that awareness of the Person of Tomorrow. He says that if the therapist is empathic, congruent, prizes, and cares for, the client, a climate will be created which facilitates the journey. He also describes something of what the journey is like, when he delineates the characteristic directions of the process of psychotherapy (Rogers, 1959). Also, his hypothesis on the outcomes in personality and behavior which result from therapy may be taken as a description of what lies ahead.

I like to think of the journey through space as in the myth of Shambala, or through time, as in Rogers' descriptions of the Person of Tomorrow, as metaphors for psychotherapy. Space and time are linear concepts which help us comprehend our present reality. I like to consider these journeys as symbolic representations of becoming aware of what already exists. In that way, becoming and being are the same, Time and Space ultimately undifferentiated.

The therapist
Using the journey to Shambala as a metaphor for pyschotherapy, I consider hiring a guide to facilitate my trip. I realize that to compare the Person-Centered Therapist to a guide might seem absurd, since to be a guide usually implies to lead, to direct, which is in contradiction with the political role played by the therapist who follows a Person-Centered philosophy. Nevertheless, it is not necessarily true in all definitions of guidance, that the power and the responsibility for the direction taken lies with the guide. If I were to hire someone to accompany me in a trek to the Himalayas, I wouldn't choose a Wall Street lawyer, as clever and resourceful as he/she might be, or a university geography professor, even if he/she is an expert on Asian mountain ranges, or a ranger in California, even though he/she has a great deal of experience with wilderness. I also wouldn't hire any of my friends, although their companionship would make the trip more fun. If I'm going to hire someone for such a journey, I want a person with certain particular characteristics which will facilitate my pilgrimage. I would do what every voyager who risks to ascend the Himalayas does: I would hire as guide a member of a mountain tribe in Northeast Nepal, a Sherpa.

Why a Sherpa?
I imagine the Sherpa as having four important characteristics which will facilitate my journey:

1) The Sherpa is willing to let the journey be mine. I'm the one who chooses the destination and the path to follow to get there. Although he may suggest ways, or show trails which I haven't noticed before, the ultimate choice is still mine. He doesn't try to impose his presence on my journey, unless it's necessary. His feelings of self-importance or success are not tied up with the way I treat him, or with any specific outcome. He's simply committed to the task of being my guide-companion in that travel, and his reward, besides the honorarium that I pay him, is to expand his awareness of himself as a guide-companion, and to increase his experience of being in the wilderness.

2) The Sherpa knows the terrain well. He might never have been on the path that I choose to follow, but the fact that he knows well the rugged mountains, and he is skilful being in the wilderness facilitates my trip. Because of those previous experiences, he may be able to discern trails which are barely visible because they are covered with snow or bushes, and show them to me, increasing in that way my alternatives as to what path to follow. He might coach me when I need certain skills to climb a mountain or ford a river. He might notice the warning signs of an impending storm, which were imperceptible to me, and help me prepare to face the storm, maybe by taking shelter while it passes. He might encourage me to go further when my imaginary fears paralyze me. He might help me identify the footprints of snow leopards or yaks, increasing my knowledge of the possibilities of the mountains. He might even, when I'm too absorbed on the path ahead of me to be able to look at my surroundings, gently tap on my shoulder and point out a higher mountain where a waterfall, cascading downstream, spreads sparkles on the air which leap at the sun in a myriad of rainbows, their colors vibrant against the lavender skies. When I start getting too high, in elevations I never have been before, and become afraid that I can't breathe, or that life might even stop, he might bring me some oxygen, and show me that it is just a question of adaptation to a higher level. I look around and see that from that altitude, the beauty is more striking and the gorges and canyons are not so terrifying. The Sherpa might remind me of the importance, when that high, of moving more slowly, with precision and mindfulness.

3) The Sherpa helps me carry the weight. By distributing the burden, the heavy load becomes bearable, and my energy is freed up to pursue the path and to learn about and appreciate my environment. My courage to proceed depends on the security I feel that we'll have enough resources to nurture us along the path. There is no way that I could, all by myself, carry enough food, oxygen, medicine, shelter, to see me through the trip.

4) The Sherpa believes that Shambala is there, and that I can only get to it through a path that I myself choose. He may know of short cuts, but they wouldn't work for me because the only way to get to Shambala is through the process of each person finding his/her own path. When we go across plateaux or through dark and narrow gorges, or when we have to descend a side of a mountain in order to start ascending again, and I lose sight of the direction I'm going in, he may reassure me that Shambala is still there despite any detours we have to take. His faith and hope encourage me to pursue my journey.

The learning

As the Sherpa learns to be a guide through his own experience, probably traveling at first under the tutelage of more experienced guides, so the training of psychotherapists is highly experiential, and also done in the context of an alliance with a more experienced psychotherapist. The therapist learning in our present-day culture has an advantage that I think the Sherpas don't have: the accumulation of knowledge, preserved and distributed in written, audio and visual forms. That allows learning from other people's experience: The creation of models and theories and the testing of them, the collection and organization of empirical data, and phenomenological accounts. Scientific methodology, although still in its rudimentary stage when dealing with human variables, may spare us from having to 're-invent the wheel', at the same time allowing us to rehearse mentally what we can't directly experience. In that way, cognitive knowledge becomes an indispensable adjunct of experiential knowledge in the learning process of therapists.

The essence of experiential knowledge is the development of self-awareness through the commitment to our own inner journey. As we go inward and increase our self-knowledge, layers of deception are lifted, perceptions get clearer, and we become more and more able to differentiate our own projections and distortions from what is. With that clarity, we become freer to let our intuition guide our process with the client. From our intuitive insights, skills and techniques spontaneously emerge in the context of what is happening at any given moment. The prior study of skills and techniques is useful as part of our repertoire of experiences from which to draw at those moments. While an emphasis only on the learning of skills and techniques may create technicians, the emphasis on self-awareness and commitment to the expansion of one's consciousness, creates freer and more aware persons, better equipped to be good therapists.

Also, the commitment by the therapist to his or her own inner journey brings at least two advantages in dealing with the client:

First, experiencing going inward, and how it affects our inner and outer lives, allows us to understand, in a deeper sense, the client's process. Secondly, if we ourselves benefit from this process, it increases our hope and faith in the benefits that the depth of inner discovery brings to one's attitude towards life.

In the learning of the therapist, the creation of a climate of Empathy, Prizing and Caring, and Congruence (Rogers, 1959), that we emphasize so much in relation to our clients, also has to be directed inward. Those qualities are intrinsically interconnected, and parts of a whole. Each one of them taken separately will not create the climate described by Rogers. The three have to coexist in order to facilitate change. It is only as an artifact, for purposes of clarity, that they may be considered separately.

Empathy

We live in a society constantly bombarded by external and internal demands. Overstimulation, achievement-oriented values, emphasis on 'shoulds', create so much noise in our heads that it becomes very difficult to find enough quietness to be able to listen to ourselves with empathic understanding. When we listen, often there is so much static created by 'what should be's', 'what could have been's,' that we're unable to recognize what is. Investment in an image, wish-fulfillment fantasies, guilt, regret and self-condemnation then become the predominant feelings, preventing us from getting better acquainted with the variety of other feelings that lie underneath. To be able to identify our own feelings and wants, to recognize when we are out of balance, or when something of importance is missing, becomes important in the learning of the therapist. It enables us as therapists to separate our own needs from those of the clients, and to recognize when our own feelings and anxieties are interfering with the client's process.

Another important aspect of the development of Empathy towards ourselves is to be able to stop the constant barrage of conscious thoughts, in order to tap that part of us which transcends the rational mind: our Inner Self (Bowen, 1982). The energy of that inner source is manifested through metaphors, dreams, visions, hunches, impulses, sudden ideas, inspirations, imageries, etc. From that deeper source emerges what I have come to call *Integrative Impressions* (Bowen, 1982) which allow us, the therapist and client, to perceive things in a new light, and to order fragmented experiences into a new pattern which moves us into a higher order of coherence and simplicity.

I consider such integrative impressions as a type of empathic response, which differs from another type of empathic response, i.e., the *Supportive Response*. While Integrative Impression leads to an immediate reintegration of experience and insight, the Supportive Response provides the client with warmth, strength, and the feeling of being connected, but it does not necessarily change the perceptions of the client. I believe that what distinguishes *Psychotherapy* from *Supportive Encounter* is that in Psychotherapy both types of empathic responses are present, while in Supportive Encounter, the client experiences the warmth and understanding of the therapist, but the therapist is not active in facilitating new integration.

In his most recent paper, Rogers (1986) describes how he feels when he operates from his Inner Self, the source from which Integrative Impressions emerge. He writes:

> Then my presence is releasing and helpful. There is nothing that I
> can do to force this experience, but when I can relax and be close to

the transcendental core of me, then I may behave in strange and impulsive ways in the relationship, ways which I cannot justify rationally, which have nothing to do with my thought processes. But these strange ways turn out to be right, in some odd way. At those moments it seems that my inner spirit has reached out and touched the inner spirit of the other. Our relationship transcends itself, and has become a part of something larger (reprinted in Kirschenbaum and Henderson, 1989, p.137).

To learn to tap into our deeper resources, to cultivate our relationship with our indwelling spirit, becomes important in the learning of the therapist. Some of the ways of cultivating this linkage, if done with intentionality and regularity, are: working with dreams, meditation, inspirational readings, journal writing, artistic endeavors, contact with nature, non-competitive physical exercises (Tai-Chi, yoga, martial arts), and one's own psychotherapy. To create rituals in which we impart our own personal meaning, with the purpose of tapping into our spiritual energy, becomes very important in the learning of the therapist. When we are able to do that, we are nurturing the deepest in ourselves. In that way, we're also creating in ourselves the second characteristic of the climate which promotes growth.

Prizing ourselves and caring for ourselves

By listening to ourselves and facing as-it-is-ness, we get better acquainted not only with the well-functioning part of us, but also with our dark side. We learn to prize and appreciate the qualities that help us to fulfil our lives and, at the same time, learn to accept the presence of our self-defeating qualities. I haven't met one human being yet who doesn't have a dark side (even the gurus have their dark sides). The challenge is to become acquainted with how those dark forces operate within us and to be in contact with the manifestations of our unconscious forces. Learning how they affect our moods and our interaction with other people enable us to witness their presences without becoming totally identified with them. Only by recognizing that those dark forces are in action can we exert any option about how to deal with them. For example, how can we possibly control our anger if we don't fully face and experience its existence? It is not by creating means of working with our 'negative' emotions that we're going to learn how to deal with them. 'I-versus-We messages', 'Non-judgmental anger', etc., are empty techniques if we don't fully experience the depth of our anger. When we do fully face the darkness within us, then, more often than not, the behavior caused by it drops away.

Congruence

The more we listen to ourselves and face what is within us with acceptance, the more we learn to differentiate what is from the creations of our mind, and the clearer our perceptions become. With that clarity, we gradually open to guidance from deeper parts of ourselves, which transcend our rational thoughts. Through that openness, our intuition guides us to act with spontaneity and appropriateness to the situation. That harmony between what is happening inside and what transpires outside is what I understand congruence to be. I do not equate congruence with spilling out what is in the mind or heart of the therapist. Sometimes that type of self-revelation serves more the needs of the therapist than the client, and can interfere with the client's process. By the same token, the therapist may choose not to reveal her/his thoughts and feelings and still be congruent. For me, the essence of congruence is to face as-it-is-ness, and to separate it from our projections and distortions. Only then does the therapist become able to differentiate intuition and the guidance of the Inner Self from that which is being driven by unacknowledged feelings or needs. In the former, one acts spontaneously and harmoniously; in the latter, one over-reacts, and disharmony and incongruence appear.

Congruence, when manifested inwardly, has the same characteristics of spontaneity and harmony when directed towards our clients. When we are congruent with ourselves, our needs, our wants, and our course of action are at one. We follow the path of the heart without being assailed by conflicts and doubts. The energy of the moment flows smoothly, taking us in the direction our path naturally leads us. In summation, the essence of the experiential knowledge in our learning as therapists is the development of self-awareness through the commitment to our own inner journey. We create a climate of empathy, prizing and caring, and congruence toward ourselves which facilitates our going into the depth of our being. This becomes the process of discovery in itself. These three characteristics are inseparably interconnected, and only for the purpose of exposition can they be taken separately. The presence of the three characteristics are essential for the climate which facilitates change and expansion.

Conclusion

Training which maximizes the learning of the therapist is one which blends well cognitive and experiential knowledge. Through cognitive knowledge the therapist expands his/her realm of possibilities through the experience of others. Knowledge of research and the ability to evaluate research results, while recognizing the limitations of current methodology, may help the therapist challenge prior conceptions of how things are, and to discard ineffective ways of operating, to re-conceptualize ideas, and to experiment with new alternatives.

The alliance with a more experienced therapist is essential in a learning program. The more experienced therapist may guide the beginning therapist in reading and research, and may share her/his cognitive formulations and experiences through supervision, courses, and seminars. Most important of all, the senior therapist hopefully will infuse the training program with a spirt of enthusiasm and appreciation, a deep sense of wonder for the therapy process, for going inward, unshakable confidence in the possibilities of therapy, and a profound sense of privilege to be invited to enter the inner world of another person and to share that person's journey.

Another important characteristic of a good training program is to constantly remind the learning therapist of the importance of one's own inner journey and how it affects one's relationship with the clients. That can be done through the modeling of the more experienced therapist, by creating opportunities for the development of self-awareness through growth groups, feedback sessions, listening to and seeing oneself in tapes, supervision etc. By stressing the importance of the inner journey, the learning therapist is reminded that both the therapist and the client have within themselves a vast source of knowledge, wisdom, compassion, and energy. When we tap that source, our work is guided in a way which transcends our intellectual comprehension, and it will facilitate healing, change, and expansion. In that way we become like Sherpas, guiding ourselves and our clients to Shambala or to the consciousness of the Person of Tomorrow.

Bibliography

Bernbaum, E. (1980) *The Way to Shambala*, New York: Anchor Books.

Bowen, M. (1982) Spirituality and Person-Centered Approach: Interconnectedness in the Universe and in Psychotherapy. Unpublished Paper.

Rogers, C. R. (1959) A Theory of Therapy, Personality, and Interpersonal Relationship, as Developed in the Client-Centered Framework. In S. Koch, (Ed.) *Psychology: A Study of a Science, Vol. 3*. New York: McGraw-Hill.

Rogers, C. R. (1980) *A Way of Being*, Boston: Houghton-Mifflin.

Rogers, C. R. (1986) A Client-Centered, Person-Centered Approach to Psychotherapy. In I. L. Kutash and A. Wolf (eds.), *Psychotherapist's Casebook: Theory and Technique in Practice*. San Francisco: Jossey Bass. Reprinted in *The Carl Rogers Reader.* (1989) (Eds) H. Kirschenbaum and V. Henderson. Houghton Mifflin.

This photograph of Maria was contributed by Suzanne Spector, a close friend of Maria's. It was taken in Scotland around the time of the ICCCEP Conference at Stirling in 1991.

Empathy at the Core of the Client-Centred Therapeutic Relationship: Contaminators of Empathic Understanding

3

Irene Fairhurst

Empathy at the core

The focus of this paper is the hypothesis that in Client-Centred Therapy, it is through experiencing empathic understanding from a credible (congruent) person that clients begin to believe in themselves as of worth. The unconditional positive regard they receive whilst in a client-centred therapeutic relationship takes the place of their embedded belief systems about themselves. Their 'locus of evaluation' becomes internalised as they begin to trust their organismic selves (Seeman, 1996).

The experience of empathic understanding reinforces the client's 'internal locus of evaluation' and this is one of the main aspects of the client-centred therapeutic relationship. Whenever therapists direct, control or treat clients they reinforce the external locus of evaluation, and if the intention is to work in a client-centred way, are wasting therapeutic time. Rogers (1980) says:

> Over the years, however, the research evidence has kept piling up, and it points strongly to the conclusion that a high degree of empathy in a relationship is possibly *the* most potent factor in bringing about change and learning. And so I believe it is time for me to forget the caricatures and misrepresentations of the past and take a fresh look at empathy (p.139).

In recent years, there has been a renewed interest in the phenomenon of empathy — the concept developed from early Greek 'empatheia' and Latin 'pathos' (feeling-perception) through aesthetic usage 'Einfühlung' (entering into feeling) in the late nineteenth century, and then at the beginning of the twentieth century it gained more recognition in psychology.

Theodor Lipps, a German psychologist, was writing in the fields of both aesthetics and psychology and seems to bridge the gap between the two:

Lipps (1903): 'Einfühlung, inner Nachahmung, und Organ-

empfindungen'. *Archiv fur die gesamte Psychologie, 2*, and 1905
'Das Wissen von fremden Ichen' *Psychologische Untersuchungen, 4*, appropriated the term for use in more psychological contexts, first applying it to the study of optical illusions and later to the process by which we come to know other people (Davis, 1994, p. 5).

In 1915, in *Beginner's Psychology*, E. Titchener translated the German word Einfühlung into the English 'Empathy' and wrote:

> We have a natural tendency to feel ourselves into what we perceive or imagine. As we read about the forest, we may, as it were, *become* the explorer; we feel for ourselves the gloom, the silence, the humidity, the oppression, the sense of lurking danger; everything is strange, but it is to us that strange experience has come . . . This tendency to feel oneself *into* a situation is called EMPATHY (Wispé, 1987, p. 22).

John Shlien (1997) remarked:

> Meanwhile, in another section of the University, empathy was a concept commonly read about and discussed by graduate students (my wife among them), in art history. One assigned reading was 'Empathy and Abstraksion' (Worringer, 1908) first published a year before Titchener introduced the term in the United States . . . The Foreword in Worringer's book describes his chance meeting with Georg Simmel at a Museum in Berlin, where they talked about the idea of empathy (p. 71).

By the beginning part of the twentieth century, the concept of empathy was widespread throughout the social sciences, including psychology and personality theories, and aesthetics, and as we moved into the second half of the century, empathy began to find its place in psychotherapy, which brings us, of course, to Carl Rogers and Client-Centred therapy. Wispé (1987) writes:

> Perhaps the most important recent work on empathy has been that of Carl Rogers (1942, 1951, 1957, 1975). He has had enormous influence in the area of individual counseling, but most people have forgotten, or never knew about, the times during which he was most influential, beginning with the 1950's when hopes for psychology ran high (p. 27).

In 1951 Rogers wrote:

> This formulation would state that it is the counselor's function to assume, in so far as he is able, the internal frame of reference of the client, to perceive the world as the client sees it, to perceive the client himself as he is seen by himself, to lay aside all perceptions from the external frame of reference while doing so, and to communicate something of this empathic understanding to the client.

Rogers goes on to quote Nat Raskins unpublished, 1947 paper:

> At this level, counselor participation becomes an active experiencing with the client of the feelings to which he gives expression, the counselor makes a maximum effort to get under the skin of the person with whom he is communicating, he tries to get *within* and to live the attitudes expressed instead of observing them, to catch every nuance of their changing nature; in a word, to absorb himself completely in the attitudes of the other . . .

Rogers continues:

> Even this description may be rather easily misunderstood since the experiencing with the client, the living of his attitudes, is not in terms of emotional identification on the counselor's part, but rather an empathic identification, where the counselor is perceiving the hates and hopes and fears of the client through immersion in an empathic process, but without himself, as counselor, experiencing those hates and hopes and fears (1951, p. 29).

Probably the most quoted of Rogers' definitions of empathy is taken from the 1959 chapter, *Therapy, Personality, and Interpersonal Relationships*:

> The state of empathy, or being empathic, is to perceive the internal frame of reference of another with accuracy, and with the emotional components and meanings which pertain thereto, as if one were the other person, but without ever losing the 'as if' condition. Thus it means to sense the hurt or the pleasure of another as he senses it, and to perceive the causes thereof as he perceives them, but without ever losing the recognition that it is *as if* I were hurt or pleased, etc. If this 'as if' quality is lost, then the state is one of identification.

In this definition, Rogers refers to 'the state of empathy', implying a static position, rather than a process. However, in the next section of the same paper under the heading 'External Frame of Reference', Rogers is beginning to describe 'empathic understanding' as an experience which can be used as a source of knowledge about the client's frame of reference. He talks about focussing on his own experience to check the reality of his feelings: 'Do I really love him? Am I really enjoying this?' then adds:

> Knowledge which has any 'certainty', in the social sense, involves the use of empathic inference as a means of checking, but the direction of that empathy differs.

Twenty years later Rogers (1980) writes:

> I would no longer be terming it a 'state of empathy', because I believe it to be a process, rather that a state. Perhaps I can capture that quality.
>   It means entering the private perceptual world of the other and

becoming thoroughly at home in it. It involves being sensitive, moment by moment, to the changing felt meanings which flow in this other person, to the fear or rage or tenderness or confusion or whatever that he or she is experiencing. It means temporarily living in the other's life, moving about in it delicately without making judgments; it means sensing meanings of which he or she is scarcely aware . . . (p. 142).

So Rogers has moved from considering empathy to being a 'state' to a 'process' and many contemporary thinkers have also developed that theme, including Barrett-Lennard (1981,1986), Neville (1994), Seeman (1995, 1996) and Shlien (1997).

The process of empathy and empathic understanding
So, where does all this leave me, in my struggle to understand my own process of empathy and empathic understanding with my clients?

In my training, some 20 years ago, I was given the 1959 definition of empathy, prior to being sent into a triad to practice empathy, or to 'be the most understanding person in the world'. As a facilitator in training programmes today, I try to offer the opportunity to participants to explore the concept of empathy and this is where I first began to feel that maybe it's not quite so simple (or perhaps my wonderings will take me back to that original position).

My hope is that by understanding my own experience more clearly, I will be as effective for my clients as I possibly can be. So, here is where I am at with my own understandings. I feel that within my 'self' there is one bank of feelings (together with their own meanings — as Rogers (1959) defines 'feeling' '. . . thus it includes the emotion, but also the cognitive content of the meaning of that emotion in its experiential context') which has to do with my own personal experience — my personal frame of reference. It also seems that maybe there is a separate bank of 'feelings' called 'empathy' which has to do with the frame of reference of another (person or object). Robert Plutchik (1994) says: 'Empathy is thus not a separate emotion by itself, but a kind of induction process by which emotions, both positive and negative, are shared . . . '(p.43).

I, along with others, am beginning to think of 'empathy' as an *innate attribute* which we are all born with, for example: Neville (1994): 'Empathy is for Gebser, a primitive phenomenon, utterly basic to the human condition' (p. 443), and Shlien (1997): 'Empathy is one of several essential forms of intelligence, an experiential form of such importance to adaptation that social and physical survival depends upon it. It is a normal, natural, commonplace capacity, almost constant, almost unavoidable' (p. 63).

So, maybe, there are in my 'self' two emotional 'banks', one to do with my own experiencing and one to do with the 'other' (empathy). If, as a client-centred therapist, I wish to access this second bank in order to develop empathic understanding of another,in order to promote the therapeutic relationship, I initiate a process which I call an *active undertaking*. One of the debates which I have discovered in my readings around this subject has been whether this process is cognitive or imaginative — for me, it is both. It requires a cognitive decision to access the second bank, temporarily putting aside my personal bank, and then, (somehow carrying memories of my own emotions with me) imagination to enter into the client's world 'as if' it were my own. James Marcia (1994) says:

> Clearly, this definition refers to both cognitive and affective aspects of empathy . . . In psychotherapy, the therapist can set him/herself to function in an empathic mode (p. 83).

I am aware that there are other aspects of empathic understanding within the client-centred relationship which are important — the 'as if' quality referred to by Rogers (1959) and the relevance of Buber's work on the I-Thou relationship (1933 and 1958), the communication of empathic understanding and how much distortion and misunderstandings of 'reflection of feelings' have contaminated Rogers's work (Rogers, 1980). Jerold Bozarth (1984) suggests that the emphasis on verbal 'reflection' as the major method of communication of empathy has distracted therapists from other more 'idiosyncratic' responses. In 1986 Rogers wrote:

> At the same time I know that many of my responses in an interview would seem to be 'reflection of feeling'. Inwardly I object. I am definitely not trying to 'reflect feelings'.
>
> Then I receive a letter from my friend and former colleague, Dr. John Shlien of Harvard, which still further complicates my dilemma. He writes: *Reflection is unfairly damned . . . But you neglect the other side. It is an instrument of artistic virtuosity in the hands of a sincere, intelligent, empathic listener . . . Undeserved denigration of the technique leads to fatuous alternatives in the name of 'congruence'* (personal correspondence, April, 1986).
>
> . . . I am not trying to 'reflect feelings', I am trying to determine whether my understanding of the client's inner world is correct . . . On the other hand, I know that from the client's point of view we are holding up a mirror of his or her current experiencing.

I will now move to the question 'Why is empathic understanding crucial to the client-centred relationship?' Or, in Margaret Warner's words 'How does Empathy Cure?' (Warner, 1994). In *A Way of Being,* Rogers (1980) states:

> First, empathy dissolves alienation. For the moment, at least, the recipient finds himself or herself a connected part of the human race . . . 'I am no longer an isolate'.
>
> . . . Carl Jung has said that schizophrenics cease to be schizo-phrenic when they meet other persons by whom they feel understood.
>
> . . . A second consequence of empathic understanding is that the recipient feels valued, cared for, accepted as the person that he or she is.
>
> . . . Still a third impact of a sensitive understanding comes from its nonjudgemental quality (pp. 151–3).

And Rogers concludes:

> The self is now more congruent with the experiencing. Thus, the persons have become, in their attitudes toward themselves, more caring and acceptant, more empathic and understanding, more real and congruent (p.159).

Margaret Warner (1994) writes:

> The communication of empathy tends to facilitate change because it generates a particular sense of experiential recognition within the other person — both the sense of being recognized in one's experience of the moment by another human being and the sense of recognizing one's own experience in the moment . . .
>
> I am speaking of the sense of recognition that one has when one feels that another has grasped, in words or in some other way, the essence of one's situation as it is currently experienced, in the absence of a sense of threat or judgement about that experience. This kind of recognition is often accompanied with a sense of slight release or relief at being seen . . .
>
> In this experience of recognition, a person momentarily lessens his or her sense of existential aloneness in the world . . .
>
> In having one's experience recognized and received by another person, one becomes able to recognize and receive one's own experience, both in a broad sense and in one's particular ability to receive one's own moment to moment experiencing . . .
>
> This openness to an ongoing experiencing allows a continuing revision of one's life narrative and the 'scripts' by which experiences are organized and interpreted, making possible more mature, differentiated ways of living in relationship with others (pp.130–3).

In addition to these findings by Rogers and Warner, which, I feel, are closely related, I reiterate my own conclusion that it is through the faithful trust by the therapist in the actualising tendency (Rogers, 1959) of the client which enables her to stay in the client's frame of reference, nonjudgementally, which reinforces the client's internal locus of evaluation (Rogers, 1959). Temener Brodley (1992) says:

> It seems to be more faithful to Rogers' theory and his therapy behavior to clarify that Rogers' empathic responses emphasize or explicitly state *the client's perceptions* and the ways in which the client is an *agent or source of reactions*. Rogers' empathic following of the client, we find, tends to pick up on the way in which the client is an *agency* or a *source* of what we have called 'actions of personality' (Brodley & Brody, 1990).

Having explored the meaning of empathy, its development in the therapy context, and considered why it is effective, my next question is, 'What gets in the way of empathy, or blocks or contaminates the process of empathic understanding?'

Possible contaminators of empathy

Throughout my own training and later readings, I have found very little in this area, particularly from the person-centred view point, and felt I should like to investigate the issue further. The issue of contaminators of the relationship in client-centred therapy has, therefore, been at the centre of the research which was the basis for this chapter. I am interested in the topic generally and more specifically around the issue of awareness in client-centred therapists of the possibility of 'unconscious' prejudice.

This central focus was prompted by my presenting my research questionnaire to an MA group at a university, during the planning stages. Of the eight students, seven, although having knowledge of the Person-Centred Approach had also trained in Psychodynamic or Analytic schools, and when answering the question: '*Are you aware of any factors about your clients which might affect your ability, positively or negatively, to be present with them?*' they spent one hour of the hour-and-a-half session, talking about 'counter transference'. My suspicion was that it would be different for groups of person-centred counsellors.

'Unconscious' and the Person-Centred Approach

It will be noted that the word 'unconscious' is written throughout this paper in inverted commas. This is because of my views around the argument of not using analytic or psychodynamic language when discussing Person-Centred theory. My view is that words in common usage such as 'unconscious', 'defences', 'resistance', 'projection' and even 'transference', were taken by Freud and given special meanings, and today it feels as if those words are taboo for anybody who does not subscribe to Freud's, or his followers' theories of personality — as if they have 'cornered the market'. So, whilst continuing to use the words, I do agree that it is important to be clear about my meanings. I am not alone in this view — in correspondence with Margaret Warner in January 1996, she writes to me:

> . . . there's a way, though, that Rogers using the word 'defences' implies that he is much more psychoanalytic than I think he really is, and I think that if it is possible for client-centered people to clarify that difference, his thinking can be linked to some very interesting current work . . . Freud is really saying that there are unconscious contents that behave as if they were real *things* under the surface or real 'people' with intentions (as when the ego tries to suppress the id). Some of the most interesting (to me) philosophers of meaning would say that meaning is partly discovered but also partly created or socially negotiated, and, of course, they have been very critical of the pseudo-mechanical, scientific ways Freud talked about human life. But I think this kind of thinking is deeply embedded in psychoanalytic theory, whereas with Rogers, it is more a surface way of talking — 'defense' was a word that people understood, that

lent an air of seriousness to his work. But, I think that at heart Rogers is much more phenomenological than that. Rogers, more than anyone, would believe in people's needing to deal with what is organismically true for them, but also having a real realm of freedom and creativity in fashioning their life stories . . .

Interestingly, it seems that it was Breuer, at that time an associate of Freud, who first used the term — 'the unconscious'. In Breuer's account of his work with Anna O. he writes (Freud, 1974):

Every one of her hypnoses in the evening afforded evidence that the patient was entirely clear and well-ordered in her mind and normal as regards her feeling and volition so long as none of the products of her secondary state was acting as a stimulus 'in the unconscious'.

In a footnote, Angela Richards comments:

The fact that Breuer puts it in quotation marks may possibly indicate that he is attributing it to Freud (p.100).

I should, therefore, like to clarify what I mean by the word 'unconscious' in the context of this paper. Rogers (1978) writes:

Whyte places this same idea in a larger context when he says, 'Crystals, plants and animals grow without any conscious fuss, and the strangeness of our own history disappears once we assume that the same kind of natural ordering process that guides their growth also guided the development of man and of his mind, and does so still.' (L.L. Whyte, *The Unconscious Before Freud*, Tavistock Publications, London, 1960.) These views are very remote from Freud's distrust of the unconscious, and his general view that it was antisocial in its direction. Instead, when a person is functioning in an integrated, unified, effective manner, she has confidence in the directions she unconsciously chooses, and trusts her experiencing, of which, even if she is fortunate, she has only partial glimpses in her awareness (p. 246).

Rogers goes on to reiterate his theory of unhealthy behaviour, namely, '. . . the rift. . . in so many of us . . . that organismically we are moving in one direction and in our conscious lives are struggling in another', is caused by conditional love by the parent or significant other:

It is only given on the condition that the child introject certain constructs and values as his own. Otherwise he will not be perceived as worthwhile, as worthy of love. Thus, for example, the construct 'you love your mother' is made a condition for a child receiving her mother's love. Hence her occasional feelings of rage and hatred toward her mother are denied to awareness, as if they did not exist.

Her organism may behave in ways that show her anger, such as spilling her food on the floor, but this is an 'accident'. She does not permit the real feeling into awareness (p. 246).

. . . The dissociated person is best described as one *consciously* behaving in terms of introjected, static, rigid constructs, and *unconsciously* behaving in terms of the actualizing tendency (p.248).

Rogers, would seem, therefore, to embrace the concept of unconscious processes affecting behaviour, but would not agree with Freud that all human behaviour is controlled by 'contents' or 'products of the secondary state' which are known only to the analyst. In the interview with Richard Evans (Evans 1975) Rogers clarifies his position:

. . . I'd prefer to think of a range of phenomena: first, those in sharp focus in awareness right now — the height of consciousness, secondly, a range of material which could be called into consciousness, that you really know and can call into consciousness but you don't have in 'figure' right now it is in the 'ground' or background; then, finally, some phenomena which are more and more dimly connected with awareness, to material that is really prevented from coming into even vague awareness because its coming into awareness would damage the person's concept of himself (p.6).

My use of the word 'unconscious' then complies with Rogers's definition and it is my view that 'unconscious' prejudice would emanate from material both in the second and third categories. My interview with the participant from Focus Group II who said 'most people do not like to admit they are prejudiced' would concur with the notion of that knowledge damaging the person's self-concept (page 31, this volume).

Prejudice

Allport (1954), quotes the New English Dictionary definition as, 'a feeling favourable or unfavourable toward a person or thing, prior to, or not based on, actual experience'. However, as Allport is mainly concerned with ethnic prejudice he argues against the concept of 'positive prejudice'. Interestingly, during my research, Focus Group II had a lot to say about it and recognised it as a possible block to empathy. Rupert Brown (1995) too, ignores the possibility of 'positive prejudice' in his definition:

The holding of derogatory social attitudes or cognitive beliefs, the expression of negative affect, or the display of hostile or discriminatory behaviour towards members of a group on account of their membership of that group (p. 8).

For the purpose of this paper, I would maintain that holding of positive or negative beliefs towards members of a group or 'types' of people without prior experience constitutes prejudice. After reading and discussion, I have reached a conclusion, at least for now, that 'unconscious' prejudice emanates from 'learned' messages from parents or significant others which signify conditional acceptance — 'think like we do, or we won't accept you'. We, therefore, take on board those messages which our parents, or significant others want us to have. Those of us who find our way into the caring professions receive a second message — 'prejudice is wrong — if you are prejudiced you are not acceptable'. So, the natural course is for us to deny our prejudices until, hopefully, we are challenged, usually in our training, and given the opportunity to allow them into our awareness. In the 1959 paper Rogers quotes E.C. Kelley and says, 'Perception is that which comes into consciousness when stimuli, principally, light or sound, impinge on the organism' (*Education in Communication,* 1955).

The research

In research recently conducted for a Masters degree (Fairhurst 1998), I identified factors which block empathic understanding in person-centred therapists and could, therefore, impede the development of a therapeutic relationship. An hypothesis within this focus is that 'unconscious' prejudice, as a block to empathic understanding, is not at the forefront of awareness in person-centred therapists.

The research project consisted of three instruments: A Questionnaire administered to a mixed group of trained client-centred therapists and non client-centred trained therapists, and two Focus Groups of trained client-centred therapists.

The questionnaire responses are summarised below in Figure 1, as a list of factors grouped under three main headings: the therapeutic relationship; factors within the therapeutic relationship; factors external to the therapeutic relationship.

Figure 1. **FACTORS IDENTIFIED AS BLOCKS TO EMPATHY**

1. THE THERAPEUTIC RELATIONSHIP

TIME ELEMENT (4) — stage of relationship; first session; long-term client; break in counselling.

CONNECTEDNESS (5) — therapist need for balanced and stimulated relationship; psychological contact; trust; safety in relationship; human contact.

DIFFERENCE BETWEEN CLIENT & THERAPIST (8) — political and social views; spiritual/psychic relationship; age difference; lack of experience of life situation; cultural difference; language; communication style; race.

COLLUSION (7) — client's view about violence or crime; racism; disability; suicide; client confusing empathy for collusion; not sure when colluding; damage to therapist.

BOUNDARIES (15) — client not accepting; client pushing boundaries; therapist extending boundaries; client manipulating; how much will therapist tolerate; flexible boundaries; client wanting friendship; exchanging gifts; interfering with private life of therapist; denial of unhealthy boundaries; difference between person-centred counselling relationship and friendship; crossing boundaries; client's understanding of boundaries; clarity of boundaries; ethics.

2. FACTORS WITHIN THE THERAPEUTIC RELATIONSHIP

A THE THERAPIST

I Emotional factors in the therapist not in relation to the client (**2**) — how therapist is feeling; anger at a social system.

II Identification of therapist with client (**5**) — unresolved issues which are similar to client's sharing similar experiences; sharing similar life experience; being able to put aside own stuff; being seduced by adulation of client; self-disclosure.

III Therapist emotional response to client (**26**) — boredom; sexual attraction; sexual arousal; fantasising; anger; not liking client; fear of client; intolerance; inhibition; dismissal; panic; responsibility; anxiety; defensiveness; guilt; abused; threatened; unsafe; approval; insular; jealousy; superiority; judgemental; disapproval; shock; horror.

IV Therapist physical condition (**12**) — tiredness; bladder control; hunger; health; over-work; stress; cold; stale; tension; hangover; psychological tension; timing of work.

V Therapist prejudice (**28**) — black people who are aggressive and who have 'chips on their shoulders'; likes and dislikes of characteristics in clients; opinions; reaction to homosexuality; awareness of reaction to sexuality; similarities to father; issues around alcohol abuse; issues around child abuse; clients who show no remorse; gender; class; being unaware of prejudice; people who are in a majority; people with speech impediments; perpetrators of child sexual abuse; people who reveal themselves sexually during counselling session; perpetrators of violence; people who are mentally disturbed; members of the NF; anti-semitism; people who exploit children; football fans; aggressive people; facial disfigurement; racism; people with criminal records; rapists; blind spots.

VI Therapist's attitude to self (**7**) — lack of experience; lack of conviction about CCT; too young; insecurity; conditions of worth; self-respect; self-confidence.

VII Therapist need (**49**) — to control client; not to be nervous; expectations of client 'improvement'; to help; not to get hooked into 'conversational' chatter; for the clients not to pre-empt their own solutions; for the clients not to deflect therapist responses; for the clients to be focussed; clients not to go too fast; clients not to be anxious about closeness; clients not to be dependent; trying to be clever; finding the client's answers first; to be appreciated; to filter responses; being chosen; being competitive with other counsellors; inner processing; to maintain a separateness from client's world; pushing too hard; being too real; holding on to inappropriate clients; not able to be congruent; fear of contaminating client's material with own; for clarity about self; for self-acceptance; to deny own shortcomings; to be transparent inappropriately; not to be judged by client; to trust the client; to be prepared for difficult material; to be focussed; to self-disclose; to express own emotions; to be able to cope with client; to be careful with client; to protect client; to demonstrate presence; to relax; clearing the air; to approve; to reassure; to promote the directional tendency; to feel concerned; to be theoretically correct; not to be conditional; to disapprove; to raise expectations; to disengage.

VIII Therapist need to express empathic understanding (**1**)

B THE CLIENT

1 Factors they bring (**30**) — clients who/who are: guarded against me; defensive; hostile; determined to keep their emotions at bay; of certain ethnic groups; smell; attractive; unattractive; physically threatening; violent; smoking; psychotic; have unpleasant disorders; boring; mad; bizarre; chaotic; dysfunctional; men; women; seductive; young; difficult; have expectations; intellectually superior; sexually threatening; counsellors; trained killers; bring their own world; bringing their belief system.

II Client prejudice (**2**) — racism; gender-based prejudice.

III Client behaviour (**3**) — demonstration of uncleanliness; fidgeting; tapping.

IV Client behaviour in relation to therapist (**11**) — pushes away; anger; aggression; rudeness; frustration; identification; sexual advances; put-downs; makes demands; makes digs; puts therapist on pedestal.

V Client content (**23**) — long silences; the presenting issue; repetitive pattern; lying; game playing; conversational; trivial; superficial; blackmailing; appalling; referring continually to the past; sexually abusive to therapist; third person; need for therapist to solve problems; overwhelming; knowledge of personalities concerned; shocking; violence; not talking about feelings; material including revelation about harm to third person; out of context; threatening to therapist; that hooks therapist's prejudices.

C FACTORS INTERNAL TO THE THERAPEUTIC RELATIONSHIP BUT EXTERNAL TO THE SESSION (7) — client has been sent; client does not want to be in counselling; client forgets to come; client is late; contracting; one-offs; contact between sessions.

3. FACTORS EXTERNAL TO THE THERAPEUTIC RELATIONSHIP

A ENVIRONMENTAL

1 General (**6**) — safety; size of the room; security; noise; interruptions; warmth.

II Home visits (**5**) — disruptive children; personal safety; not knowing the situation in advance; threatening situations; being in the family situation.

III Working at home (**7**) — threatening clients; family in house; too small; feeling of invasion; being alone in house; interruptions; being in own home.

B ORGANISATIONAL (9) — responsibility for success of service; responsibility for people who support; no control; personal safety; conflicting schools of therapy; professional responsibility; policy of agency; assessment procedures; clients in work situation.

C EXTERNAL INFLUENCES ON THE CLIENT (6) — other therapist; assessment; faith healer; specialist; psychiatrist; friends.

Total factors: 270

There are many ways in which the findings in this project could be analysed further, however, readers might be interested from the general point of view of comparing with their own experience, or using the list for discussion in training situations. Here, I will confine myself to identifying a few of the most obvious areas for discussion.

The list of factors is not intended to be definitive, but rather representative of client-centred therapists working in a range of situations. However, one important manifestation of certain of the identified factors, was not mentioned: namely, therapist asking questions. A possible reason for this omission could be that the participants in the focus groups were experienced, well-trained client-centred, therapists, whereas the questionnaire respondents were a mixed group and therefore not so representative of a well trained client-centred group. As a trainer, I have found that counsellors who have trained in counselling skills courses purporting to be person-centred have been advised that a 'technique' in counselling is to ask 'open-ended' questions, and without knowing the training background of the participants in the questionnaire, it could be that they would not identify asking questions as a manifestation of a block to empathy. Some of the factors identified which could lead to this behaviour would be:

- stage of relationship (therapist seeking information);
- break in counselling;
- cultural difference;
- therapist need to control;
- therapist need to help.

It is my view that whenever a therapist asks a question, particularly *about* feelings, such as 'How are you feeling now?' she takes the client out of their feelings into 'cognitive mode'. It could also be a method the therapist employs to control the level at which the work progresses (usually unknowingly). For example, if a client is talking about an issue which is close to the therapist's unresolved material, an effective way of avoiding going too deeply into content is to ask questions about the client's process.

Asking questions also results in 'therapist direction' which is in opposition to 'entering the client's world'. An exception to this position is usually 'questions asked for clarity' and, of course, occasionally it is important for the client that the therapist is clear about what they are saying. However, as explored in the section on 'Empathy' it is important that the client *feels* understood. A therapist who is continually asking questions (even for the sake of clarity) is giving a message: 'You are not understandable', so whichever of the factors are present and which are causing the therapist to ask questions, they need to be identified and dealt with.

Although I do not intend to attempt to quantify the order of interest or importance of the factors identified (this is a qualitative research project), it became evident that 'The Need of the Therapist to Verbalise Empathic Understanding' was of great interest to the first Focus Group. This raises important points for this paper. In his 1959 paper, after proposing the six necessary and sufficient conditions of the therapeutic process, Rogers says:

> The point which is most likely to be misunderstood is the omission
> of any statement that the therapist *communicates* his empathic
> understanding . . . to the client. Such a statement has been omitted
> only after much consideration, for these reasons. It is not enough for

the therapist to communicate, since the communication must be received . . . to be effective. It is not essential that the therapist *intend* such communication, since often it is by some casual remark, or involuntary facial expression, that the communication is actually achieved. However, if one wishes to stress the communicative aspect which is certainly a vital part of the living experience, then condition six might be worded in this fashion:

> *That the communication to the client of the therapist's empathic understanding . . . is, at least to a minimal degree, achieved.*

He was certainly right about the point being misunderstood.

A second important point raised in the first Focus Group was that of being 'too empathic' and the example was given of the therapist 'reducing macho young men to tears, challenging their masculinity and taking away all their identity of a really hard, tough person, man'. I would agree that this is a good example of a situation where the need of the therapist to express empathic understanding blocks the *client's receiving* any empathy which might be present. I would further suspect that in this particular case (involving recounting experience of child sexual abuse), the therapist was focussing on the content of what the client was saying and missing the feelings (or lack of them) being expressed in the moment.

When I suggested in my original hypothesis that 'unconscious' prejudice, as a block to empathic understanding, is not at the forefront of awareness in person-centred therapists, I was not implying that client-centred therapists *deny* the presence of 'unconscious' prejudice. Rather, that such a possibility is not at the height of awareness for many and is, therefore, either not considered when encountering problems in their work, or recognised as an unintentional method of directing clients. From the 28 responses to the questionnaire, four expressed the possibility that there might be something in their own 'unconsciousness' which could block their empathy and a further nine mentioned that they were aware of their own prejudices.

In Focus Group I (see Figure 2.), seven statements were made about therapist prejudice before I 'funnelled' them into the area, of which, five could have had implications of a possible 'unconscious' element. After the 'funnel', a further 48 statements were made about therapist prejudice, but it was not until after the end of the structured group, when I declared my interest, that two comments were made around their possible 'unconscious' prejudice.

In Focus Group II, 49 statements were made about therapist prejudice before the funnel, of which 13 included a possible element of 'unconscious' prejudice, 84 additional statements were made after the funnel, which included 54 around possible 'unconscious' elements. One further comment was made after the structured group — 'Whether we like it or not, most of us do it a lot of the time'. It needs to be mentioned that in this group, there was one participant who seemed particularly interested in his 'unawareness' and determinedly returned to the topic, again and again. In fact he made an appointment to speak with me and said that he

Figure 2. *Number of Statements per Category*

Category	Quest-ionn-aire	Focus Grp I	Focus Grp II	Total
1 THE THERAPEUTIC RELATIONSHIP				
A TIME ELEMENT	None	12	02	14
B CONNECTEDNESS	05	04	02	11
C DIFFERENCE BETWEEN CLIENT & THERAPIST	02	37	None	39
D COLLUSION	02	24	19	45
E BOUNDARIES	None	21	78	99
2 FACTORS WITHIN THE THERAPEUTIC RELATIONSHIP				
A THE THERAPIST				
I Emotional Factors in the Therapist, not in Relation to the Client	None	14	03	17
II Identification of Therapist with Client	03	29	31	63
III Therapist Emotional Response to Client	05	37	50	92
IV Therapist Physical Condition	01	22	18	41
V Therapist Prejudice	18	58	133	209
VI Therapist Attitude to Self	02	20	35	57
VII Therapist Need	12	36	154	202
VIII Therapist Need to Express Empathic Understanding	1	146	20	167
B THE CLIENT				
I Factors they Bring	19	23	14	56
II Client Prejudice	None	20	33	53
III Client Behaviour	None	10	None	10
IV Client Behaviour in Relation to Therapist	08	33	01	42
V Client Content	10	50	10	70
C FACTORS INTERNAL TO THE THERAPEUTIC RELATIONSHIP BUT EXTERNAL TO SESSION	02	12	01	15
3 FACTORS EXTERNAL TO THERAPEUTIC RELATIONSHIP				
A ENVIRONMENTAL				
I General	01	13	02	16
II Home Visits	01	27	None	28
III Working at Home	None	10	14	24
B ORGANISATIONAL	None	26	None	26
C EXTERNAL INFLUENCES ON THE CLIENT	None	08	None	08

felt one of the 'problems' is that most people don't like to admit that they are prejudiced. We talked for a while about different sorts of prejudice, sharing personal experiences, and I said that I felt that I had suffered more from prejudice around class than from sexism — he looked surprised, and said, 'How would you have experienced sexism as prejudice?' After I had given him a few examples he said, somewhat sheepishly, 'You know, Irene, when we started talking, I wouldn't have thought of sexism as prejudice, but now I think about it, of course it is.' I feel he illustrated his own point! Possibly, as a male, he was not aware of his own prejudice around sexism and how that might have affected his therapeutic relationships.

Conclusion

I struggled and searched inside myself to find how my own empathy relates to my empathic understanding of my clients. I believe I discovered a model which is true for me, which was informed by my extensive reading around the issue. This work will change the way I introduce trainees to the concepts in future and also will inform my work with supervisees, as well as enhancing my own work with clients.

In my explorations (often informal) with dozens of people around these issues of blocks to empathy and 'unconscious' prejudice, I feel I have confirmed for myself that for a significant number of client-centred therapists the concept is a new one and that it does exist within themselves.

References

Allport, G.W. (1954) *The Nature of Prejudice* (3rd edition). USA: Addison Wesley.

Barrett-Lennard, G.T. (1981) The Empathy Cycle: Refinement of a Nuclear Concept. *Journal of Counseling Psychology.* Vol.28, No.2.

Barrett-Lennard, G.T. (1986) The Relationship Inventory Now: Issues and Advances in Theory, Method, and Use. Reprinted from *The Psychotherapeutic Process: A Research Handbook*, Greenberg, L.S. and Pinsof, W.M. (Eds). New York: Guilford Press.

Bozarth, J. (1984) Beyond Reflection: Emergent Modes of Empathy in *Client Centered Therapy and the Person Centered Approach,* Levant R.F. and Shlien J. M. (Eds). New York: Praeger.

Brown, R.(1995) *Prejudice: Its Social Psychology*. Blackwell.

Buber, M. (1933) *Between Man and Man.* London: Kegan Paul.

Buber, M.(1958)*I And Thou* (2nd edition). Edinburgh: T & T Clark.

Davis, Mark H. (1994) *Empathy: A Social Psychological Approach.* Brown & Benchmark.

Evans, Richard I. (1975) *Carl Rogers: The Man and His Ideas.* New York: E.P. Dutton.

Freud, S. (1949) *An Outline of Psychoanalysis.* (J. Strachey, Trans.) Norton.

Freud, S. and Breuer, J. (1974) 3 Studies on Hysteria, in *The Pelican Freud Library* Richards, A. (ed.) London: Penguin.

Marcia, J. (1994) Empathy and Psychotherapy, in *Empathy and Its Development.* Eisenberg, N. and Strayer. Cambridge: Cambridge University Press.

McLeod, J. (1994) *Doing Counselling Research.* London: Sage Publications.

Neville, B. (1994) Five Kinds of Empathy. In *Client-Centered and Experiential Psychotherapy: A Paradigm in Motion.* Hutterer, R., Pawlowsky, G., Schmid, P.F. and Stipsits, R. (Eds). Frankfurt: Lang, 1996.

Plutchik, R. (1994) Evolutionary Bases of Empathy. In *Empathy and Its Development.* Eisenberg, N. and Strayer, J. (Eds). Cambridge:Cambridge University Press.

Raskin, N. (1947) The Nondirective Attitude. Unpublished paper.

Rogers, C.R. (1951) *Client-Centered Therapy, Its Current Practice, Implications and Theory.* London: Constable.

Rogers, C.R. (1959) Therapy, Personality, and Interpersonal Relationships. In *Psychology: A Study of a Science, Study I. Conceptual and Systematic, Vol.3. Formulations of the Person and the Social Context.* Koch S. (Ed). McGraw-Hill.

Rogers, C.R. (1978) *On Personal Power.* London: Constable.

Rogers, C.R. (1980) Empathic: An Unappreciated Way of Being. In *A Way of Being.* Boston: Houghton Mifflin.

Rogers, C.R. (1986) Reflection of Feelings and Transference. In *Person-Centred Review* Vol.1.No.4. New York: Sage.

Seeman, J. (1995) *A Human-System Model of Psychotherapy)* Paper delivered at the Annual Meeting of the Association for the Development of the Person-Centered Approach, Tampa, Fl.

Seeman, J. (1996) On Connectedness: A Review and Essay. *The Person-Centered Journal, Vol3, No.1.* USA: Elliott & Fitzpatrick, Inc.

Shlien, J.(1997) Empathy in Psychotherapy: A vital mechanism? Yes. Therapist's conceit? All too often. By itself enough? No. In *Empathy Reconsidered.* Bohart, A. and Greenberg, L.(Eds) Washington: APA.

Temener Brodley, B.(1992) Empathic Understandings and Feelings in Client-Centered Therapy. In *The Person-Centered Journal. Vol.1.No. 1.*

Warner, M. S. (1994) How does Empathy Cure? A Theoretical Consideration of Empathy, Processing and Personal Narrative. In *Client-Centered and Experiential Psychotherapy: A Paradigm in Motion.* Hutterer, R., Pawlowsky, G., Schmid, P.F. and Stipsits, R. (Eds) Frankfurt: Lang, 1996.

Wispé L. (1987) History of the Concept of Empathy' In *Empathy and Its Development.* Eisenberg N. and Strayer, J. Cambridge: Cambridge University Press, 1994.

The photograph was taken at the ball held at the First World Congress for Psychotherapy in Vienna. I was enjoying myself, relaxing and dancing with good friends — integrating business and pleasure in the best ways possible.

CHALLENGE AND THE PERSON-CENTRED APPROACH

4

MARY KILBORN

Introduction

Challenge is not a term that is often heard in relation to the person-centred approach. It was not, to my knowledge, used by Rogers. Person-centred practitioners aim, on the whole, to take a warm and accepting stance rather than a challenging one. For them, empathy means entering the inner world of the client and moving around in it with ease; unconditional positive regard means valuing the person of the client whatever the attitudes and behaviour. The therapist is concerned to understand and respect the client's frame of reference, without imposing her/his own. Challenge, however, must perforce stem from the therapist's frame of reference. The therapist is using her/his perception of reality to react to that of the client's. This is covered by the third condition, that of congruence, which enables the therapist to monitor her/his experiencing in the session and to share it with the client if s/he feels it to be beneficial to the therapeutic process. The therapist can therefore offer feedback on the 'here and now' in a session. However, as Germain Lietaer (1984) points out, this can involve a loosening of the client-centred principles of continuously staying in the experiential field of the client. There can therefore be a tension between unconditional positive regard and many forms of challenge.

The aim of the study

As a person-centred practitioner, I aim very much to stay within the experiential field of the client. Does this mean that I feel unable to challenge my clients? Person-centred therapy is often criticised for being too 'soft', for not really addressing all the issues, the therapists for being too self-effacing and not really committed. How often have I heard therapists from other orientations say that they take a person-centred approach, then they use further techniques and understanding to get on with the real business of therapy! Many would see challenge as one of their tools. Person-centred therapists will know how hard it is to show that the core conditions are indeed sufficient and that the approach is by no means as 'soft' as it appears.

With these issues in mind, I concluded it would be very beneficial to my practice if I focused on the question of challenge, to find out more about just how challenging I am as a therapist and how beneficial this is to my clients. I planned a small-scale research study.

Preparing the study

I decided I would collect data from two sources, clients and other person-centred therapists.

I wanted to find out how challenging my clients perceived me to be and whether they welcomed this or not. I also wanted to collect the views of other person-centred therapists on the role of challenge in the person-centred approach.

I decided to collect my data in the form of a questionnaire. I felt this would be the most effective and allow the respondents to reply at their leisure. I made the questions as open as possible in the hope that those answering would be able to bring in their own ideas and not feel in any way directed. I explained that I wanted a personal response and was not looking for specific answers.

I approached 15 clients to respond to my questionnaire. These were all clients who had been working with me for a while (all over six months). I knew that being asked by your therapist to give feedback would have an influence on the counselling process and I wanted to ensure as much as possible that the impact would be beneficial rather than detrimental. I felt that the clients who had not worked with me for a long time might find a questionnaire on challenge a rather threatening experience. I carefully explained the aims of the study to each client at the end of a session and made it clear that there was no obligation to take part. In the event, all the clients whom I asked responded, some quicker than others, and a number of them used their response to the questionnaire as a basis for discussion concerning our relationship and our work together. Some of them claimed that taking part in the study had made them think and helped them focus on the counselling process. A couple of them said they had found the openness of the questions difficult and they had not always been sure what to say.

A small sample of therapists was chosen, therapists known to me and therapists I work closely with. Rather than a broad spread, I aimed to get the views of therapists with whose practice I was familiar and who would be able to respond to the open nature of the questions. The number who filled in the questionnaire was ten.

Client questionnaires and responses

• *Client Question 1: Person-centred counselling/therapy is sometimes criticised for being 'soft', too warm and accepting. Can you say something of your experience?*

This opening question to the clients led to very similar responses. They all felt the 'warm and accepting' nature of the approach to be beneficial. One put it rather graphically: 'I need warmth and acceptance to help heal the brutal emotional assault that has taken place inside my body'. Another commented that 'Feeling that my way of being is valued has enabled me to feel safe enough to explore possible changes in myself and my relationships'. However, they all rejected the word 'soft'. One client commented she had felt uncomfortable in the earlier sessions: 'just being accepted and cared for'. She had come, nevertheless, to experience the safety of the warmth and acceptance as 'powerfully enabling'. Another client said she had struggled with feeling that counselling was an indulgence, that she needed someone to tell her to 'pull my socks up and get on with it'. Such a feeling, however, did not come from the type of counselling being too accepting and soft but from her inability to accept herself.

One of the clients pointed out that he needed not only warmth and acceptance but also 'transparency — genuineness — truth and if this means contradicting the client, then so be it. The honesty will be appreciated.' This client was prepared to risk what he called the counsellor 'contradicting' him in his desire for a real relationship with his counsellor. He said that the counsellor 'agreeing with everything and smiling at the appropriate moments is not enough'. Another client said that the acceptance had been very important in helping her in her struggle to accept herself and that now she was looking for more of a two-way process, for a feeling that we are 'looking at things together'. These two clients were making it clear that empathy and unconditionality are necessary but not enough. They also want congruence and a sense of mutuality between counsellor and client.

Two clients alluded to the non-directive nature of the counselling. One said 'being denied direction and conditionality is not a soft option for me. It is the most difficult task that I have ever faced — to reconsider my values and expectations.' Another client: 'My difficulty with person-centred therapy is not that it is too soft but that it leaves the direction entirely up to me. This leaves me fearful that I am going round in a circular path.'

The general view was that the warmth and acceptance offered a challenge in themselves. One client saw it in terms of confronting herself and said, along with a number of other respondents, that this was the hardest thing she had ever done.

- *Client Question 2: Do you feel that I challenge or confront you in any way? If possible, give examples and say how you experienced this.*

A number of the respondents added to the responses to Question 1 by stating that the approach itself was challenging to them. As one put it: 'Your whole approach challenges my own life experience of trusting others'. Another introduced the concept of love: 'Mary, your unconditional love challenges me to the very core of my being'. A further client stated that 'the challenge is in the acceptance . . . as bits of me emerge and are accepted even when these are the bits that fight against me being there in the first place and that become frustrated with all my circling around and angry because you just let me drift'. The theme of the client taking the helm, choosing the direction, came up again and again. Clients found it a real challenge that I, the therapist, stay with them on their circular path, allowing them to find a way of moving on. I would like to say here that although a client may feel s/he is going round in circles, I, the therapist, may not have the same perception. The 'circles' are always slightly different, with the client revisiting the same subject from a slightly altered angle.

Although most clients felt comfortable with the concept of challenge, a number thought that the word 'confrontation' was too strong: they do not see our meeting in terms of confrontation. As another put it: 'I am not aware of being challenged or confronted in a conscious or deliberate way, although I have come to expect a consistent level of integrity in Mary which encourages me to look squarely at each issue as it arises'. Again, the suggestion arose that the task is not an easy one.

What interested me by the responses to this question was that, on occasions, clients do feel that I am the one who is challenging their way of being, or at least holding up what they say for them to look at. I am not seen as confronting in the traditional sense or arguing or putting a different point of view, but rather by encouraging the clients to question themselves. One client felt that I sometimes reflect back with a questioning tone of voice, which makes her consider what she has said and reflect more on her 'attitude'. This sounds like me offering an invitation for the client to challenge herself.

One client said I challenged quite subtly: 'when I have tended to drift off in head-thought rather than hanging onto gut feelings of where I am. It has been helpful almost always to be shown that this is what seems to be happening.' Another client spoke of my having pointed out her tendency to focus on others in the sessions and she took this challenge as permission to stay with herself. It seems that my challenge in these cases came in the form of 'here and now' reflections.

Whereas the above two clients stated they felt the challenge to be beneficial, another spoke of my having, on one occasion, brought 'realism' into the discussion. She had been talking of how unbearable her life at work was for her and how she would have to leave. I must have lost my focus, as I apparently made some remark about her having to live without a salary. Not surprisingly, she noted that she was not sure that what she called my 'rational challenge' helped at a deeper level!

What has particularly interested me in the responses has been how clients have a vivid memory of any time they have felt challenged by me, whether they have felt the challenge to be useful or not. This shows me the importance of creating a safe, trusting environment where clients feel held and supported in the challenge, able to share what the challenge has meant to them.

• *Client Question 3: Would you welcome it if I challenged or confronted you more? Can you give reasons?*

Two clients gave a resounding 'no' to this question. One client put it thus: 'I don't think I could cope with more challenge or confrontation from you or our relationship'. Another put it in terms of having failed in many of life's situations. She sees counselling as a means of achieving a greater degree of self-acceptance and she does not feel she would get this through my challenging her. These two clients find the counselling challenging enough as it is!

A lot of the clients felt that I had the balance about right. Quite a few spoke of the importance of having enough trust in the relationship to accept challenge. One client who gave a tentative 'yes' to welcoming more challenge put the rider: 'Just be genuine and try to empathise whilst you are challenging me!' He added that he wanted me to give more of myself away, which would help him understand where the challenge was coming from. He also commented that he wanted challenge only to help him get deeper into feelings not as a basis for an intellectual debate. Another client, who was not sure whether she wanted more challenge or not, said what she was looking for was the opportunity to test 'the real me'.

One thing, which stood out from the answers to this question, was that many clients had mixed views. They did and did not want more challenge at the same time. Some felt almost that they *ought* to want it. 'There is some part of me that thinks my participating in counselling could be justified if it were more "painful"!' Another put it this way: 'Sometimes I think so, but then you would be playing the role of the authority figure, which seems to be such a big part of my anxieties. In fact, what makes the relationship unique is that it is "authority neutral".' For one client, who was getting very frustrated with what she perceived as going round in circles, 'Challenge to get on with it would be enough'. She then added: 'But I realise that I would then lose all respect for you, because I would have won yet again, discovered your conditionality'. These three answers give an indication as to just how delicate the balance is and how important it is for clients to trust the relationship with the counsellor. The responses also show an awareness on the part of some clients as to how their reactions to me offer them more self-awareness.

> • *Client Question 4: Have you ever felt I have challenged or confronted you because I was considering my own opinions or point of view rather than yours? How was this for you?*

The answers to this question were very varied. A number felt I did not do this and that if I ever offered a point of view, I was careful to acknowledge that it was mine. One client felt that it only happened on the occasions when my reflecting back had not been accurate and he had then mistakenly taken my reflecting back as an opinion of mine. However, he felt we usually managed to sort it out. Another client remembered a time when I had appeared to be offering an opinion but she felt our ensuing discussion of it had been very beneficial.

One client argued that when I did challenge from what appeared to be my own point of view, I come across as more human! 'You sometimes seem a little apologetic about using your own form of words to get at what is going on, particularly if you get it wrong. But when it is wrong, you tend to backtrack very quickly and it certainly does not worry me, because I generally see that I am not coming across very clearly and there is some room for working a little harder to get closer to whatever it is'.

In fact, a number of clients felt that getting something of me helped them know me better, that my getting something wrong often brought us closer together. One client said he would prefer it to be 'a little more two-way' but then added: 'that is probably because I have not yet completely let go of seeking approval'.

A couple of clients could remember specific times when they had felt I had been coming from my own opinions, my own reality. One client, whom I have found very challenging to me, felt, on the occasions when our perceptions of what was happening between us differed, that I was saying to her 'speak for yourself'. She said that made her feel very alone.

Another client spoke of a time when she had felt I was reacting from my own opinion. She spoke in terms of a stumbling block between us: 'I felt alienated from you. I had little self-esteem to see me through this sense of total alienation. I felt under pressure to live up to your expectations, afraid of disappointing you.' This indeed sounds very strong, yet at the time I had no idea that the client was feeling this.

Finally, a client spoke of the occasion I had said something like: 'So you are not sure you want to have a baby with him?' The client experienced this as out of context, out of the blue, something that had not come out of what she had been saying. Again, I was unaware at the time of the impact this had had on the client.

What was really encouraging about the feedback was that clients, by filling in the questionnaire, had been able to realise which of my responses they had had trouble with and not forgotten. It enabled us to focus on these occasions and strengthened our relationship. However, it also shows that a comment which the therapist may see as a reflection, can be seen by the client as a challenge and even the personal opinion of the therapist. As one client put it: 'Sometimes I think your responses are not so consciously thought through or deliberate'. Although I feel that I *do* try to monitor every response, it would appear that I do say things that may not always come from heightened awareness!

• *Client Question 5: I aim to be open and genuine with you. Is this your experience of me? Can you mention any times when you have felt this to be challenging?*

The general response to this was that I *am* experienced as open and genuine. As one client expressed it: 'Your being open and genuine is a constant feature of our relationship'. Or another: 'Oh, Mary, you're as open and genuine with me as I think possible for you to be and sure, that often is very challenging. Basically it challenges me to be open and genuine with you, it challenges me to risk being myself and that is both terrifying and exhilarating and ultimately very liberating.'

Other clients were not quite so enthusiastic. One said: 'I have no sense of whether this is empathy from the depths of you or simply you just being good at your job. I suspect both combined, the one being necessary for the other.' *I* find such a comment very challenging, one which makes me look closely at the level of empathy I am offering this client!

Another client admitted to finding my constant acceptance a bit 'unreal'. She said: 'I know I feel more relaxed when you share bits of your own weaknesses or fears with me but this doesn't happen very often'. It would appear that it helps this client to know something of my own vulnerabilities.

One client who said he experienced me as open and genuine added: 'But sometimes I think you are feeling something, say for example, a little anxious and you don't talk or say anything about it . . . Then again, *I* sometimes have so little trust that I need people to scream, two inches from my face: "I am being genuine" before I can believe them.' Here it would seem that the client felt he was picking up anxiety from me and yet he was not sure whether it was his anxiety or mine.

The majority said that they did find my openness and genuineness challenging but not in an uncomfortable way. However, one client referred to the time I had acknowledged that something she had said had affected me quite powerfully: 'This presupposes a relationship between you and me and this necessitates a challenge to me of having to accept my responsibility and power to affect others, rather than being "a *passive* client"'.

Another client spoke of how challenging she found it that I accepted 'this and that part' of her. 'You also say that you don't have the answers. I find that scary and frustrating too! I want answers. Again, maybe that says more about me than you!'

The clients' growing sense of self-awareness was very evident in many of the answers as was the struggle of some of them to determine which was my responsibility and which was theirs.

Therapist questionnaires and responses

• *Therapist Question 1: What place do you think there is for challenge in the person-centred approach?*

All the therapists felt that challenge had an important place in the person-centred approach, indeed the word 'integral' was used by a number of them. 'It creates opportunities for reflection and new understanding' was the way one therapist expressed it; another spoke of it promoting clarity and health in the relationship. The point was made that the aim is for the client to feel the *engagement* of the therapist as a separate person. Challenge may then be accepted as part of an authentic and trusting relationship. Indeed, empathy is an implicit challenge — it basically asks the question 'Is it like this?', inviting the client to empathize with himself, inviting him to confront parts of himself and to relate. One therapist linked challenge specifically to congruence and said that there were times when it was appropriate to confront the client with an experience coming from one's own locus of evaluation. However, a number of the therapists mentioned the need for sensitivity and care and keeping in mind that there is a risk in such an intervention.

Some of the therapists' responses related specifically to particular comments or contributions of their own. However, a number of them pointed out that the challenge comes from the whole approach. As one put it: 'The whole approach is a challenge — to many cultural and societal norms and, often to the whole previous experience of the client'. Many of them linked challenge to the fundamental nature of the core conditions in the approach and this leads us to Question 2.

• *Therapist Question 2: How does challenge fit in with the core conditions?*

Here the therapists were very much in agreement that the core conditions, by their very nature, constituted a challenge to the client. **Unconditional positive regard** challenges the basic assumption that the client is worthless. Clients of low self-esteem may find that the therapist's acceptance increases dissonance and be extremely challenging to their conditions of worth. Deep **empathy** can challenge the assumption that nobody can understand the client. Or as another therapist put it: 'Clients who feel unheard and misunderstood will find this introjected belief constantly challenged by the therapist'. The therapist's **congruence** challenges the basic assumption that others are untrustworthy and unwilling to be involved. For clients with an externalised locus of evaluation, the therapist's congruence offers a powerful confrontation with 'reality'.

One therapist brought in the notion of the client challenging the therapist, saying that she considered it her professional duty not to be on the defensive herself. This opens up the whole area of the challenge of the approach to the person-centred therapist.

• *Therapist Question 3: Do you aim to challenge your clients and in what way do you do this?*

None of the therapists felt that challenge was a specific aim of their therapeutic work but was often perceived as such by the clients. All of them reiterated the need for any kind of challenge coming from the therapist's congruent self to be done in a climate of acceptance and empathy. A number said that there needed to be a high level of trust in the relationship. Another said that the timing had to be right, which links back to one of the clients saying it depends how vulnerable she is feeling as to how much she welcomes a challenge from the therapist.

Opening up the relationship between the client and the therapist can sometimes be perceived as challenging by the client. One therapist said it was her way of positioning herself within the relationship. She would sometimes express directly what she feels or sees or may express an underlying feeling concerning the relationship and then ask the client for feedback. Here she spoke of the need of gentleness.

The conclusion which all the therapists came to was that challenge must come within the context of a trusting relationship in which the core conditions are offered to a high degree. Indeed, challenge then becomes an integral part of the therapy and flows from it.

• *Therapist Question 4: Would you wish to be more or less challenging? Please explain.*

The majority of the therapists stated that they had the balance about right. They did not see challenge as something separate but something that came out of their offering the core conditions.

One therapist expressed it as follows: 'I have learned to trust myself in the way that I am in a therapeutic relationship and that is how it must be for me. It means of course that my personal integrity is at stake all the time in every relationship which is very challenging for me!' Another therapist said that whether he is challenging or not depends on the client: 'If my client's locus of evaluation is very externalised, my challenge is gently through empathy, staying very close to their own expression, but using one part of them to challenge another. If the locus of evaluation is very internalised, my challenge may be flamboyant and even eccentric at times.'

Two therapists said they would like to be more challenging, one with certain clients where she tended to feel protective or responsible for them in some way. She would like to be more forward on this but was aware it felt risky for her. Another therapist saw it more in terms of the quality of his presence: 'I wish to be more challenging in the sense that if I can be fully present to my client, I am more likely to enable both of us to move into the slightly altered state of consciousness where spiritual reality is apprehended'.

• *Therapist Question 5: Can you give examples of when you feel challenge has worked with a client or when you feel it has not?*

Like the clients, the therapists mentioned times which had been particularly significant for them; either times where the challenge had been too much for the client and this had, on occasions, caused the client to leave therapy, or where the challenge had really moved things on. It appears to be a very delicate balance. In retrospect, for example, the therapist may have to concede that the relationship was not robust enough for the level of empathy, acceptance or congruence offered by them. However, at the time they took the chance or risk. Sometimes it is only the challenge of this which can reveal just how much trust there is in the relationship. I would like to end with a comment by one of the therapists on the subject of his anger. As an example of when challenge can work for him, he said that pure, loving anger, congruently expressed, constitutes for him the challenge which was nearly always productive: 'I feel myself enraged at the power within you that threatens to keep you from the truth that you are lovable and loved'.

Conclusion
From this small study, it would appear that challenge, which is not normally associated with the person-centred approach, is an integral part of it. Challenge, not in terms of the therapist confronting the client's reality with her/his own, but

challenge in terms of the opportunities and freedoms offered by the core conditions. As we have noted, the person-centred therapist aims to create an environment in which the client experiences the therapist's empathy and unconditional acceptance so that trust can be built up. The client then feels safe enough to accept the therapist's authenticity, the therapist's positioning her/himself in the relationship. The client can then risk a new way of relating to others and to the self — a new way of being. The ultimate challenge!

References

Lietaer, G. (1984) Unconditional Positive Regard: A controversial basic attitude in client-centered therapy. In Levant, R. and Shlien, J., *Client Centred Therapy and the Person-Centred Approach*: *New directions in theory, research and practice*. New York: Praeger.

My photograph was taken by my daughter at my home. I like it because it shows me relaxing and taking time with someone I love.

In You There Is a Universe: Person-Centred Counselling as a Manifestation of the Breath of the Merciful

5

Mhairi MacMillan

Introduction

During the winter of 1997–8, I spent six months in a school where the writings of the thirteenth century Andalusian Sufi mystic Muhyiddin Ibn al'Arab, were a central element in the course. At first I was struck by many parallels between Ibn 'Arabi's work and the principles of the Person-Centred Approach as set out by Carl Rogers. Subsequently I have come to see them not so much as 'parallels' but as signposts pointing in the same direction, which converge on the Unity, the One from which all being emanates and to which *all* returns. My intention in this chapter is to try to articulate what these two major influences mean to me and whatever synthesis I can make of them.

In so doing, I hope to be able to explore some questions which have arisen for me in relation to the person-centred approach. Carl Rogers asked: 'What permits the therapist to have deep respect for and acceptance of another?' (Rogers, 1951, p. 22). We have become used to reeling off the 'core conditions' (whether three or six) as if their articulation actually explained the reality of the person-centred approach. A noun has been fabricated — 'person-centredness' — as if it were something that has an existence of its own, and can be used as a standard to judge whether people come up to it or not. At this time, I would rather consider: How *does* the Person-Centred Approach *work,* and what is its source?

Unity of Being, Ibn 'Arabi and Carl Rogers

Muhyiddin Ibn al-Arabi was a Sufi mystic whose earthly life spanned the twelfth and thirteenth centuries CE. Known to Sufis as 'the greatest master', *al-shaikh al-akbar*, he brought together in his teaching much that was implicit in the doctrine of earlier Sufi mystics from the time of the Prophet Mohammed onwards. Ibn 'Arabi himself, in teachings made known through the large number of his books and writings that are extant — only some of which are translated into western languages — influenced both eastern and western thought and spirituality down to the present day (Addas, 1993). More and more of his writings and ideas are currently making themselves known.

Ibn 'Arabi's metaphysics — called *wahdat al-wujud*, usually translated as 'Unity of Being' — admits of essentially only one Being, whether existent or non-existent. One of the first problems for our normal minds to grasp is the idea of 'existence' and 'non-existence'. That which is existent (literally, 'standing out') is manifest as a phenomenon in the world, that which is called 'immanent'. That which is non-existent and transcendent remains latent and unknowable.

Here is one description of Unity of Being:

> There is one Reality which reveals or manifests itself in an infinity of forms, not one that produces or creates, or one from which anything other than itself emanates.
>
> The self-revelations of the One, thus understood, are as follows: When we conceive the One as apart from all possible relations and individuations, we say that God has revealed Himself in the state of Unity or is in the Blindness ('ama', non-communication) — the state of the Essence. When we regard it in relation to the potential existence of the phenomenal world, we say that God has revealed Himself in the state of the Godhead. This is the state of the Divine Names. And when we regard it in relation to the actual manifestation of the phenomenal world, we say that God has revealed Himself in the state of Lordship.
>
> (*The Twenty-nine Pages,* Beshara Publications, no date.)

Here is explained how multiplicity emerges from Unity as an array of revelations of Being (or Reality, or Truth or God). Ibn 'Arabi's Sufism (like Islam, in which it is embedded, as well as Judaism and Christianity; and unlike, for example, Buddhism and Taoism) is *theistic*, that is, it embodies a personal God who actively manifests in the world.

Thus, three aspects, or states of Reality (God) are described above. First the totally transcendent aspect — in 'the blindness', like a newborn before its eyes are opened. This is the Essence, sometimes designated the Ipseity or Self of God. The Essence is unmanifest, without quality, and thus cannot be described or known. The second aspect (the 'Godhead') is full of potential, ready — through the 'Divine Names'— for full manifestation.

Thirdly, in the phenomenal world, the aspect of Reality is 'the Lord'. That world, therefore, is in a state of servanthood in regard to God, each created (i.e. manifested) thing being the servant of its own particular Lord. When Ibn 'Arabi uses the term 'Lord' he means that essence which is deep in the interior of a person, not an external, separate entity. A translator of Ibn 'Arabi's Fusus al-Hikam puts it thus: '"Lord" (*rabb*). . . denotes a private and special relationship between a particular creature and its corresponding archetype in divinis' (Austin, 1980, p. 31). The 'archetype in divinis' corresponds to that 'Divine Name' through which a thing is manifest. Ibn 'Arabi also uses the term 'latent (or "fixed") potentiality' (*ayn i thabita*).

Carl Rogers made the following statement in the theoretical paper, 'A Theory of Therapy, Personality and Interpersonal Relations': 'I share with many others the belief that truth is unitary, even though we will never be able to know this unity' (Rogers, 1959, p. 121). Ibn 'Arabi might well have said the same thing.

The Breath of the Merciful — from non-existence to existence

In the Unknowable station of complete Unity, the Reality is 'rich beyond need of the universes'. In this state of Absolute Transcendence, nothing can be said of Him. Why, then, should the universes be brought into existence? A *hadith qudsi* (extra-koranic word of God) states: *'I was a hidden treasure and I loved to be known, so I created the world that I might be known'*. In the poetic language which is necessary to even approximate happenings at this level, another way of saying this is that God (Reality) wished to behold Itself and created the cosmos as a mirror in which Its own reflection might be seen. This desire first caused God to emerge from (but not leave) the Unity. Therefore, *Love* (or longing or desire) is the cause of creation, and *knowledge* ('to be known') is the purpose of creation.

Concomitantly, the process of creation is one in which God's *Mercy* predominates. There is no essential separation between the organismic self, its valuing and its archetype or 'mentation in the mind of God', the *'ayn i thabita'* or 'fixed potentiality'. The myriad of created things (the 'ten thousand things' that the Tao refers to) demand, as the *a'yan i thabita*, to come into existence and God, in response to the demand (which, remember, is from within Himself) releases them on the exhalation of the Breath of the Merciful, *nafs i rahman*.

Ibn 'Arabi's description of this process, necessarily metaphorical, is startlingly akin to the process that occurs within a person in 'giving birth' and to Gendlin's description of the realisation of the 'felt sense' (or client's client, as he calls it) and how the 'change-steps' in therapy come about (Gendlin, 1984).

Compare this description:

> Having stated that the origin of the divine longing to be known is love, he [Ibn 'Arabi] goes on to describe the precreative state of the Reality as one of anxiety or distress (*karb*), of a primordial labour pressing for birth and manifestation. Ibn 'Arabi describes the relieving of the distress as a breathing or sighing (*tanaffus*) which at once expresses and relieves the distress (Austin, 1980, p.28),

with these remarks concerning 'the felt sense':

> While people think of a problem, or have troublesome feelings, they are usually uncomfortable in their bodies This bodily unease turns out to be less intense and not as rough on the person as the strong feeling.
>
> There is typically also a sort of gratitude that comes from this bodily discomfort, as if it were thankful for one's attention (Gendlin, 1984, p. 78),

and,

> When therapy is effective, the client does something more with a

listening response than just checking the words. We hope and assume that clients will check the response . . . against . . . 'the felt sense'. An effect might then be felt, a bit of inward loosening, a resonance . . . For some moments there is an easing inside (Gendlin, 1984, p. 82).

The 'loosening' or 'easing' is often accompanied by an exhalation of breath — analogous to *tanaffus* (see above).

What is implied for the nature of human beings?

In you there is a universe

Every human being is a 'microcosm' of the universe. Each and every individual is created from God's Self and, like a hologram, each fragment also contains the whole. One esoteric axiom is 'as above, so below'; this means that the processes described in 'universal', 'cosmic' or 'God-related' terms, are the same processes that we can observe occurring within ourselves.

> You thought yourself a part, small
> Whereas in you there is a universe, the greatest
> (Ibn 'Arabi, *Kernel of the Kernel*, p. 14).

However well you know yourself, there remain mysteries and hidden — latent or unmanifest — aspects of 'you'. Some of these aspects become apparent if circumstances call them forth: unexpected courage in a time of danger, for example; grieving for the first time; ability to steal, or lie, or kill when it is a necessity. A cruel streak you never knew you had. All the 'highest' and the 'lowest' attributes of a human being are there — in you — but most are latent for most of your life (for most people). Extreme situations, whether entered into voluntarily or, as in most cases, by force of circumstance, can bring out the latent qualities. Wilson (1986) tells how G. I. Gurdjieff pushed his pupils into performing more and more extraordinary tasks. One of these pupils describes a time when he 'was filled with an influx of immense power' in the course of a day which started with him feeling so weak that he could not stand up (Bennett, 1974). A more usual example is the experience of an athlete who must break through the pain barrier to produce a great performance. The greatest 'veil' over these unmanifest aspects is your self-concept or conditioned self, what or who you 'think' you are.

Humanity's special place

There are two primary implications for the nature of human beings. The first is that humankind holds a special place in the universes, standing as the bridge or isthmus — which both joins and separates — the unseen world (which is our origin and from where revelations are continually coming) and the world of phenomena, the material world of which we are part and on which we also depend. Humanity is the synthesis of 'spirit' and 'nature', and in this resides the dignity of humankind. Without this synthesis, humanity is an absurdity.

The created world (cosmos) enables God to see God. The metaphor of the mirror is central. It is said: 'In the mirror of the universe He sees His reflection and in the mirror of Adam [humanity] He looks upon Himself exactly and sees Himself' (*Kernel of the Kernel*, p.46). Humanity, in its highest state, is the vice-regent of God (*khalifa*), that is, God's representative in the cosmos.

> Man is the highest and most venerable creature God ever created.
> He should be guarded and honoured, for 'he who takes care of Man
> takes care of God' (*Twenty-nine Pages*, p. 19).

Most of us forget this or are only dimly aware of it. The Great Ones of Humanity — for example, Moses, Buddha, Mary, Jesus, Mohammed — were fully aware of their status as representatives of Truth in the world. As are those known as a 'True Human Being' or 'Perfect Man', those who are the perfect servants.

Human beings are uniquely placed to receive the knowledge that is constantly sent out from the Unknowable to the phenomenal world. This is not philosophical or 'head' knowledge but the knowledge of the heart intuitively received. Such intuitive knowledge is valued by mystical traditions and largely undervalued in contemporary intellectual circles and education systems. As an example of an exercise designed to stimulate the heart as a receptor of knowledge, Assagioli (cited in Neville, 1989, p. 235) suggested that one meditate on the words 'I know'.

Although in person-centred counselling, 'reflection' has been somewhat downgraded (see, for example, Rogers, 1980: chapter 7), one function of a person-centred therapist is to act as a mirror for the client and to reflect without the colour of interpretation or the distortion of personal bias. Such reflecting is a far from easy thing to do, and can be both a most challenging and releasing event for any client; really looking at oneself in a mirror can be a true confrontation with oneself.

No independent 'self'

Who am I? A person may find themselves addressing this fundamental question about identity many times in their lives. There are many responses to it concerning different aspects of identity — personal, social, cultural, 'false', 'true' and so on. Ibn 'Arabi distinguishes all constructed identities ('selves') — who one 'thinks' one is — from the essential identity which is none other than the One Being, God.

> Thou thoughtest, a-thinking, that thou wast thou,
> And thou art not thou and never wast thou.
> For if thou wert thou, then wert thou a Lord
> And a second of Two. Leave what thou art thinking.
> There is no difference between the beings of Him and Thee:
> He is not distinct from Thee nor Thou from Him.
> (Ibn 'Arabi, 1976, p.19)

There is no separate, individual 'self' that does not depend on Reality for its existence, sustenance and support. The most obvious way in which we are dependent is that we have no power over when we are born and when we die.

The 'self' and the nafs

Of course, our usual experience in the world is that of being an individual self or 'soul'. In Sufism, the word for 'self' and 'soul' is the same — *nafs*. *Nafs* is a complex idea with many aspects, the two most relevant in this discussion being the 'animal soul' and the 'conditioned self'. The *nafs* is needed as a vehicle for us to traverse the physical world. It is not, however, our 'real' self and may (in fact, does) prevent the real self's realisation, just as the conditioned self-concept can prevent the clear experiencing of the organismic self from coming into awareness.

The self in person-centred theory

One of the earliest published attempts of Carl Rogers to define the 'self' is in chapter 11 — 'A theory of personality and behaviour' — in *Client-Centered Therapy* (Rogers, 1951). Rogers clearly found it difficult to produce an entirely satisfactory definition: he tells us that he had revised and reworded propositions IX and X (which deal with the self) over several years, and had still not reached an adequate statement. Nevertheless his ideas about the self have proved both extremely durable and remarkably useful over the years in developing theory, and have been tested and ratified in practice.

The 'self-structure' is, Rogers writes, a 'fluid, but consistent conceptual pattern', formed 'as a result of interaction with the environment . . . and with others'. He separates out values attached to 'direct organismic experiencing' and 'distorted perception of introjected values'. Later, the phrase 'conditions of worth' takes over from 'introjected values' (Rogers, 1959, p. 225). Rogers emphasises again that 'reality' for the infant (and for any person) is that person's perception of their environment, internal and external, and is indeed 'of his own creation . . . regardless as to how this relates to some "real" reality which we may philosophically postulate'.

'Know thyself'

Most people live in a world of their own creation most of the time in accordance with their socialised or 'conditioned' self-structure. This is the 'theatre' in which the unique essential self lives out its Reality in the phenomenal world. But Ibn 'Arabi quotes the *hadith* (saying of the Prophet Mohammed) 'Whoso knoweth himself knoweth his Lord', meaning that if you 'know' your essential self, your true reality, you know 'your Lord', the inner core of guidance.

Traditionally, steps involved in knowing yourself include:
- To be able to separate out — distinguish between — the 'essential self' and the 'conditioned self'. Or, in counselling terms, between the 'self-concept' and the 'organismic self-experience'.
- To acknowledge and discipline (lovingly) the 'animal soul' — bodily and psychological appetites and drives.
- To challenge (and loosen) the self-concept (who you 'think you are') and aim to surrender it completely.

This is primarily a process of 'disidentification' or 'dying to what you thought you were'. A modern psychological variant describes the following steps:

I *have* a body but I *am not* my body

I *have* emotions but I *am not* my emotions

I *have* a mind but I *am* not my mind

(Assagioli, 1990, pp. 215–6).

Assagioli suggests that what 'remains after having disidentified myself from my body, my sensations, my feelings, my desires, my mind, my actions' is 'the essence of myself — a center of pure *self-consciousness*' (Assagioli, 1990, p. 216, italics in original).

The 'ego' (or self-concept) is a good servant, but a bad master, it is said. The conditioned self is necessary for survival in this world, so it is not a matter of getting rid of it. The Dalai Lama's words and Ibn 'Arabi's are strikingly similar on this point:

> Selflessness is not a case of something that existed in the past becoming nonexistent. Rather, this sort of 'self' is something that never did exist. What is needed is to identify as non-existent something that always was non-existent (Tenzin Gyatso, 1984; cited in Epstein, 1996, p. 98).

> For the knowledge of God does not presuppose the ceasing of existence nor the ceasing of that ceasing. For things have no existence and what does not exist cannot cease to exist. Then, if thou know thyself without existence or ceasing to be, then thou knowest God; and if not, then not (Ibn al-Arabi, 1976, p. 5).

This is not easy, as anyone who has tried to get out of the grip of the self-concept knows! 'Beware the dynamics of self-concept change' (Mearns, 1994: chapter 22) In Sufi terms, the self-concept may be worked on to change little by little until surrendered completely in Truth or Reality (alternative terms for 'God'). That is: 'Die before you die'. Self-concept change can be viewed as a primarily psychological process, whether the change is gradual or 'seismic' (Mearns, 1994, p. 92). The 'death' of the self (self-concept) is a spiritual process of mystical dimensions not granted to (or sought by) many.

> The man of knowledge in these affairs is lost and buried in nothingness . . . All the qualities inside him and outside him are changed. That day the earth becomes another earth, equally the skies . . . (Ibn 'Arabi, *Kernel of the Kernel*, p. 35).

The One and the Many

Sometimes we need to see things from the point of view of Unity — Wholeness, holistically; sometimes from the point of view of the Many — acknowledging each part, taking every individual into account. In other words, we see 'multiplicity in Unity or 'Unity in multiplicity'. Both views are valid. The relationship between them is something like a change of focus. Ibn 'Arabi always takes the point of view from Unity (the One) into multiplicity (the Many) — as if from the top of a pyramid, out of the Unseen into manifestation and 'down' to the phenomenal world. He sees multiplicity in the light of unity; i.e. the individual is *the place for the presencing of the whole.*

This distinction is important in regard to one's approach to counselling. For example, counsellors at one time attend carefully to the details of the client's story in order to hear and understand all the parts of it. At other times, their focus shifts to seeing a whole — the person, the person's life and its wider context.

John Wood puts it like this:

> When Rogers (1980), perceiving profoundly his client as a unique person, also perceived 'what is universally true', it was because the individual was a place for 'presencing' the whole, not a generalization arrived at by seeing many instances. Although Rogers succeeded in this realization, many counselors do not, since they continue to look for a unity in multiplicity instead of the multiplicity in unity (Wood, 1999, p. 159).

One of the most popular 'Rogerian tags' is 'What is most personal is most general' (Rogers, 1961, p. 26) — sometimes he is quoted as saying 'most universal'. Here is what Rogers says in explanation of this: 'There have been times when I have expressed myself in ways so personal I have felt I was expressing an attitude which it was probable no one else could understand, because it was so uniquely my own'. Rogers found, however, that this 'most private, most personal' material was that 'for which there is a resonance in many other people'. (Rogers, 1961, p. 26). He goes on to say that 'what is most personal and *unique* in each one of us' (my italics) is what connects at the deepest level with others. He then speaks of poets and artists as people 'who have *dared* to *express the unique* in *themselves*' (again, my italics). But he notes that this 'most personal' material was rejected by book publishers and many academic psychologists.

Compare this with the following:

> Consider then how wonderful is God in His Identity and in His relation
> to the Cosmos in the realities inherent in His Beautiful Names:
>
> Who is here and what there?
> Who is here is what is there.
> He who is universal is particular
> And He Who is particular is universal.
> There is but one Essence,
> The light of the Essence being also darkness.
>
> (Ibn 'Arabi, 1980, p.150)

Ibn Arabi's teachings and person-centred theory
1. *The actualizing tendency*
Rogers writes: '. . . the substratum of all motivation is the organismic tendency

towards fulfilment' and 'The individual has an inherent tendency towards *actualizing* his organism' (1980, p.123). The 'formative tendency' within the universe not only provides but *is* the motivational direction (Rogers, 1980, p.114).

For Ibn 'Arabi and the Sufi mystics *Love* is the motivation for all that happens in the Universe. It can be hard to accept that all human motivation arises from love — so many actions seem completely devoid of love. Love as the cause is often hidden from an observer by 'secondary causes' (Ibn 'Arabi, 1980, p. 257; trans. Austin). Love can also be distorted and limited almost to the point of disappearing. Similarly, the actualizing tendency may be masked, but not destroyed, by the organism's response to deprivation or limiting conditions.

The primary determining factor (or tendency) in our lives, according to Ibn 'Arabi, is not our past childhood experiences — which are themselves 'effects' as much as 'causes' — but the *ayan 1-thabita*, the latent potentialities, our images in the imagination of God (Truth). A person becomes closer and closer to the utmost that they can be. This does not mean being fatalistic: it is a question of receptivity and of aptitude. What we can become is essentially out of our hands, but we still have our part to play. The essential goal and direction is 'to be that self which one truly is' (Rogers, 1961, chapter 8).

2. *The 'fully functioning person', and the 'gnostic'*
Muhyiddin Ibn 'Arabi put it like this:

> . . . everything is tied to his aptitude, a man will do what he has to do accordingly . . . He finds things happening within himself, one after the other, each in its own time. If that man thinks his aptitude in this is short, then he suffers. (Ibn 'Arabi, *Kernel of the Kernel*, no date).

This is very reminiscent of what Rogers (1961, p.188) writes of the 'fully functioning person': 'What I will be in the next moment, and what I will do, grows out of that moment, and cannot be predicted in advance either by me or by others'. Guy Claxton, in a penetrating commentary on Rogers's thought, remarks: 'the fully functioning person realizes that his organism can cope on its own' (Claxton, 1981, p.126). The person who thinks their aptitude is short — who is beset with doubts and worries — is not fully functioning'.

For Ibn 'Arabi (and other Sufi mystics) *fulfilment* is realised in the return to the Origin i.e. the return to non-existence, being withdrawn from the phenomenal world to the Ipseity. Since one has, of course, never left the Ipseity (the Self) at the station of Unknowableness, 'return' can be equated to the *realisation* of this essential Oneness. 'I am closer to you than your jugular vein' (Koran, 50, p. 16). Ibn 'Arabi, in his *Book of Theophanies* (self-revelations of God) says: 'I am closer to thee than thine own self'.

3. *Congruence*
'When self-experiences are accurately symbolized, and are included in the self-concept in this accurately symbolized form, then the state is one of congruence of

self and experience' (Rogers, 1959, p. 206). He used 'integrated, whole, genuine' as synonymous with 'congruence'. This definition depends on what is meant by 'self' and experience'. What happens to congruence when the idea of 'self' is extended? What happens when 'experience' is extended? In meditation, following many different traditions (see, for example, *Thoughts without a Thinker* [Epstein, 1995] on Buddhist practice), the meditator typically becomes aware of levels of being not normally present in ordinary daily life. And what can be said of congruence when the concept of self actually disappears?

I am not always conscious of being 'congruent' but 1 can be aware of my incongruent functioning. The more I 'know myself' the more likely I am to spot incongruence. At a deep level, Ibn 'Arabi enjoined upon his disciples the need for them to observe themselves in every degree. He (and they) followed the exacting spiritual practice of *muhasaba* (examination of one's conscience) not only recording all of his actions during the course of a day, but examining all his *thoughts* as well (Addas, 1993, p. 164). This is because 'those who have arrived at closeness to God are responsible for untoward thoughts that come into their hearts'. By examining one's thoughts, a person can distinguish between that which is from God — or, we might say, from the authentic self — and that which is from the 'lower self', the *nafs*, the ego. 'Even though God is the creator of all thoughts, all the same, the servant is subject to questioning due to his own unmindfulness' (Ibn 'Arabi, *Kernel*, p. 42).

4. *Empathic understanding*

Another mystery that is seldom addressed is that of empathic understanding. How can it be possible for one person to understand another? What lies behind Rogers's experience (and, more significantly, the experience of each one of us) that at a deep level, there is a 'resonance' between people (Rogers, 1961, p. 26)?

From Ibn 'Arabi's teachings, we see, hear and understand each other within the Oneness of Being. We are only able to see each other through reflection in the mirror of the Ipseity, God the One and Unique *(Wahid al-Ahad)*, in a way analogous to the kind of mirror device that enables seeing round corners.

Yet we are 'unique' as well as 'one'. Thus the inner experience of 'understanding' — resonance or whatever that means — is unique or idiosyncratic, and so is the expression of this experience (Bozarth, 1984), not a parroted formula.

5. *Unconditional positive regard*

A therapist strives to engender a basic attitude of acceptance and respect (Rogers, 1951, p. 20). The attitude is described as 'warm, positive, acceptant', meaning that the therapist 'prizes the client in a total rather than a conditional way'. 'The term we have come to use for this', writes Rogers, 'is unconditional positive regard' (Rogers, 1961, p. 62).

In the view of a foremost exponent of client-centred therapy and the person-centred approach, unconditional positive regard is the primary condition for constructive change to occur (Bozarth, 1992). He explains, quoting Rogers (1959):

'The experience of threat is possible only because of the continued unconditional positive regard of the therapist, which is extended to incongruence as much as to congruence, to anxiety as much as to absence of anxiety'. In other words, the message that the therapist gives is, 'You are all right as you are'.

When those aspects of the client that have been blocked, denied or distorted are enabled to become, the process is the intrapersonal equivalent of the original act of bringing the manifest world into existence on the Breath of the Merciful. Unconditional positive regard, then, is a manifestation of the Mercy that englobes and maintains the universe.

Lietaer (1984, chapter 3) calls unconditional positive regard 'a controversial basic attitude'. The problem is in the unconditionality of the attitude. In Lietaer's view unconditionality calls upon the therapist for 'a devoted self-effacing that often leads to a compensatory reaction' in which 'confrontation becomes a form of self-assertion'. From Ibn 'Arabi's teaching, there are several ways of supporting this 'devoted self-effacing'. First of all, one comes to realise that there is no 'self' to assert, and that self-effacement is constantly practised, not only at times of the therapeutic encounter. Do not imagine that this leads to an insipid, passive presence of the therapist (or the person). What arises in the therapist is likely to surprise the therapist as much as the client. The therapist is not only transparent to the client but transparently allows the unconditional positive regard — the unconditional Mercy of God — to be manifest. The therapist is not striving to reach a new or forced state. It is rather a return to the original state of non-existence.

Secondly, gnostics, we are told are 'not tied to one form of belief; their circle is large', since 'Whichever way you turn there is the face of God' (Koran 2, p. 115). A person as an individual 'self' is not large enough to hold unconditionally all that is perceived in the client, nor is a 'belief system', such as client-centred therapy or the person-centred approach large enough. Only something that Itself englobes the system can hold the unconditionality. A Japanese therapist has written: 'Actually in the midst of a counselling session I sometimes feel that it is not me who accepts my client but the living force of nature itself which through me that does so' (Morotomi, 1998, p. 28).

There are two aspects to the Mercy of God corresponding to the Name 'the Compassionate, the Merciful'. The first is the Mercy before creation; the second, the Mercy after creation. The breath of the Merciful corresponds to the order of the Ipseity 'Be' which confers existence upon — gives life to — the latent possibilities, the potentialities implicit in the Ipseity, which they yearn for and as they have demanded from God. The second aspect of the Mercy of God is inherent in the return to Him — the Cosmos must 'yield its being back to its sources in Him' (Austin, 1980, p.187). All living creatures must eventually die.

6. *The problem of 'evil'*

Both good and evil have their origin in God; 'all things are manifestations of God and all actions are His actions, only we call some of them good and others bad' (*The Twenty-nine Pages*, p. 38). The Ipseity in the Absolute Unknowable is without quality

or determination. But in the phenomenal world the polarities arise, each quality
with its polar opposite. As part of the created world, this also holds for human beings.
Not surprisingly, in this view, since it is also found in Kabbalistic thought, Ibn 'Arabi
appears to be closer to the position of Martin Buber than to that of Carl Rogers — at
least as far as Rogers expressed it in the 1957 dialogue with Buber. As the very basis
of human nature, Rogers takes into account only one 'pole' namely, a 'constructive'
one:

> **Rogers**: . . . my own experience, which is that when you get to what
> is deepest in the individual, that is the very aspect that can most be
> trusted to be constructive . . . Does that have meaning for you?
> **Buber**: . . . I would put it in a somewhat different manner . . . And
> my experience is . . . if I come near to the reality of this person, I
> experience it as a *polar* reality There is again and again in different
> manners a polarity, and the poles are not good and evil, but rather
> yes and no, rather acceptance and refusal this polarity is very often
> directionless. It is a chaotic state. We could help bring a cosmic note
> into it. We can help put order, put a shape into this. Because I think
> the good, what we may call the good, is always only direction. Not a
> substance (Kirschenbaum and Henderson, 1990, pp. 58–9).

The difference is a subtle one ,[1] as all polarites, which Ibn 'Arabi and Buber perceive
manifested in the phenomenal world, are ultimately resolved in the Essence (God).

Order

Ibn 'Arabi's teaching is based on the certainty of an order (*amr*) in the universes.
Rogers wrote of his continuing effort 'to discover the order which exists in our
experience of working with people'. He confirms that this order was not something
other than the experience: 'I was beginning to sense a discoverable orderliness in
this experience, an orderliness which was inherent in the experience and . . . did
not have to be imposed *on* the experience' (Rogers, 1959, p. 187, italics in original).

Again: ' . . . any theory, derived from almost any segment of experience, if it
were complete and completely accurate, could be extended indefinitely to provide
meaning for other very remote areas of experience' (Rogers, 1959, p. 191). This is
surely an extraordinary statement, implying once again that the specific is the
place for presencing the universal.

The proper study of a phenomenon is through the phenomenon itself, seeing
the phenomenon in depth, 'feeling' yourself into it, loving it (O'Hara, 1995, p.109).
This was the view of Johan Wolfgang von Goethe, whose essay *The Flowering
Plant*, did not treat the plant as 'an external assemblage of different parts' —
dissecting it in order to know it. Perceiving the plant holistically he saw each
organ intimately related and each containing within it all the others. Again, he
saw the *multiplicity within unity*, that is the perception of the universal coming
through or shining in the particular (Bortoft, 1996, p. 88).

Change or 'coming into existence'?

When a client comes to counselling they want to be something more than what they are now. The universes come into existence on the Breath of the Merciful — *nafs ar-rahman* — each created thing demands its existence from Being and is granted that existence in time out of Love, in Mercy. Being (Truth, Reality) does not impose or force existence on to the 'latent essences'. There is a resonance between the unmanifest thing and its manifestation.

> Were it not in the nature of a thing to be at the moment of God's command, it would never be. Nor even would God command it to be. So, nothing brings a thing into existence (i.e. makes its existence manifest) except itself (*Twenty-nine pages*, p. 7).

Change, seen in this way, consists of the coming into existence of an aspect of your universal Self unveiled, active. It is brought into existence by its own essence at the word of its Lord, 'Be'. Ibn 'Arabi said, 'God creates His own Being'. Each of us creates our own being. The question is: do we try to make it (our being) conform to our conditioned view or do we give the word that brings into existence that aspect of our Self that is demanding to be released?

Conclusion

There really is no conclusion. Carl Rogers, academic psychologist, scientist, twentieth-century secular humanist and Muhyiddin Ibn al-Arabi, thirteenth-century Sufi mystic would appear to have little in common. However, once you start looking and take the point of view from Unity, they are like rivers flowing in the same direction. There are no particular implications for practice, whether for person-centred counselling or client-centred therapy, whichever you prefer. Rogers's theoretical propositions are not invalidated. There is room within Rogers's legacy to expand the idea of what a human being is. 'He turned the best part of himself toward the best part of the other' (Wood, 1995); he looked toward the greater rather than the lesser. To encapsulate, for a moment, Carl Rogers's work within Ibn 'Arabi's terms, he did indeed release a Breath of Mercy upon the world.

Notes

1. An illustration of how this subtle difference operates in therapy is given by Maria Bowen in a letter to Rogers expressing her reaction as she listened to a tape of a therapy session of Rogers and a client who refers to a 'monster' inside herself. In the session, Rogers appears to consider only one 'pole' of the person's self expression. Bowen wrote: '. . . you seemed to act as if the monster was a figment of her imagination . . . and the tone of your voice seemed to convey how absurd it was for her to think that she had such a monster within . . . my approach would have been different. I would have tried to facilitate her facing that monster.' In his reply, Rogers acknowledged the difference (Barrett-Lennard, 1987).

References

Addas, C. (1993) *Ibn 'Arabi or the Quest for the Red Sulphur.* Cambridge: Islamic Texts Society.

Assagioli, R. (1990) *The Act of Will: a guide to self-actualization and self-realization.* Wellingborough, Northants: Crucible.

Austin, R.W. (1980) Preface, Introductions and Notes to *Fusus al-Hikam.* London: SPCK.

Barrett-Lennard, G.T. (Ed.) (1987) *The Ceshur Connection,* 2, 1 , pp.25–8. Perth, W.A: The Centre for Studies in Human Relations.

Bennett, J.G. (1974) *Witness.* London: Turnstone Press.

Bortoft. H. (1996) *The Wholeness of Nature: Goethe's Scientific Consciousness.* Edinburgh: Floris Books.

Bozarth, J (1984) 'Beyond Reflection: Emergent Modes of Empathy' in R.F. Levant and J. M. Shlien (Eds) *Client-Centered Therapy and the Person-Centered Approach.* New York. Praeger.

Bozarth, J. (1992) *A Theoretical Reconceptualization of the Necessary and Sufficient Conditions for Therapeutic Personality Change.* Paper presented at the Fifth International Forum on the Person-Centred Approach; Terschelling, Netherlands.

Claxton, G. (1981) *Wholly Human.* London: RKP.

Epstein. M. (1996) *Thoughts Without a Thinker.* London: Duckworth.

Gendlin, E. (1984) The Client's Client: The Edge of Awareness. In R. Levant and J. Shlien (Eds) *Client-Centered Therapy and the Person-Centered Approach: New Directions in theory, research and Practice.* New York: Praeger.

Gyatso, Tenzin, 14th Dalai Lama (1984) *Kindness, Clarity and Insight,* (trans. and ed. Jeffrey Hopkins). Ithaca, N.Y.:Snow Lion.

Ibn 'Arabi, M. (no date) *Kernel of the Kernel*; Beshara Publications.

Ibn 'Arabi, M. (no date) *The Book of Theophanies*; Beshara Publications.

Ibn 'Arabi, M. (1976) *Whoso Knoweth Himself*; (trans. T. H. Weir) Beshara Publications

Ibn 'Arabi, M. (1980) *Fusus al-Hikam*; (trans. R. W. J. Austin). London: SPCK.

Kirschenbaum, H. and Henderson, V. (Eds) (1990) *Carl Rogers Dialogues.* London: Constable.

Lietaer, G. (1984) Unconditional Positive Regard: a Controversial Basic Attitude in Client-Centered Therapy. In R. Levant and J. Shlien (Eds) *Client-Centered Therapy and the Person-Centered Approach: New Directions in theory, research and Practice.* New York: Praeger.

Mearns, D. (1994) *Developing Person-centred Counselling.* London: Sage.

Morotomi, Y. (1998) 'Person-Centred Counselling from the Viewpoint of Japanese Spirituality; *Person-Centred Practice,* 6 (1).

Neville, B (1989) *Educating Psyche.* Melbourne: Collins Dove.

O'Hara, M.M. (1995) Streams — on Becoming a Postmodern Person. In M. M. Suhd (ed) *Positive Regard: Carl Rogers and Other Notables He Influenced.* Palo Alto: Science and Behaviour Books.

Rogers, C.R. (1951) *Client-Centered Therapy.* London: Constable.

Rogers, C. R. (1959) A Theory of Therapy, Personality and Interpersonal Relations, as Developed in the Client-Centered Framework, in S. Koch (ed.) *Psychology: A Study of a Science, Vol. 3.* New York: McGraw-Hill, pp. 184–256.

Rogers, C.R. (1961) *On Becoming a Person.* Boston: Houghton Mifflin.

Rogers, C.R. (1980) *A Way of Being.* Boston: Houghton Mifflin.

Wilson, C. (1986) *I.Gurdjieff:the war against sleep.* London: The Aquarian Press.

Wood, J.K (1995) The person-centered approach: toward an understanding of its implications. *The Person-centered Journal, 2, 2, pp 18–35.*

Wood, J.K. (1999) Toward an understanding of large group dialogue and its implications, in C.Lago and M.MacMillan (eds). *Experiences in Realatedness: Groupwork and the Person-Centred Approach.* Ross-on-Wye: PCCS Books.

The photograph was taken by my grand-daughter, Michelle, on a fabulous trip we took together in Greece in 1998; so it carries memories of our travels and trevails in that ancient sun-drenched land.

Moments of Eternity: Carl Rogers and the Contemporary Demand for Brief Therapy[1]

6

Maureen O'Hara

Introduction

It is now over a decade since Carl Rogers died, so perhaps this is a good time to revisit his work with a degree of perspective that only distance from the man himself can provide. I offer this as a homage to my friend and mentor, and as encouragement to those therapists who have grown tired of the seemingly endless claims for new approaches and miracle fixes in their search for a way of being with their clients that heals the soul and expands human possibilities.

My other agenda is to propose to those of us who became psychotherapists not merely to work on 'cases' and DSM categories in order to alleviate abstract sets of symptoms, but to help whole persons become more fully realized, that it is long past due to take back our profession. It is now urgent that we rescue our calling to care from the behavioral engineers, the physician 'wannabes' and the pharmaceutical companies they are in bed with. From people everywhere, there is emerging a call for relief from the culture of alienation and cynicism and a recommitment to the cause of human emancipation. These calls arise from the schools, the streets, business organizations, from the poor and destitute, victims of abuse, forced refugees, countless other victims of oppression, and as we saw recently in the massacre at the high school in suburban Littleton, Colorado, the time-strapped culturally overwhelmed middle class. As we search for a way to address human suffering and to enhance our capacity for joy and creativity, I believe we have a good deal to gain from revisiting Rogers' elegant yet demanding pathway to psychological healing and transformation.

Carl Rogers is arguably the most influential American psychologist and perhaps the least understood. His work spanned sixty years, from the later 1920s to the late 1980s, and participated in three radical philosophical shifts that occurred in

---

1. Adapted from a presentation given at the Brief-Therapy Conference, New York, August 1998.

twentieth century psychology. He started out as a logical positivist and ended up as a post-modern romantic.

Rejection of Medical Model

Rogers was among those early humanistic psychologists who rejected the medical paradigm of psychotherapy, where people called 'patients' are seen as suffering from something labelled a medical pathology and where the effective therapeutic agent is thought to be therapist-delivered treatment, applied in prescribed doses and according to predetermined protocols to specific diseases or disorders exhibited by a 'patient'. In place of this 'allopathic' view of 'treatment from without', Rogers, along with many others in the founding generation of humanistic psychologists, saw healing as something intrinsic to the client and regarded the client as an active agent in his or her own change. He sought not to impose some externally originating 'treatment' but to align himself with the self-healing powers of individuals and groups. Rogers and his humanistic colleagues were, in effect, homeopathic psychologists.

Formative tendency

More radically, although he might have balked at the word, Rogers held the metaphysical belief that the inborn capacities for self-healing and creative agency are reflections of a formative tendency in the universe impelling all of nature — from molecules to galaxies — to evolve towards greater complexity and expanded levels of consciousness. In Rogers' view (and the view of those of us who worked closely with him on the development of what in 1975 we named the 'Person-Centered Approach'), to establish the kind of relationship with people in which they can make an experiential shift towards greater awareness and higher orders of consciousness is, in some minuscule way, to participate in the evolution of consciousness and the process of matter becoming conscious of itself.

Attitudes not techniques

During the 1940s and early '50s Rogers and a large team of co-investigators conducted a massive and systematic study to identify key techniques and interventions that would provide a standardized approach to therapy and counseling. The further into the project the team got, the more they were forced to admit that what seemed to bring about significant shifts in therapy was not the technical expertise of the therapists, but a certain set of attitudes, values, and personal qualities, which he later came to call 'ways of being', which they bring into their relationships.

   Central to these attitudes are:

1. A faith that 'each person has within himself or herself vast resources for self-understanding and for constructive changes in ways of being and behaving', and,
2. The ability to create with clients a relational bond with certain definable qualities.

These qualities are 'realness, caring, and a deeply sensitive, non-judgmental understanding', and the willingness and ability to enter into an experiential empathic connection with clients. The goal is to sense the internal experience, the frames of reference and flow of feelings and meanings, moment by moment, as if from the point of view of the client.

Research on therapeutic effectiveness over the past forty years has pointed to these attitudes as the bedrock of the therapeutic presence, even for the proponents of the more instrumentalist approaches to therapy such as the solution-focused brief therapists.

When asked about the place of Carl Rogers' methods in his work, solution-focused brief-therapist guru William O'Hanlon replied, 'That's the first five minutes. If you don't do that stuff, I don't think you are going to get anywhere' (O'Hanlon, 1993).

What 'stuff' is O'Hanlon speaking about?

He's talking about the special way client-centered and person-centered therapists and counselors trust the growth and self-healing capacities of their clients and are willing to be in relationship with them. That's it, nothing more, and nothing less. No bells, no whistles — just faith in human beings and their striving to become, and the healing effects that derive from the basic human capacity to enter into a deep authentic connection with each other.

Over the decades since Rogers' research was conducted, a wealth of outcome and process studies have been conducted which have largely confirmed Rogers' discoveries (Bohart, 1999).

The 'common factors' research points to the remarkable stability over the decades of Rogers' basic constructs. Whatever therapists think they are doing, client resourcefulness, agency and capacity for self-directed growth, in the context of a relationship characterized by warmth, respectful and empathic understanding, overpowers any other variables — including technique, theoretical orientation, diagnosis or experience level of the therapist.

It is perhaps an irony, then, that just as there seems to be a convergence of evidence that supports the client-centered attitudes as the basic therapeutic stance, the approach is rarely the therapy of choice with insurance companies or the new Health Maintenance Organizations offering 'managed care': which appear to favor any therapy with the words 'brief', 'short term', 'strategic', or 'medication' in its name regardless of evidence about effectiveness!

It is doubly ironic since Rogers pioneered research on brief therapy. As early as 1942 he wrote: If we can recognize this [time] limit, and refrain from playing a self-satisfying Jehovah role, we can offer a very definite kind of clarifying help, even in a short space of time (Rogers, 1942).

But Rogerian approaches are rarely considered as 'brief approaches', and more often than not are caricatured as interminable navel-gazing. In preparation for this article I wanted to find out where today's client-centered therapists 'fit' on the 'snap out of it' brief-therapy — 'Woody Allen' endless talk therapy spectrum. I decided to conduct an informal, not very scientific, email survey of client-centered therapists from across the world.

Who does what in the real world?

Responses came from Latin America, Australia, Europe and North America, from younger practitioners and old hands. It may not have been a representative survey in the statistical sense but a wide range of diversely situated people responded. In fact the first thing that surprised me was the diversity of settings in which client-centered therapists are working. Most respondents worked at least some of the time in settings where the number of sessions was tightly restricted. These included employee assistance programs, college and university counseling centers, on-call emergency psychiatric clinics, residential treatment centers, orphanages and HMOs.

Most respondents said they did not favor the artificially imposed time limits determined by extra-therapeutic factors, but they nevertheless felt that under the right circumstances, even with externally imposed time limits, it was reasonable to expect positive results in several sessions (six to sixteen was the typical number); some reported significant effects in as little as three sessions, and one reported positive changes after an allotted single assessment interview. Even therapists in private practice, who were under no externally imposed time constraints, reported that the typical number of sessions was in the same range. Some of these therapists, however, did report that sometimes clients remained in therapy up to fifty sessions and beyond.

Another set of responses came from therapists who pointed out that in intensive small and large-group encounter settings, significant life-changing effects could be experienced in short-term encounters. Rogers described the long-term impact of single sessions done as therapy demonstrations (Rogers, 1980, pp. 207–234; Rogers, 1989). In a study co-authored with Rogers and others, we had reliable, independently corroborated reports of radical life changes that occurred for some of the participants of a two-day encounter with several hundred people (Bowen, 1979). Follow-up reports indicated that the changes persisted over time (Rogers, 1980, p. 316).

It seems quite clear from these reports that person-centered therapy in its theory and as it is practised, not just the first five minutes, but throughout the whole therapy has as much grounds to think of itself as an effective brief therapy as any other modality.

So why do contemporary person-centered therapists, including myself, not identify with the brief-therapy movement? And why are we not busy promoting client-centered therapy and the Person-Centered Approach to the managed care industry and financially strapped social service agencies as a cost-effective method of delivering short-term 'quality care' that research studies show (Seligman, 1995) have the added value of receiving high satisfaction ratings from 'customers'?

It's the paradigm

The answer, I believe, is that most client-centered therapists and certainly most practitioners who refer to their work as the 'Person-Centered Approach' operate within a different paradigm.

As Rogers said:

The single element that most sets client-centered psychotherapy apart

from the other therapies is its insistence that the medical model —
involving diagnosis of pathology, specificity of treatment, and
desirability of cure — is a totally inadequate model for dealing with
psychologically distressed or deviant persons (Rogers, 1989,
p. 1483).

Put simply, the reason person-centered therapists are not lobbying to be recognized
as practitioners of one of the brief therapies is because most do not think of their
practice in the terms of the contemporary medical discourse, and especially not in
the aggressively manipulative expert-focused stance of brief-strategic approaches
(Cade, 1993). In the Kuhnian sense, they inhabit a different paradigm (Kuhn,
1970).

Practitioners of person-centered therapy believe they are not there to solve the
problem or to heal the client, but to help build a space in which clients can heal
themselves. Their goal is to, as far as possible, open themselves to be present to
Being, and to join with people — clients — in ways that facilitate their achievement
of the same kind of openness.

Rogerian therapy recognizes and aligns itself with the self-healing properties
of living systems. At the core of the tradition is an invariant radical faith in a self-
organizing emergent vector at work in nature. Rogers described it as:

an evolutionary tendency towards greater order, greater complexity,
greater inter-relatedness (Rogers, 1980, p. 133).

Like the scientist, who would find it impossible to proceed without a faith in an
ordered universe, the person-centered facilitator would not be able to practice
client-centered approaches without this faith in a self-ordering or self-righting
human psyche.

Moments of eternity

Much of mainstream psychotherapy, in keeping with the medical tradition, trusts
a mechanistic world of diagnosis and a linear sense of cause and effect. Person-
centered therapists, on the other hand, trust the life process — a non-linear,
indeterminately causal reality — and then try to serve it. Their focus is on learning
a million and one ways, from any wisdom tradition they can borrow, of opening
sacred space and time — moments of eternity — within which the self-organizing
formative tendency in nature can become manifest and effective in the world.

Whether with a single individual, a family or group, and whatever the degree
of pain and disturbance, healing becomes not a matter of what one does but of
who and how one is in relationship to the world, including the world of the Other.

Once this is admitted then the nature of the transformational encounter shifts.
No longer as Buber would say, I-It — 'me doctor, you case' — but I-Thou, in
which a true encounter between Beings of infinite complexity and infinite
possibilities can occur. When we meet in Being, the next moment and all future
moments are radically open. The work of the therapist shifts from techniques to

apply to the client, to focus on developing greater capacities to be spiritually open and present. The work of the client is to use the hour and any techniques offered and the relationship, to allow themselves to think differently, to open themselves to a more vivid quality of experiencing, to feel more fully, focus more directly on their own inner and contextual resources, and to experience themselves no longer alone, but deeply met by an enthralled and invested other. For some clients this might be the first time in their entire lives that they have ever been met by someone else in this way.

For Rogers and other person-centered practitioners this accepting, non-judgmental and non-directive attitude is the bedrock of their work, out of which comes the courage to listen deeply, to enter into an empathic attunement with the Other, to surrender separate individual consciousness, and enter and participate in the phenomenal world of the other. In doing so, they attempt to become one with the emergent edge between the known and the unknown. Wood (1997) describes the 'mediumistic' quality of Rogers' level of empathic connections, even from an early stage in his career. Rogers and others came eventually to call these states (after Buber) 'presence'. Rogers exquisitely captures this presence as follows:

> I find that when I am closest to my inner intuitive self, when I am
> somehow in touch with the unknown in me, when perhaps I am in a
> slightly altered state of consciousness, then whatever I do seems to
> be full of healing. Then simply my presence is releasing and helpful
> to the other. There is nothing I can do to force this experience, but
> when I can relax and be close to the transcendental core of me, then
> I may behave in strange and impulsive ways in the relationship, ways
> which I cannot justify rationally, which have nothing to do with my
> thought processes. But these strange behaviors turn out to be right,
> in some odd way: it seems that my inner spirit has reached out and
> touched the inner spirit of the other. Our relationship transcends itself
> and becomes a part of something larger. Profound growth and healing
> and energy are present (Rogers, 1980, p.127).

When clients or groups sense that they are being received with this kind of openness they too are more willing to open up to the greater resources within them, within the relationship and in the greater contexts of their lives. With this kind of focus they may discover what David Bohm has referred to as 'the tacit infrastructure of thought' (Bohm 1980) and almost miraculously, sometimes, come upon creative and unpredicted responses to what challenges them.

Moments like these seem regularly to involve altered states of consciousness — altered that is from the ego-bounded state that is valued in contemporary 'professional' scientific discourse, but entirely recognizable to shamans, hypno-therapists, ministers, poets, mothers, lovers and other kinds of healers. There is a sense of alert patience — waiting. (The origin of the word 'therapy' is to wait.) It is common at such moments to lose the sense of separation between self and Other and instead experience oneself, and all other existence, as unique local manifestations of the whole, part of one indivisible and endlessly generative whole. In wisdom traditions these moments of eternity are sought as intimations of enlightenment, in religious traditions as glimpses of God, and in shamanic traditions as moments of healing.

Although patient, such states are not passive. Practitioners who can be there in this way have achieved the discipline to be wide awake, aroused, and fully there. They are not thinking, judging, evaluating, diagnosing, but simply available. Those of us who wish to be with our clients in this way must wait until the spirit moves us, and move us it will. We move towards or away, we hear a new note, we sense new symbols, we see an opening, we encounter a boundary, we are filled with pain, we are teased, we are swallowed up, we are seduced, repulsed, encouraged, and plunged into despair.

This degree of openness, especially in relationship with a person or situation which is chaotic or dangerous, is no job for the faint-hearted. Nor for the naive, poorly trained or inexperienced. To meet another, available to be moved by their story, means opening oneself to all the pain and nastiness that life can hurl at us (Neimeyer, 1999). Murder, rage, greed, rape, trickery, madness, terror, despair, loss, confusion, incoherence, numbness and death all move through us as if it were our own — because it is. To be able to tolerate such confrontation with human suffering, without exploiting or violating the vulnerability of the other takes maturity and, like any other advanced skill, it takes practice and good teachers (Gilligan, 1997).

We are not needed to 'fix' anything, to perform, or to intervene. Our clients need us for our humanness. They need us to bring to the encounter our hope, courage and energy and love to accompany them in their journey which for the moment is too hard for them to bear alone. We provide the safe, protected 'working space' and an attentive helper, and then let the client get to work thinking and feeling through their dilemmas.

Our significance to our clients, particularly those who are very troubled or very perplexed, is as constant and loving witness to their existence. They need us to care, to stand alongside as they struggle with the happenings of their lives, to love them, to be at least one significant Other who regards them in return — with all their difficulties and flaws — as another significant Other. In the mutual recognition of one human being for another comes the possibility to go beyond I-It, and even beyond I-Thou to become a 'We' (Schmid, 1997).

By both parties being willing to risk even temporarily becoming a 'we' a new never-before-existent universe is created between therapist and client. For those who feel separated and alone, cut off from themselves and from fellowship with the rest of the human race, the bridge back from exile into a world of relationship and of infinite possibility is what Gilligan calls 'sponsorship' or non-possessive love (Gilligan, 1997).

Transformational andragogy

All effective therapy by whatever name always involves a shift towards greater mental capacity — a transformation.

Practitioners of consciousness traditions East and West have invested centuries studying transformational moments, both the details of how they are experienced and on how they can be facilitated.

At the beginning of this century American psychology abandoned studies of consciousness, which had been begun by William James, in favor of a materialist psychology that was indistinguishable from biology. Humanistic psychology stood in opposition to this. But finally this is changing. The recent convergence of findings in neuropsychology, mind-body interaction, phenomenology and existential psychology, cognitive psychology, developmental psychology, psychophysiology, epistemology, systems science, complexity science, and depth psychology has revitalized interest in consciousness. It has also provided new non-religious but definitely spiritual languages with which to speak about consciousness change and its facilitation in therapy and other settings. It is once more respectable to speak of consciousness and to try to understand the process of its expansion and evolution.

Whether gradually over a period of time, or apparently in an instant, deep irreversible, transformational change in the way human beings experience their world, make meaning and act upon it, occur all through life — sometimes quite quickly. Sometimes this happens through therapy and sometimes it just happens.

When Jenny first came to see me, she was forty years old, with a highschool education. She was suffering from acute debilitating panic attacks of recent onset and complained that 'instead of getting more self-confident with age', she was 'losing ground'. She blamed other people for her difficulties. She blamed her father because he had abandoned her and a sister when he divorced their mother; she blamed her step-father for being a 'drunk', her husband for being a 'workaholic'; she even blamed psychologists for not having diagnosed her dyslexia as a child. Her thinking was one-dimensional and she jumped around from topic to topic, never able to reflect on her story, only to recount it.

She was the mother of two teenagers — an older boy and a younger girl, the wife of a distant overworked husband, and she had a small, not too successful, jewellery design business. She admitted that she was often close to despair and told me that she had flirted with a neighbor but backed off at the final hour. She was 'disgusted with herself', was feeling 'old, unattractive and ripped off by life' and was contemplating divorce and occasionally suicide.

During the first two sessions she spoke of her pent-up frustration; of her many attempts to solve her problems herself — self-help books, assertiveness training classes, journaling, Oprah, a women's support group and so on; and of her self-diagnosis as a 'chronic under-achiever who had married out of her intellectual class'.

The third session Jenny arrived in a highly agitated state, she had obviously been crying in the waiting room. She began to cry again as she started to speak and was obviously fluttering on the brink of an anxiety attack. Her tears were angry. She was 'livid', 'incensed', and she would like to 'tear the face off' her son's high school principal. Apparently he had just announced a new policy that only students with grades B or better could play baseball. Her son Ryan (also dyslexic), whose grade-point average was a B minus, had been kicked off the team and he was, in his mother's words, 'devastated'.

This affected the whole family since she and her husband, and the daughter were heavily involved with Ryan's team. Jenny had wanted to storm off to speak with the principal on her son's behalf but he begged her not to. This left her even more furious and impotent. At first she ranted, alternately blaming herself, then the principal, then her son, then her husband. She felt completely stuck, overwhelmed by emotions but not knowing what to do. 'I'm damned if I do, and screwed if I don't.'

I simply listened — there was no need (or room) for me to say anything for quite some time. Occasionally I asked for clarification, expressed surprise, sympathy, or curiosity like any engaged listener would. Once, in frustration, she demanded angrily that I 'earn my fee' and give her some advice, 'Should I go see the principal even though Ryan said not to?' she asked. 'Shouldn't a mother intervene for her son when injustice has been done?' 'Won't he be scarred by being rejected like this?' I responded quite honestly to Jenny's legitimate request for 'expert' advice by saying that I had more faith in her ability to work this through than I had in any counsel I might offer. Once or twice I expressed my confidence in her and my admiration for her fierce support for her son. But mostly I just listened attentively and appreciatively as she explored the multiple dimensions and meanings of her predicament. Gradually she developed deeper and more nuanced understanding of the complex basis for her rage, the way it related to her own childhood experiences, separating these transferred feelings from the problem for her son, his need to not be seen as a mama's boy, her own beliefs that baseball had been the reason her son was willing to try to succeed in school, and her fear that he would now withdraw his efforts the way she had, her anger at her husband because 'as usual he won't do anything', her anger at male authority, and so on.

Eventually the flow of her words slowed down and with my gentle prompting she began to listen to herself, and to correct herself as she did so.

J: The principal's a fucking asshole. He's on a big power trip (Pause). No, that's not really true, it isn't all the principal's fault, he has a job to do and he's probably under pressure to improve kids' grades so they can go to college. I seem to be looking for a villain. I am noticing now that I do that when I don't know what to do. That's what Mark always says I do. It really pisses me off when he says it, but he may be right. (She smiles, I smile back.) (Pause.) Hmmm. Sometimes there isn't one, right? No easy answers? Wow!

T: You are beginning to see just how complicated the situation is, not so easy to see what to do, but now you have noticed a pattern, and you seem to be willing to go beyond your usual search for someone to blame. That seems like something important!

J: Yeah, it does. Finding a villain only makes me feel like a victim. It's even worse when I decide the villain is me, then I just want to go away and shoot myself. It's like right now I can see it in bigger perspective, somehow. You know, when Mark would say 'you're losing perspective', I didn't really know what he meant, like there was right and there was wrong and you had to do what was right. But it's not so clear, is it?

As Jenny's exploration of the issues continued, her one-dimensional 'victim' story gradually became elaborated into a new and much more complex grasp of the situation. This understanding extended beyond herself to include empathy for all the participants, including the high school principal. As we approached the end of the session she seemed different. She was more relaxed, she sat quietly, her face calm and her eyes wide. She sat silently for several moments (the first long silence of the session), and then said:

J: Something incredible has just happened. I don't feel angry anymore, I don't feel afraid, I don't feel inadequate, I don't feel anxious. It's as if I am seeing all of this in a new way — like instead of it all happening to me, I am part of a whole lot of other people's lives and they're part of mine, and what I do affects them and what they do affects me. I suddenly feel a sense of confidence in my own position on this baseball and grades thing. I feel like I am a part of it all somehow, not just a bystander. I feel like an adult — like I understand why the principal thought it was a good idea. I just don't agree. And maybe Ryan needs his friends' respect more than he needs baseball, and maybe he needs baseball so much because he thought it meant so much to his dad and me. I don't know, but I am going to talk all this over with him.

Between that session and the next, I was to learn, Jenny had conversations with her family and with Ryan alone. With Ryan's blessing she paid a (calm) visit to the principal at which she expressed her disagreement with his educational strategy while affirming his responsibility to 'call 'em as he sees 'em', but she did feel that their dialogue may have made some difference. She shared with me that her entire family seemed to be taking her more seriously and that her customary sense of dread had evaporated. She was laughing a lot more.

Next session:
J: In that last session, it was as if all these years of struggling to come to terms with my shitty life had come to a head over this one issue. I just couldn't hide behind the history, the 'molest' thing anymore, making excuses for not standing up for myself. Even as I talked, part of me knew more was at stake than Ry's baseball. I think that's why I came. I could either walk away from it and say

it's too hard, like I have a thousand times, or I could face it and do something else. But now, I am seeing a whole lot of interconnecting lines going everywhere — to Ry, to Kimberley, to Mr. Boyd, to my dad — it's all one big bundle of people and everyone has their point of view. It could be easy to get lost, but somehow I seem to have my own opinions as well.

Because you were so there for me . . . in a funny way you were more help because you didn't try to help, you never gave an opinion about what I should do, but you did seem genuinely interested in me and my situation and that made me take myself more seriously. Usually, with Mark, he either takes over or won't get involved — so he tries to talk me out of my feelings. What you did and what you didn't do was just right. It gave me the space to see the bigger picture, I guess.

The next week Jenny arrived with a basket of vegetables from her garden, and a decision to end therapy.

J: I can do it myself, I think. You said you had confidence in me, and I thought when got home, 'Heck, if she sees me like that, why don' t I just do it.' So I tried it, and it is working out. If I can't do it sometime, I'll come back. OK?'

She didn't. She did, however, keep in touch by Christmas card and the occasional letter. Over the decade since I last saw her she went to college, finished a fine arts degree, began to design for a major jewellery house, and rebuilt her relationship with her husband. Now at fifty-one, she has a business making a good income and is close to her family in a way she had never been. She has not needed any further psychotherapy, she experiences occasional stage fright before making a major sales presentation, but otherwise is anxiety- free. More importantly, she still feels 'like an adult'. She says she is 'a deeper person, somehow' and is beginning to think she is going to make a 'pretty awesome old lady one of these days.'

Jenny had a transformative experience — apparently in just four sessions — a brief- therapy success. But it wouldn't matter whether it had taken ten sessions or even thirty, it was the quality of the change that marks it as significant. It would miss her achievement altogether to think of what occurred in terms of 'number of sessions', 'symptom reduction', 'problem-solving', and certainly not in terms of the managed care industry's favorite standard 'returning her to pre-morbid functioning'.

Who Jenny was after the third session, was qualitatively altered from who she had been just the week before and this change permeated her whole existence. She had not only changed what she thought about the situation she was facing, she had changed how she was thinking. She had made an epistemological leap.

Jenny had been operating from within mental processing frameworks inadequate to the complexity of the situation she was facing. It was as if she was attempting to navigate the complex psychological terrain of adult life with the very primitive maps she had drawn as a teenager. She herself realized that she needed capacities she did not (yet) possess and had worked furiously to find her own remedy. All those books, classes, talk shows and her women's group had certainly expanded her repertoire of conceptual options in important ways, but had up until then added more to the 'quantity' of her knowledge-base rather than to the quality of how she processed it.

When faced with life-challenges, such as her unsatisfactory marriage and her commitment to being a good mother, in which several of her well-established but adolescent cognitive-emotive patterns were in conflict, it seemed to Jenny that any solution from within one pattern would violate the requirements of another. The crisis over Ryan's baseball had kicked the whole dilemma into high gear. She had been running around in mental circles looking for ways out of the impasse and not finding one and this had precipitated her anxiety attacks. Her level of physiological arousal had been raised significantly, and this had activated many if not all the mental possibilities she had accumulated over a lifetime of experience. At home, without a supportive context in which to permit this process to take its own course, she was flooded with unbearable anxiety, but within the special conditions of the therapeutic setting, where she experienced herself as being met in the appreciative context of an unconditionally accepting 'we', she was able to resist her impulse to retreat, and instead of another failure, she was able to find her way out of the impasse.

As artists, scientists and mystics have long known, states of high mental arousal, when not accompanied by too much fear or sense of threat, permit us to bring into focus all at the same time, ordinarily disparate and disconnected fragments of knowing; and context-specific schemas; tidbits; unrelated ideas; narrative repertoires; oddball possibilities; unconscious connections; strange and creative associations, and to make new connections. Neural pathways and cognitive sub-routines, which develop separately at different stages of development and in response to specific experiential challenges, become available to each other in such altered states, cognitive and even neurological reorganization can take place, and higher orders of mental functioning can be achieved. By accepting errors in her characterization of the situation, taking them as a challenge, getting perspective on a broader more comprehensive level, and by becoming aware of her own existential involvement in the flow of her life, Jenny's breakthrough is archetypal of all higher orders of psychological growth.

Jenny is navigating a transformation from a way of being in which she is a passive recipient of life to one in which she is an active agent, from what Belenky et.al. call a 'subjective knower' — where the only truth is her own personal feelings — to something approaching a 'constructive knower' where reality is seen as a co-construction among multiple players (Belenky, et. al., 1986).

In this one series of statements we can hear her begin to see her connectedness to larger systems, her existential limits and the dialectical relationships among the systems she is involved in. She can see the tension between Ryan's membership in the family, his relationships with peers, and their relationship to the high school culture. Jenny begins to 'dis-identify' with her own emotional responses — 'getting perspective' — which she can now see are contaminated by out-of-awareness associations from her own (very different) childhood. She also begins to see that she had choices in the way she construes the world — 'no right answers' and begins to accept personal responsibility for the way she sees things, while accepting others will make different choices.

Whether such transformations occur through psychotherapy, education, the ordinary challenges of life, through participation in enlightenment traditions, rapidly during a crisis or over the long haul is incidental, Jenny is becoming what Rogers called 'a person of tomorrow'.

Rogers believed that unless prevented by overwhelming aversive circumstances, leaps of consciousness such as these could be expected to occur in therapy, in encounter groups, in community workshops, at home, at work, in church, temple or mosque — whenever two or more are gathered in healing's name, because it is the nature of Being to become. Rogers believed that complex systems — especially living systems — do not obey the laws of entropy, but rather move towards higher levels of organizational complexity. In his view, this 'formative tendency' of the cosmos is eternally waiting for opportunities whereby the unseen, 'implicate order' (as David Bohm terms it) of the not yet Being, can become.

So here's the challenge. Therapists practising in today's contexts are faced with a deep epistemological choice. We can do what the HMOs want us to do, namely take the instrumentalist approach and align with the rampant medicalization which is overtaking the psychotherapy world. Or we can chart our own path — which is both ancient and growing edge — and align with the intrinsic self-healing forces that reside within each and all of us. In one direction lies the way of the expert, in the other lies the path of the servant and participant in the great mystery of the unfolding of the world's story.

If you are ready to try out the latter and have the courage to enter naked into a true encounter with the enigma of Being, the work of Carl Rogers deserves consideration as a simple, accessible way in. If you choose a person-centered path, and learn how to be open to the moments of eternity waiting each time you meet another soul to soul and to be taken by unexpected moments of divine presence, you will have the added satisfaction of knowing that in addition to the transformational possibilities immanent at such times, most of the therapy outcome research is on your side too.

References

Belenky, M. F., Clinchy, B. M., Goldberger, N. R., & Tarule, J. M. (1986) *Women's Ways of Knowing: Development of Self, Voice, and Mind.* New York: Basic books.

Bergen, A. E., & Garfield, S. L. (1994) Overview, trends, and future issues. In A. E. Bergin & S. L. Garfield (Eds.), *Handbook of Psychotherapy and Behavior Change* (pp. 821–830). New York: Wiley.

Bohart, A., O'Hara, M., & Leitner, L. (1998) Empirically Violated Treatments: Disenfranchisement of Humanistic and Other Psychotherapies. *Psychotherapy Research, 8,* 141–157.

Bohart, A., & Tallman, K. (1999) *How Clients Make Therapy Work: The Process of Active Self-healing.* Washington DC: American Psychological Association.

Bohm, D. (1980). *Wholeness and the Implicate Order.* London: Ark Paperbacks.

Bowen, M., O'Hara, M. M., Rogers, C. R., & Wood, J. K. (1979) Learning in Large Groups: Implications for the Future. *Education,* 100,108–117.

Buber, M. (1970) *I and Thou.* (W. Kaufman, Trans.). New York: Scribner's Sons. (Original work published 1923).

Cade, B., & O'Hanlon, W. H. (1993) *A Brief Guide to Brief Therapy.* New York: W.W. Norton & Company.

Gilligan, S. (1997) *The Courage to Love: Principals and Practices of Self-relations Psychotherapy.* New York: W. W. Norton.

Kuhn, T. S. (1970) *The Structure of Scientific Revolutions.* (2nd. ed.). Chicago: University of Chicago Press.

Mearns, D. (1994) *Developing Person-centred Counseling.* London: Sage.

Neimeyer, R. A., & Stewart, A. E. (1999) *Constructivist and Narrative Therapies.* In press.

O'Hanlon, W. H. (1993) Possibility Therapy: From Iatrogenic Injury to Iatrogenic Healing. In S.Gilligan & R. H. Prices (Eds.), *Therapeutic Conversations.* New York: W.W. Norton.

O'Hara, M. (1995) Carl Rogers: Scientist or Mystic? *Journal of Humanistic Psychology,*35 (4), 40–53.

O'Hara, M. (1996) Rogers and Sylvia: A feminist Analysis. In B. A. Farber, D.C. Brink, & P. M. Raskin (Eds.), *The psychotherapy of Carl Rogers: Cases and commentary.* (Pp. 284–300). New York: Guilford Press.

O'Hara, M. (1997a) Emancipatory Therapeutic Practice in a Turbulent Transmodern era: A Work of Retrieval. *Journal of Humanistic Psychology,*37(3), 7–33.

O'Hara, M. (1997b) Relational Empathy: From Egocentric Modernism to Socio-centric Postmodernism. In A. C. Bohart & G. L.S. (Eds.), *Empathy reconsidered: New directions in psychotherapy.* (Pp. 295–320). Washington D.C.: American Psychological Association.

Rogers, C. R. (1942) Counseling and Psychotherapy: *Newer Concepts in Practice.* New York: Houghton Mifflin.

Rogers, C. R., & Dymond, R. F. (Eds.) (1954) *Psychotherapy and Personality Change: Co-ordinated Research Studies in the Client-centered Approach.* Chicago: The University of Chicago Press.

Rogers, C. R. (1957) The Necessary and Sufficient Conditions for Therapeutic Personality Change. *Journal of Consulting Psychology,* 21, 95–103.

Rogers, C.R. (1969) *The Person of Tomorrow.* Sonoma State College Pamphlet.

Rogers, C. R. (1977) *Carl Rogers on Personal Power.* New York: Delacorte.

Rogers, C. R. (1978) The Formative Tendency. *Journal of Humanistic Psychology,* 18, (1), 23–26.

Rogers, C. R. (1980) *A Way of Being.* Boston: Houghton Mifflin.

Rogers, C. R., & Sanford, R. C. (1989) Client-centered Psychotherapy. In H. I. Kaplan & B.J. Sadock (Eds.), *Comprehensive Textbook of Psychiatry.* (Pp. 1482–1501). Baltimore: Williams & WIlkins.

Schmid, P. F. (1997) In N. Andrade (Ed.), *IV International Conference on Client-*

Centered Therapy and Experiential Psychotherapy, (p. 30). University Católica Portuguesa, Lisbon, Portugal.

Seligman, M. E. P. (1995) The Effectiveness of Psychotherapy: The Consumer Reports Study. *The American Psychologist,* 50(12), 965–974.

Shlien, J. M. (1957) *An Experimental Investigation of Time-limited, Brief, Client-centered therapy.* Doctoral dissertation, University of Chicago.

Wood, J. K. (1984) Communities for Learning: A Person-centered Approach. In J.M. Shlien & R. F. Levant (Eds.), *Client-centered Therapy and the Person-centered Approach: New Directions in Theory and Practice* (pp. 297–316). New York: Praeger.

Wood, J. K. (1997) *Carl Rogers and Transpersonal Psychology.* Invited presentation at the VI International Holistic and Transpersonal Congress, Aquas de Lindoia, Brazil.

This photograph was taken by the editor at the 'Large Group Workshop' in Sedona, 1998, which Maureen helped to organise. It was taken when she was dancing at the final night party.

THE MEANING OF CARL ROGERS AT THE OPENING OF THE 21ST CENTURY

7

RUTH SANFORD

What is the distilled essence of the life and work of Carl Rogers that is relevant to our life as we pause on the threshold of the 21st century? To answer this question I relived my experience with Carl Rogers the man and reviewed my knowledge of his work. After meditating at length I entered into a deeply empathic process. The words came to me: 'power and the use of power'. 'But,' says another voice, 'it is about deep listening with a will to understand. It is about caring and accepting the other as a person as that person is. It is about being real and open. It is about being nonjudgmental in my acceptance of others as persons. It is about a way of being.'

'True,' says the first voice, but as Carl stated in *On Personal Power* 'it is personal power, inner power, inner strength, power within rather than power over.' It is about the healing power of deep empathic listening, of the extension of caring to the point where it genuinely tries to understand. It is listening to and trusting the power and the efficacy of the self-actualizing tendency at work in all of nature, including the human organism. This tendency can be perverted or damaged but not destroyed as long as the organism is alive. This was substantiated by rigorous research. We have strong evidence that this tendency toward realization of full potential is functional in all aspects of our society by releasing the inner power of the individual.

Extended to the universe it is called the formative tendency. Carl described it in *A Way of Being*:

> We are tapping into a tendency which permeates all of organic life — a tendency to become all the complexity of which the organism is capable. And on an even larger scale, I believe we are tuning in to a potent creative tendency which has formed our universe, from the smallest snowflake to the most gifted of persons. And perhaps we are touching the cutting edge of our ability to transcend ourselves, to create new and more spiritual directions in human evolution. This kind of formulation is, for me, a philosophical base for a person-centered approach (Rogers, 1980, p. 134).

If this tendency is working in plants and animals and the human organism, we know it is working in groups and other larger social organisms. Far from being simple and easy, it is probably the most rigorous way of life and of self-discipline, the most exacting test of coming to maturity as a fully functioning person.

After writing these preliminary notes, I decided to reread — via Talking Books — *Carl Rogers on Personal Power*. I found Carl saying:

> I believe that individuals are culturally conditioned, rewarded, reinforced for behaviors that are in fact perversions of the natural directions of the unitary actualizing tendency . . . This dissociation that exists in most of us is the pattern and the basis of all psychological pathology in humankind, and the basis of all his social pathology as well (Rogers, 1977, pp. 247–248).

This statement is central to the message of Carl Rogers to the world and it poses a question and a challenge to all of us in the western world. Unfortunately, many countries including the United States seem to have adopted in the name of democracy some of the patterns which Carl referred to as perversions. Businesses and large corporations, driven by the profit motive, depend on power over others and the power of money.[1]

National governments in the name of economics tend to yield to the widespread influence of high-powered lobbyists representing big corporations, with the result that the responsible electorate is sacrificed to the power of corporate money. There is evidence, however, that in the United States common citizens are becoming more aware of the displacement of power and are responding actively via the ballot box to choose leaders who will listen to the people and will not be bought.[1]

We may be reaching a critical point. My research with Bob Barth on the inner process of significant change in the individual found that when individuals reach a critical point they're most likely to change (Barth and Sanford, 1994, pp. 19–37).

This finding is in agreement with the contemporary work of researchers in complexity and their findings concerning 'the edge of chaos' as well as earlier work on open systems. At that critical point, the organism moves toward self-destruction or to reorganization at a higher, more complex level (Sanford, 1993).

One important example of shared power helping to bring about such a critical point in US national politics is the emergence of volunteer groups (including Vote Smart) that publicize the voting record of every legislator so that the public is informed systematically of their representatives, enabling the active participation of the American people in the political process. With this information the voters are better able to inform their legislators of their needs and they demand accountability of their legislators. Shared power has also been the goal of John Vasconcellos. As a member of the State Assembly of California for thirty years,

---

1. Limitations in my knowledge of political structure in other countries makes it impossible for me to draw parallels but citizens of other countries can look for similar applications or take initiatives appropriate to their political structure.

and founder of the Task Force on Self-Esteem, he has had wide influence on the direction of the state budget and legislation, on the openness of contact between the elected official and so-called ordinary citizens.

There is strong evidence that members of the electorate are beginning to rebel against government by lobbies protecting special interests. This is one of the reasons that has led John Vasconcellos to find that person-centered politics is the wave of the future.[2]

An increasing number of pro-active citizens are involving themselves in a diversity of causes aiming to increase the freedom and responsibility of the electorate in determining political values and directions, such non-partisan volunteer organizations as Common Cause, Greenpeace, Environmental Defense Fund, Physicians for Social Responsibility, Public Citizen, to name a few.

There has been an improvement in the political and social coverage of national public TV and radio programs who are increasingly relying on public contributions rather than federal funding or corporate money.

South Africa with its 'people-driven government' or 'people's government' is another rich example. Educators, social workers, helping persons in the health care professions are striving together to make their services available to all South Africans.

In contrast to the quote on psychological and social pathology, I wish to place a very positive quotation of Carl's, often repeated, which lies at the core of the client-centered therapy/person-centered approach to relationships:

> . . . the individual has within himself vast resources for self-understanding, for altering his self-concept, his attitudes, and his self-directed behavior — and these resources can be tapped if only a definable climate of facilitative psychological attitudes can be provided (Rogers, 1980, p. 115).

Carl also quoted Gertrude Stein on Paris ['It is not what Paris gives you; it is what she does not take away']. Carl continues (Rogers, 1977):

> Rather than empower the student, the teacher as facilitator does not take away the student's freedom to be a full partner in the *learning process* (p. xii).

In the marriage relationship each partner respects and shares with the other, power and responsibility within the relationship. The administrator and employer share power and responsibility with employees. Shared power has already been demonstrated in situations of ethnic, racial, cultural and religious conflict. In the words of Carl Rogers:

> Small-scale examples exist in abundance to show that improved communication, reduction in hostility, steps toward resolving the

---

2. More about John Vasconcellos' program can be found on his world wide web homepage at http://www.webcom/-smartpol.

tensions are entirely possible and rest upon tried intensive group approaches (Rogers, 1977, p.289).

In politics we're becoming aware of the challenge to extend similarly the sharing of power and responsibility in regional, national, and international politics. We need not wait for a new millennium or even for tomorrow to experience this 'quiet revolution'. In Carl Rogers' own words '[the PCA] changes the very nature of psychotherapy, of marriage, of education, of administration, even of politics'.

The person-centered approach is available for the use of everyone who has the understanding, the courage, the self-discipline, the will, the commitment to use them in whatever field — professional or personal — is his or hers to practice.

> This can be paraphrased to become a definition of the person-centered approach... It is not that this approach gives power to the person; it never takes it away. That such a seemingly innocent base can be so truly revolutionary in its implications may seem surprising. It is, however, the central theme of what I have written (ibid).

In the person-centered way of being the therapist does not empower the client, but does not take away the power of the client by controlling, advising, analyzing, interpreting. The therapist trusts the client as another person who can find his/her own way of changing and growing toward realization of his/her potential. The therapist respects and accepts the inner strength of the client.

These changes indicate that a quiet revolution is already under way. They point to a future of a very different nature, built around a new type of self-empowered person who is emerging. What's most important for the future is that each person recognize the areas in which they can best function, can best use their talents and abilities, can apply and extend a trust in the actualizing tendency, and consciously apply the concepts of the Person-Centered Approach in their own lives every day with everyone they meet. I want to return to and emphasize the issue of power and the radical implications of sharing power, and more importantly, creating the conditions for our own and each others' power to flourish in personal relationships and endeavours and in all spheres of political and social life.

In the chapter entitled *The World and Person of Tomorrow*, Carl said:

> The winds of scientific, social and cultural change are blowing strongly. They will envelop us in this new world, this world of tomorrow . . . Central to this new world will be persons, the persons of tomorrow . . .
>
> This is the person-centered scenario of the future. We may choose it, but whether we choose it or not, it appears that to some degree it is inexorably moving to change our culture. And the changes will be in the direction of more humanness (Rogers, 1980, p. 356).

References

Barth, R. and Sanford, R., (1994) Human Science and the Person-Centered Approach: An Inquiry into the Inner Process of Significant Change within Individuals. *The Person-Centered Journal, 1, (2),* 9–37

Rogers, C.R., (1977) *Carl Rogers On Personal Power: Inner Strength and Its Revolutionary Impact.* New York: Delacorte Press.

Rogers, C.R., (1980) *A Way of Being.* Boston: Houghton Mifflin.

Sanford, R., (1993) From Rogers to Gleick and Back Again: The Theory of the Person-Centered Approach and the Theory of Chaos. In D. Brazier (Ed.) *Beyond Carl Rogers: Towards a Psychotherapy for the 21st Century.* London: Constable.

Carl took his favourite picture of me in Mexico. He described it as 'listening, caring and thoughtful'.

A Client-Centered Demonstration in Hungary

8

Barbara Temaner Brodley

The following interview took place in Szeged, Hungary at a Cross-Cultural Workshop, in July of 1986. John Shlien had convened a small group to learn about client-centered therapy and I volunteered to do a demonstration. A young European woman who had recently completed Master's studies in the United States volunteered to be my client. There were eight or ten Hungarians and several English-speaking participants in the observing group. The Hungarian participants clustered together in a corner so as not to disturb the interview while they were receiving a simultaneous translation. The interview was scheduled for twenty minutes, more or less, depending on the client's wishes.

The Interaction

Barbara: Before we start I'd like to relax a little bit. Is that all right with you? (Spoken to the client who nods.) I would like to say to the group that I'm going to attempt to empathically understand my client — to do pure empathic following. As I have the need, I will express my empathic understanding of what she expresses to me about her concerns and herself. (Turns to Client.) I want you to know that I am also willing to answer any questions that you might ask (C: O.K.) if it happens that you have a question.

Client 2 : You are my first woman therapist. Do you know that?

Therapist 1: I didn't know.

C2:   And that's important for me because . . . uh, it sort of relates to what I'm going to talk about. Which has been going on in my mind since I decided to spend the summer in Europe. (T: Uhm-hm.) Um . . . I spent the last two years in the United States studying, and (pause) when I left _____ [her home and country of birth] in 1984, I was not the same person I am right now.

T2:   Something has happened to you.

C3:   A lot of things have happened to me (laughs). And, I'm coming back to Europe this summer primarily to see my parents again. When I had left _____ [home] two years ago, I had left in a state of panic. Promising almost never to go back. Promising never to see them again. And . . .

T3:   Escaping and going to something.

C4:   Yeah, yeah, yeah. Getting away from . . . and I had never expected that I would reach this point, that I would be able to go back and see them again.

T4:   Uhm-hm. You were so sure, then.

C5:   I was *angry.* (T: Uhm hm.) I was *so angry.* (T: Uhm-hm.) And it's good for me that I'm taking all this time before I go back to _____ [home]. I mean this workshop now, and then I'm going to travel. And then I'm going to go to _____ [home] at a certain point in August. (T: Uhm-hmm.) But sometimes, I just, I'm struck by the fact that, *gosh,* I'm going to see them again, and how would that be? How will that be?

T5:   You're making it gradual and yet at a certain point you will be there, (C: Uh-huh.) and what will that be?

C6:   Uh-huh.

T6:   Is? . . . you have, uh, an . . . anticipation or fear (C: Yeah.) or (C: Yeah.) something like that . . .

C7:   Yeah, and I guess . . . I was thinking about my mother the other day, and . . . I realized, in the States I realized that she and I had a very competitive relationship. And . . . it was interesting but, three days ago in Budapest, I saw a lady in the street who reminded me of my mother. But, my mother, not at the age which she has right now. But my mother twenty years from now. And, I don't know why. I was so struck by that, because I saw my mother being old and weak. So she was not this powerful, domineering person that she used to be in _____ [home]. Who I was so much afraid of.

T7:   Uhm-hm. But old and weakened and diminished . . .

C8:   Diminished. That's the word. (T: Uhm-hm.) That's the word. (C begins to cry).

T8:   It moved you to think of that, that she would (C: Yeah.) be so weak and diminished.

C9:   And I think there was something in that lady's eyes that reminded me of my mother which (voice breaks — crying) I was not aware of when I was in _____ [home]. And it was fear. (T: Uh-huh.) I saw fear in the woman's eyes. (T: Fear.) Yeah. And, I was not aware of that.

T9:   You mean, when you saw this woman who resembled your mother but twenty years from now, you saw in this woman's eyes something you had not realized was in fact in the eyes of your mother. (C: Yeah.) And that was the quality of fear. And that had some great impact on you.

C10: Yeah. Because I felt that this woman needed me. (Crying.) (Pause.) It feels good that I am crying now. (T: Uhm-hm.) I'm feeling very well that I am crying. (T: Uhm-hm.)

T10: (Pause.) It was a sense of your mother at the future, and that your mother *will* need you.

C11: You got it! The future stuff. It's not the present stuff. (Pause.) It feels right here. (She places her hand over her abdomen.) (T: Uhm-hm.)

T11: The feeling is that your mother will have, *has,* fear and will have great need for you, (C: Yeah.) *later on.*

C12: Yeah. (Pause.) And as I am going back to _____ [home], I don't know if I'm ready to, if I'm ready to take care of her. I don't know if I'm ready to see that need expressed by her. (Continuing to cry.)

T12: Uhm-hm, uhm-hm, uhm-hm. (Pause.) You're afraid that when you get there that will be more present in her. Or you will see it more than you did before, now that you've seen this woman. And that that will be a kind of demand on you and you're afraid you're not ready to meet that.

C13: That's it, yeah, and it's gotten too much for me. Or, right now in Hungary, I perceive it as being too much. (Crying continues.)

T13: Uhm-hm. At least, you're saying you're not sure how you will feel there, but it feels now like if that comes forth, if you see that, you, you, won't be able to . . . (C: Take it.) respond — be able to take it.

C14: Yeah, yeah. It was interesting. I kept looking at her, you know. And it's like I was staring at her and she was staring at me. She was Hungarian. She didn't know why I was looking at her and I didn't know why I was looking at her either. But it's like I wanted to take all of her in, and make her mine, and prepare myself. And suddenly I realized that all this anger I had was gone. There was nothing left. It was gone. (Crying.)

T14: Uhm-hm. You mean, as you and this older woman looked at each other, and you had the meaning that it had for you about your mother, you wanted to — at that moment, you wanted to take her in, and to give to her. To somehow have her feel that you were receiving her.

C15: Yeah. (Expressed with a note of reservation.)

T15: The important thing is that — out of that you realized that you weren't afraid of your mother anymore, you weren't afraid of her dominance or . . .

C16: Yeah. Yeah.

T16: And that's a kind of incredible (C: Discovery.) discovery and an incredible phenomenon that that (C: Yeah.) fear and oppression could drop away so suddenly.

C17: And I guess, another feeling that I had also was, I felt sorry for her.

T17: Your mother.

C18: Yeah. (Pause.) And I don't like feeling sorry for her at all. (Crying.) I used to a lot. For a long time when I loved somebody I used to feel sorry for them at the same time. I couldn't split those two things. (Pause.) I don't know what I'm trying to say right now, I don't know if I'm trying to say that I felt that I was loving her or that I was feeling sorry for her or both.

T18: There's a quality. Pity, or feeling sorry for her, that was strong but which you
did not like. And then you don't know whether there was a quality of love that was part of that pity?

C19: Yeah.

T19: So both the feelings are mixed and confusing (C: Yeah.) and then the reactions of, of having the sympathy and then having the (C: Uh-huh.) pulling back (C: Uh-huh.) from it.

C20: And, I don't know if the woman did really resemble my mother or if it was my wish to make her resemble my mother. Maybe I'm ready (pause) ready to get there. I'm ready to see my mother as a person, and not — I can't put a word because I don't know how I was perceiving my life so far. But, I had never perceived her as a woman in the street, just a woman, just another woman in the street, (her voice quakes with feeling) vulnerable and anxious and needy, and (softly) scared.

T20: You don't know whether you had changed and therefore saw, experienced, this woman *from* the change, of being open to seeing all of that in your mother. (C: That's right.) Or whether she really, when you looked at her, looked very much like your mother and how *she* would look. Is that right? (C: Yeah.) You don't know which?

C21: Yeah.

T21: I guess that the really important thing is that you saw her, your mother, in your mind through this woman in a completely new way. As a person, as vulnerable, as afraid, as in need.

C22: Uhm-hm, uhm-hm. And that made me feel more human . . .

T22: Made *you* feel more human. (C: Uh-huh.) To see *her* as more human (C: Also) made you feel more human in yourself.

C23: Yeah. (Reserved or thoughtful tone.)

T23: Uhm-hm, because the force of how she *had* been to you — the tyrant or something . . .

C24: She had a lot of qualities. Some of them I don't remember anymore.

T24: But not a whole person to you, not a vulnerable person.

C25: Uhm-hm, yeah. (Pause.) I said at the beginning that you were my first woman therapist, (T: Uhm-hm.) I was avoiding women therapists like hell. (T: Uhm-hm.) All the therapists I had were men so far and now I know why. I can't put why to words but I know why.

T25: That some of your feelings about *her* made you avoid a woman therapist and choose men?

C26: Yeah. (Pause.) And lots of other things. But at this point um, I, I'm perceiving everybody as another person, and that makes me feel more of a person as well.

T26: Uhm-hm. You're perceiving everybody, (C: Everybody.) as more rounded . . . um, (C: Yeah.) including the therapist.

C27: Therapists were big, were a big thing for me for a long time. Very big authority figures and stuff like that. (T: Uhm-hm.) So I guess I was afraid that a woman therapist — a woman therapist was very threatening to me. (T: Uhm-hm.) Four years ago, three years ago. But at this point I feel everybody's a person.

T27: Everybody's a person. So that among the many transformations that have occurred since you left home (C: Yeah.) for the United States. That's a big one. (C: That was . . .) That people have become persons to you instead of figures of various sorts.

C28: Absolutely true. I *mean* that's absolutely right. And it happened after I left _____ [home]. (T: Uhm-hm.) (Pause.) And I feel . . . (looking toward observers).

T28: And you feel it's about time . . . ?

C29: (Client nods.) Thank you.

T29: You're welcome. Thank *you*. (Client leans towards therapist; they embrace affectionately and with smiles.)

C30: Thank you very much (continuing to embrace).

Commentary
I evaluate client-centered therapy interviews by making a basic distinction between (1) errors of attitude and (2) errors of understanding:

Errors of attitude occur when the therapist's intentions are other than maintaining congruence, unconditional positive regard and empathic understanding or when the therapist has adopted *other* than a nondirective attitude in relation to the client. For example, the therapist is emotionally disturbed, confused or not integrated. Or the therapist has lost unconditional acceptance of the client and reveals this in the tone or content of his or her communications. Or the therapist is distracted and failing to try to empathically understand the client. Or the therapist is attempting to influence the client to accept a particular interpretation of his behavior.

Errors of understanding occur when the therapist is experiencing the therapeutic attitudes and is attempting to acceptantly and empathically understand, but misunderstands the client, or fails to grasp what the client is getting at or intending to immediately express.

In this brief interview, out of a total of twenty-nine therapist responses, twenty-five (93%) can be considered empathic following responses. Four responses (7%) are responses from the therapist's frame of reference. Response T1 is a therapist-frame response — an answer to a question. Responses T23 and T25 are therapist-frame responses that are explanations. Therapist response T29 is a common-courtesy therapist-frame response; it is responsive to the client's appreciation and expresses my gratitude to her. Only responses T23 and T25 represent errors in attitude in the interview. Responses T1 and T29 are appropriate deviations from empathic following that take account of the social context.

All of my other responses in the interview are empathic understanding responses that follow the client and intend to express the acceptant, empathic understanding attitude. One empathic response (T8) has an element of comment from the therapist's frame and another (T10) has an interpretive element although both were intended to check understanding. My T17 follows the client, but it is only an informational response. I classify it as of this type because it does not contain the element of communication that expresses something about the relation of the client to what she is talking about. It does not reveal anything about the client's self or the client as an aware agent of actions, reactions, feelings or personal meanings. Response T20 ends with a question for clarification ('Is that right? You don't know which?') that expresses my uncertainty as well as the client's. The response was not wholeheartedly accepted (C21) but my correction in T21 was better received. The client did not accept my non-empathic explanation response (T23). This, however, was corrected by the empathic response (T24) I expressed immediately after the explanation, according to the client (C25). Response T28 is an empathic guess — a kind of following response — based on my sense of the elapsed time and the client's nonverbal behavior.

I felt *present* and attentive to the client throughout the session. Although I could vaguely hear the soft voice of the translator in the room speaking Hungarian, it distracted my attention from the client only slightly. My therapeutic attitudes were very consistent, although not perfectly so, during the interview.

My accuracy of empathic understanding the client seems fairly high when therapist responses are compared with prior client statements and to judge on the basis of the client's frequent affirmations. Four of my responses are at least in part inaccurate in understanding. One response (T14) is partly inaccurate because it does not respond to the client's change — a release from fear of her mother. The client's lukewarm reaction (C15) confirms that it was unsatisfactory. I correct it in T15 and the client accepts the improvement (C16). Empathic response (T18) is inadequate because it is vague and it is inaccurate in respect to the client's uncertainty about love feelings towards her mother in the present rather than in the past. I also missed acknowledging (in T20) the client's sense of never having perceived her mother as a regular person that she expressed in C20. The client did not accept (C24) my error-of-attitude, explanation response (T23), that included the word 'tyrant' to describe her previous perception of her mother.

It is impossible to judge how much my relatively accurate following of the client contributed to her movement. It is also impossible to be sure how much my considerable attunement facilitated her to new awareness and new expression. Certain of my responses obviously had emotional impact. The word 'diminished' (T7) struck her hard, stimulating her to cry. My T10 response appears to have felt very right (C11) and her reaction had a strong physical quality. Her emotional and physical expression towards me — her warm thanks to me at the end of the interview — suggests she felt it was a good experience. Whether it was truly therapeutic is difficult to know. At the time, immediately after the session, the client told me it was helpful. I was certainly functioning as a client-centered therapist, as I understand and practice the approach.

My demonstration client was in her mid-twenties and I was in my mid-fifties when the interview took place. I don't know how much her experience of my age being close to her mother's age may have influenced the content of the interview. I do know that we had a good chemistry; we were attracted to each other as persons. The client and I had briefly encountered each other the evening before the interview. After the interview, she told me she had experienced a positive reaction to me that previous evening (as I had toward her) and that she volunteered to be a client for the demonstration because I was to be the therapist. She had felt there was a warmth about me and thought she could trust me.

In the interview I felt open to her and emotional as she unfolded her narrative. One of our Hungarian observers commented to me after the interview, 'now I understand client-centered therapy' because he saw tears in my eyes at some moments as I worked with her. He had apparently not realized from his readings that the client-centered therapist's presence may reveal authentic emotional experiences.

This photograph was taken at my daughter Noah's wedding. It is my husband Bob's favorite picture of me.

The Person-Centred Approach and its Relevance to Substance Users

9

Sue Wilders

My background in working with drug and alcohol users

Since 1992 I have been working with people experiencing problems related to drug or alcohol use. To begin with I had the advantage (and I use this word deliberately) of knowing very little about substances, their effect on individuals, or why people became dependent upon them.

Consequently, I concentrated my efforts on really trying to listen to and understand my clients and their experience. I genuinely felt accepting of my clients and the choices they made. In addition I had never learned the 'skill' of hiding myself behind a professional veneer.

Of course, I have since learned that, although undefined and unrefined, and often inconsistent, I was attempting to work with my clients in a person-centred way, offering, to the best of my ability, the core conditions of unconditional positive regard, empathic listening, and genuineness.

The training in the Person-Centred Approach I have since taken part in has given me a theoretical framework that has led to greater consistency in my work. My observations on the impact of the Person-Centred Approach in the lives of my clients has led me to the belief that this approach is better suited to work with substance users than any other.

What is the Person-Centred Approach and how does it relate to work with clients who use a lot of alcohol or drugs?

> It has been my experience that persons have a basically positive direction. In my deepest contacts with individuals in therapy, even those whose troubles are most disturbing, whose behaviour has been most anti-social, whose feelings seem most abnormal, I find this to be true (Rogers 1961, p. 26).

The above statement from Rogers matches my own experience of working with substance users. However, it is a world away from the beliefs and attitudes of most people who work with substance users, regardless of their theoretical stance.

Since amongst the many people who use substances are individuals who appear not to care either for their own well-being or the well-being of others, to say that they have a basically positive direction is an extremely challenging statement. This statement runs in opposition to the generally held view that substance users are moving in a basically negative direction, engaged in harmful and destructive activities from which they must be wrenched.

The Person-Centred Approach holds a belief which *appears* to fly in the face of reality and which requires an understanding of the personality theory of Carl Rogers if one is to make sense of it. Therefore, I shall briefly outline the theory using quotations from Rogers. In 1959 he wrote:

> The individual, during the period of infancy perceives his experiences as reality. He has a greater potential *awareness* of what reality is for him than does anyone else, since no one else can completely assume his *internal frame of reference.* (p. 244. All *italics* in Rogers' quotations appear as such in the original text.)

Seen from this perspective, the notion that someone *other* than the individual in question could be able to understand the needs of that individual *better than she herself* is a ludicrous idea. Since, for example, only a hungry individual can *experience* the feeling of hunger in her belly, no one else can be so intimate with that experiencing. I may *think* that you are hungry but I cannot feel your hunger. If I am truly empathic I will be so close to your hunger that I will come to know how it feels *as if* it were my hunger — only it is not my hunger and I cannot feel it as *mine*.

Rogers (1959) continues:

> He has an inherent tendency toward *actualizing* his organism. He interacts with his reality in terms of his basic *actualizing* tendency (p. 244).

Having experienced her hunger, the infant strives to have her needs met and will cry out for food even without the capacity for conscious thought. In so doing, she is striving to meet her organismic needs:

> . . . the human organism itself has a directional goal of growth, process and change, and that this drive is the only motivation for health in the individual (Fairhurst, 1994).

If an infant were allowed to develop amongst caring individuals who did not attempt to re-interpret her world but walked in her world with her, who did not judge her but truly accepted her, then her actualizing tendency would continue without obstacles.

However, this is a purely theoretical point. In reality a person will throughout childhood invariably find his natural organismic self under threat. For example, he may be told 'eat, you're hungry' although he is NOT hungry, and 'bad boy for not eating your food' although he felt no organismic need to eat at that time.

Why does the child pay any heed to attitudes or opinions, which are not in accord with her organismic growth tendency? Rogers believed that all human beings have the need for positive regard:

> As the awareness of self emerges, the individual develops a need for positive regard. This need is universal in human beings and that the expression of positive regard by a significant social other can become even more compelling than the organismic valuing process . . . (Rogers, 1959, p. 245).

Consequently, a child's feelings around food become a response to the needs of her adult carer(s), rather than a felt organismic need. This is a process common to human beings in our present culture, we all need positive regard — yet this is rarely offered unconditionally in our infanthood.

In common with other people in this culture and as far as I am aware, none of my clients were offered unconditional positive regard as children. Furthermore, many of the substance users I have met described infanthoods where they were raised in brutal and abusive families in which extreme means were used to hurt, control, and disempower them as children. Others described childhoods of extreme neglect in which their needs were unseen and unmet. Clearly for many substance users even *conditional* positive regard was not available to them as children.

Rogers described the process by which people adopt *conditions of worth* in response to conditional positive regard, and negative regard:

> A *need for self-regard* develops as a learned need developing out of the association of *self-experiences* with the satisfaction or frustration of the *need for positive regard*. When a *self-experience* is avoided (or sought) solely because it is less (or more) worthy of *self-regard*, the individual is said to have acquired a *condition of worth* (ibid, p. 246).

Thereafter Rogers says that *only*:

> Experiences which are in accord with his *conditions of worth* are *perceived* and *symbolized* accurately in awareness. Thus from the time of the first selective *perception* in terms of *conditions of worth*, the states of incongruence between self and experience, of psychological maladjustment, and of vulnerability exist to some degree (ibid, p. 247).

Rogers believed that through the provision of certain specific conditions a person's actualizing tendency can be released. These conditions are acceptance, or unconditional positive regard, and empathic understanding from a significant and congruent other. He wrote:

> . . . when I hold in myself the kind of attitudes I have described, (empathy, unconditional positive regard and congruence) and when

the other person can to some degree experience these attitudes, then I believe that change and constructive personal development will invariably occur (Rogers, 1961, p. 35).

and he continues:

. . . the individual has within himself the capacity and the tendency, latent if not evident, to move forward toward maturity. In a suitable psychological climate this tendency is released, and becomes actual rather than potential (ibid).

The actualising tendency will be freed as a direct consequence of provision of the core conditions, and, once freed it will enable the organism — the whole person — to continue its process of positive growth.

The overwhelming majority of my clients had never felt genuinely seen and accepted before entering 'treatment'. Once they are offered the core conditions they frequently recognise for themselves the benefits of the Client-Centred Approach, often expressing their appreciation in terms which could have come directly from a person-centred handbook. These quotes are typical of comments I have received from clients:

• 'No one has ever really listened to me before.'
• 'Thank you for listening to me and not treating me as a total nut case – which my behaviour definitely warrants. I don't understand myself, so I certainly don't expect anyone else to.'
• 'Thank you for listening to me and not judging me'.

Yet even in person-centred circles there are doubts expressed over the appropriateness of the Person-Centred Approach with this client group. In December 1998 a discussion on these issues ensued in a person-centred Internet group for practitioners, theoreticians, and people interested in the Person-Centred Approach.

Many of the writers in this debate, although adherents of the Person-Centred Approach, made exceptions when it came to working with substance users. For some writers the actualizing tendency was called into question in respect to substance users per se. For others the usefulness of the approach was called into question because of the clients' altered states of consciousness, conscious memory loss, altered personalities, or degrees of self-harm. Value judgements were made in respect of the extent of substance use by individuals, and the therapeutic relationship itself was questioned.

During this debate I described 'a lack of unconditional positive regard from the therapist who values her client sober more highly than when intoxicated ' and wrote: 'I can't see the therapist's trust in the actualizing tendency in this. Surely the client is smart enough to know what's best for her and find her own way to get there?'

Richard Bryant-Jefferies' response clearly questions the existence of the actualizing tendency in substance users. He replied to the above with the following: 'Here we get into whether the actualizing tendency can operate through the chemically affected central nervous system.' And in a later message (with reference to Rogers' example of the actualizing tendency of a potato): 'What if the chemicals [drugs and alcohol] have the effect of killing the potato's growth urge?'

Yet Rogers himself had complete confidence in the existence of the actualizing tendency in all clients:

> This tendency may become deeply buried under layer after layer of encrusted psychological defences; it may be hidden behind elaborate facades which deny its existence; it is my belief, however, based on my experience, that it exists in every individual, and awaits only the proper conditions to be released and expressed (Rogers, 1961, p. 351).

From my own work with substance users I have come to the conclusion that the actualizing tendency exists in substance users as it does in all other human beings. Substance users do not constitute a separate life-form and to suggest that their process is unlike that of other clients seems highly discriminatory to me.

Certainly the freeing of the actualizing tendency is difficult to assess accurately in another individual. Clients I have worked with often move in the direction of a decrease or cessation of their substance use or a change in their lifestyle. Yet if we measure 'success' with a client in this way we may be missing the whole truth for our clients. I strongly believe that the client knows best what is right for her. Substance use by a client may be as much evidence of her actualizing tendency as cessation of use may be for her partner.

One example of this can be seen in the case of R., a client I worked with for two years. R. had come to see me because her children had been taken into care by the Social Services and her Social Worker had told her that unless she gave up her substance use, and also attended contact sessions with the children punctually, they would not be returned to her.

When she first came to see me, her substance use was quite small and fairly manageable in that she could easily access drugs, and neither purchasing them, nor the use itself, caused her major problems in other areas of her life. Her attendance with me was quite unpredictable, sometimes she attended punctually, sometimes late, sometimes early, and sometimes not at all. During the sessions she spoke quite superficially and as if she was performing for me rather than being real. I provided the core conditions to the best of my ability.

R. did not attend the contact sessions with her children punctually, and the only change in her drug use was a slight increase. Eventually her children were put up for adoption.

So does R. provide evidence that even when the core conditions are present, some people's actualizing tendency cannot be freed, does not exist, or some other such interpretation, all of which could point to R. 'failing' as a person-centred client?

I would say the opposite was true. That her time with me was freeing for her actualizing tendency and indeed all of her actions were evidence of a healthy actualizing tendency.

In this case I was fortunate to have had one session with R. during which she was the most congruent I had ever known her to be. Her words and emotions seemed to match exactly and she seemed in strong and meaningful contact with me.

R. described her current relationship with the father of her children. He was frequently violent towards R. and she acknowledged in this session that the behaviour of her partner made the home an unsafe environment for the children.

The things in R.'s life, that she held dear and gave her hope for the future, were her children who she clearly loved very much. This session was the only time that R. did not maintain that she wanted the children to come home, and that it would kill her if they did not come home. She described her own childhood in which she suffered emotional abuse from her mother and sexual abuse from her uncle. Her mother had been unable, or unwilling, to protect her from her uncle and she recalled her feelings of lack of protection and emotional abandonment.

I believe that her decision to not comply with Social Services in order to bring the children home, and to in effect, sabotage the opportunity for their return, was, in fact, evidence of her actualizing tendency. Although she was grief-stricken at the prospect of the permanent loss of her children, enabling them to be protected during their childhood was healing for her, it gave her hope for the future and some peace from the past. I believe it was evidence of a positive directional force.

I was fortunate, firstly, in that R. was able to access into her awareness her very deep feelings in relation to these events, secondly, that she was able to articulate these feelings, and finally, that she felt heard enough by me to be able to trust me with hearing them.

Had she never expressed these thoughts and feelings to me I would not have understood why she *appeared* to be on such a downward spiral of self-destruction. Yet I believe that the road to recovery does not merely lie through the conscious understanding and articulation of a person's experience.

I believe that just such a mistaken approach, built on these type of *appearances,* was expressed by the eminent person-centred theorist and practitioner, Barbara Temaner Brodley during the Internet Group debate. She wrote, starting with this value judgment: 'with many people who are over-using alcohol' and continued: 'the therapeutic benefits of the relationship [are much diminished]'.

There can be a tendency in person-centred circles, as in other approaches, to doubt that we can trust our clients to know what is best for them, and this seems especially to be the case with substance-using clients, due to their altered states of consciousness. I believe that if a client attends a session, something in her organismic self is finding value in being there — it is not my job, nor necessarily my prerogative to know what that value is.

As well as the client's internal lack of self-worth, society in general does not value the lives of substance users, often turning them away from hospitals, refusing to carry them in ambulances, imprisoning them, denying them homes and employment. There is a condition of worth on all substance users if they use more than socially acceptable quantities, or certain specific substances. That is the condition to change their substance use.

I, therefore, believe that the most useful thing that a therapist or drug/alcohol worker can offer a substance-using client is unconditional positive regard, and this I try to do.

Despite my approach at times being undermined by my work colleagues, and even ridiculed, clients who are deemed too damaged or chaotic to be worked with successfully, or too violent or abusive, unstable or self-harming will frequently be offered to me in team meetings, as a client.

In a sense, my colleagues are agreeing with me that the Person-Centred Approach *is* beneficial to all clients. I believe that the Person-Centred Approach is the most appropriate approach for work with substance users because it puts its trust in the client.

But is it really possible to do therapeutic work with people who cannot remember the sessions?

Professor Doutor Joao Hipolito raised this question during the Internet Group debate, writing:

> When people are in an altered state of consciousness with alcohol or drugs there is most of times a discontinuity on their perception and consciousness. I believe the actualizing tendency is at work but there are some situations where our therapeutic relationship presents a problem: we might be in psychological contact with the 'intoxicated' self, at other times with the 'sober' self, but there is no communication between both. There is a great difficulty to integrate both . . .

I would agree with Doug Bowers' response:

> My position is that there is always some sort of contact in the therapeutic setting. That a person is intoxicated only alters the nature of the contact.

In addition, I do not believe that my role is to in any way attempt to 'integrate' the different parts of a person, although this may happen in the course of the therapy.

Whether a person's failure to remember a session is purely due to substance use, or whether that person has dissociating parts, the same conditions should exist as for clients who do remember each session since the only relevant continuity is the presence of the organismic self.

Conclusion

The Person-Centred Approach meets the client where she is at, makes no judgments or has no expectations of the client and frees the client to find her own path. I can think of no better approach for work with substance-using people.

References

Fairhurst, I.M. (1994) The Actualizing Tendency as the Sole Precept for Client-Centred Therapy. Unpublished paper.

Rogers, C.R. (1959) A Theory of Therapy, Personality, and Interpersonal Relationships, As Developed in the Client-Centered Framework in Kirschenbaum, H. and Henderson, V. (Eds), Boston: Houghton Mifflin, (1989) *The Carl Rogers Reader.* Originally published in Koch, S. (Ed), *Psychology, A Study of a Science, Vol.3 — Formulations of the Person and the Social Context.* New York: McGraw-Hill.

Rogers, C.R. (1961) *On Becoming a Person.* London: Constable.

I love this photo! I'd just run up a (small) hill. I was feeling happy and free and enjoying nature in the company of my beautiful girlfriend. Bliss!

Subtle Energy Exchanges in the Counselling Relationship[1]

10

Rose Cameron

In this paper I would like to talk about personal energy, a concept I find really useful in thinking about the therapeutic relationship. I'd like to begin by introducing myself so as to give you some sense of where my ideas have come from.

I work as a person-centred counsellor, supervisor and trainer in Manchester, UK. I also practise healing by laying hands, and have done so for as long as I can remember. It is a relief to me that in very recent years — particularly since the Japanese system of healing, Reiki, has become so popular — people are generally less likely just to look alarmed when I say I am a healer, and more likely to respond by asking what kind of healer I am. When first giving this paper as a lecture, I was asked to describe myself for the publicity. I finally settled on describing myself as a 'Scottish healer' — a description which is in some senses daft as I doubt that Scottish healing, were there such a thing, would differ significantly from any other kind of healing. It is my belief that the ability to alleviate physical, mental, emotional and spiritual suffering by laying hands is a universal human attribute — something that we can all do. I believe that the process of becoming a healer is a process of remembering rather than learning anew.

However, I do think it is partly due to growing up in Scotland that I managed not to forget. There, as in many cultures that have undergone a conversion to new religious beliefs, the old system of spiritual beliefs and the traditional ways of helping and healing continue to exist underneath the new belief system. In Scotland the deal with the Kirk — the Church — seems to be that you can practice the older ways but not talk about them. So when it came to laying hands, I didn't talk about it, or think about it, and I somehow didn't fully register what I was doing. I suspect this was partly due to the attitude of quiet acceptance I encountered and partly due to a paucity of words and concepts with which to think about it.

This lack of words with which to think or talk about healing did not matter much

This chapter is adapted from an article published in the *Race Multi-Cultural Journal* No 16 pp 16-19, reproduced here with kind permission of the publisher, the British Association for Counselling.

to me for a long time. However, after I'd moved down to England I found many people suspicious of healing unless I could give some explanation of what it was and how it worked. I also found what seemed a sudden need within myself for some framework within which to think about it. I joined a group of healers, and found lots of concepts and the words to explore them with. I found a vocabulary for my experience.

The lack of such a vocabulary had previously rendered me unable to speak up in defence of my experience. 'Hands up those of you who can see the air,' my teacher asked us in my first year at school. Obediently I stuck my little arm in the air. I saw, and still see, a constant vibration and pulsation everywhere I look, and assumed that this must be the air. My teacher told me not to be silly, that nobody could see air.

These days I think of that constant vibration as ch'i, prana, tondi or eckankar. I know that there are at least 79 cultures that have a name for it, and that the concept of a universal energy is intrinsic to the psychology and spirituality of those cultures. Ch'i, prana, energy, life-force is within us and all around us. The practices of yoga, tai ch'i, ch'i kung and healing, to name but a few, are about becoming more able to absorb this energy, to the eventual end of becoming absorbed into it. Being absorbed into it is an experience going beyond unity within oneself to a state in which there is no within and without.

You may or may not have had, or desire, such an experience. Perhaps you are more likely to have sensed a flow of energy between yourself and your environment, between yourself and a client, which you may not have been able to name. As a healer, I think of myself as channelling energy that comes through me, but is not from me. It does not matter, when I lay hands on someone, whether we have spoken or whether the person receiving healing knows that they are being treated by me rather than someone else. I am there simply as a channel. My job as a healer is to stay out of the way and let it happen. In some ways I think the discipline of person-centred counselling is also about not getting in the way whilst healing takes place, but as a counsellor my own personal energy is also involved — I give of myself as well. I believe this means that I have a responsibility to be aware of how I interact with clients on an energetic level, and that I have a responsibility to look after myself energetically.

Our energetic response in relationship

The traditional systems of psychology and medicine of a great many cultures recognise not only an all-pervasive, universal energy but also that we are each surrounded by a moving field of energy which is essentially an expression of our own life-force. I am not talking about a projected, or dissociated part, but about a part of ourselves whose rightful place is 'out there', beyond our skin, a part that we only contain within the boundaries of our skin when we are feeling defensive. It can be photographed (using special equipment), and some people can see it.

In the esoteric tradition of the West this is called an aura, but I know of no term for it in mainstream European psychological thought. The disharmony between European psychological and esoteric thought is such that many of us who wish to be taken seriously as psychologists, psychotherapists and counsellors may be prone to dismiss the very concept as New Age claptrap without giving serious consideration to an idea that exists in the psychological thought of practically every other culture I can think of.

The idea that we absorb universal energy through our aura, our energy body, and that it flows through us is the basis of not only the healing practices of many traditions, but also the basis of their spiritual practices. It is through our aura that we are profoundly connected with the world that we think of being outside ourselves. It seems no accident that the systems of psychological thought that recognise such a concept have grown out of cultures which value interconnectedness more highly than individualism and personal autonomy, cultures in which psychology and spirituality have not been wrenched apart.

A huge amount is known about alleviating physical, emotional and spiritual distress by working directly with the energy system. Hands-on healing, acupuncture, yoga, shamanic practice, tai ch'i, ch'i kung, crystal therapy, many dietary systems, and homeopathy are all ways of working directly with a person's energy system. In addressing problems at an energetic level the practitioner affects body, psyche, spirit and community. I believe that whether we conceptualise our own way of working as being focused primarily at a physical, psychological or spiritual level, it will inevitably affect the person receiving in a holistic way because we are indivisibly whole people.

However, what I am concerned with here is not working with a client's energy field or the holistic nature of counselling, but the importance of being aware of how we interact with clients energetically. At workshops I suggest some simple exercises that enable participants consciously to experience their aura expanding and contracting. These exercises demonstrate how our personal energy field generally expands towards what we like, and contracts away from that which we dislike and with which we want to avoid contact. Sensing someone energetically expanding towards us is part of our experience of feeling received, and of experiencing the person we are with as fully present. What we are doing energetically has an impact on clients. We have an energetic relationship with our clients, which may or may not be congruent with the relationship we intend. It seems to me terribly important that we are aware of, and able to reflect on, our part in that relationship.

Most of us will have experienced knowing that someone's response to us has changed even if that person continues to make the right noises during a telephone conversation — we can sense that they have closed down, withdrawn their energy. We know if we are being watched. We know when someone's attention has wandered long before we see them glaze over. We pick up 'vibes' that feel very real, even if they are not congruent with the person's behaviour towards us. However, if the reality of something is not confirmed by our culture and language, it can seem secret, known only to us. I suspect many of us, although acutely aware of other people's energetic reactions, imagine that our own energetic reactions will not be sensed by others.

Our clients are, of course, every bit as perceptive as ourselves, and will be aware of our energetic reactions even if they do not have the words with which to name them. If we, as person-centred counsellors, want to be trustworthy, it is really important that we are aware of our energetic responses and willing to acknowledge them. When we do so we affirm our clients' ability to trust their own perception as well as our willingness to be honest.

Sensing energetic incongruence — perhaps somebody's energy field being contracted and withdrawn whilst their behaviour is welcoming and friendly — alerts us to inauthenticity. We may, as counsellors, think we are being warm and open, but if we have withdrawn energetically, our client is unlikely to experience us as such. They are likely to sense our withdrawal and feel out of contact with us. They may feel rejected, disapproved of, disliked. Their perception that we have withdrawn will almost certainly be accurate. Their interpretation of our withdrawal — that we dislike or disapprove of them — may or may not be accurate.

I believe that most of us accurately perceive energetic change in other people, but then go on to interpret that change with reference to our own habitual reactions. My own tendency is to withdraw energetically when I'm angry, but not when I am frightened. I puzzled for years over what it was I was doing that irritated so many people till I noticed my therapist energetically withdraw from me. I was surprised to find that he felt frightened rather than angry. My perception that he had withdrawn was accurate, my interpretation as to why he had done so was not.

Developing awareness and choice

Our energetic reactions are usually instant, and therefore we may feel as if they are beyond our control and choice. They are not. Contracting and withdrawing our energy or allowing it to be open and expansive is something we do, and we can choose to do otherwise if we want to. I noticed, when working in a fairly violent setting that fights tended to worsen if I contracted my energy whilst intervening. I began trying to stay energetically available. When I managed to do so I was able to make full enough contact with the people involved to bring a fight to a more rapid end.

Separating our energetic reaction from our emotional response may seem a very strange thing to do if we strongly associate particular energetic sensations with particular feelings. Not tightening up and withdrawing energetically when frightened may seem impossible, unwise, or plain incongruent. Having made a point of not energetically withdrawing when scared, I can report that I still feel frightened, but not panic-stricken. If I remain energetically available when angry, I still feel angry, but not hostile, and, I believe, am much less likely to be experienced as such.

We have every right to withdraw energetically when frightened, hurt, offended or uncomfortable, and may well choose to continue doing so. What I believe is important is that we are aware that this will have an impact on the person we are with. Most of us probably already have a reasonably well-developed awareness of what we are doing energetically, although this may be genuinely difficult to acknowledge due to our lack of words. We know when we feel distant or when we surge forward to make contact with someone we really want attention from.

We can bring our awareness more sharply into focus by just paying attention to what we sense happening beyond our skin (for some people this may be a fair distance beyond their skin). Paying attention to the rhythm of our breath may also give us clues as to how we are reacting energetically. Our energy field will generally contract as we inhale, and expand as we exhale.

We usually contract our energy in an effort to protect ourselves. However, we may well find that the armour-plated and utterly isolated type of protection that contracting gives us is not really what we want.

Maintaining our own energy

Although expanding our personal energy field sensitises us in both senses of the word — we become better equipped to pick up what is going on around us and also more vulnerable to its impact upon us — energetic expansion does not have to render us too tender to be touched. It is possible to be solid in our expansion rather than insubstantial. I think of it as the difference in quality between a thin mist that drifts and doesn't hold its shape or space and a jelly that is transparent, flexible enough to be impacted, yet has enough substance to bounce back into its own shape. Such substantial flexibilty can be built by expanding and contracting our energy field just as we would stretch and contract a muscle in which we wanted to build substance, flexibility and strength.

Until a couple of years ago, I recognised no particular need to protect myself from the energetic impact of working with counselling clients. I was shocked into acknowledging the need after seeing my osteopath one Saturday morning. He had been asking what I thought were pretty inappropriate questions about my counselling clients — was I working with anyone who was very depressed? Did any of my clients have high blood pressure and such-and-such a physical condition? Just as I was about to get shirty with him he asked if I was seeing anyone who sat in a particular position. I immediately recognised a client I had been seeing for a long time, who was very depressed, and who did have all the physical symptoms he'd asked about. He took my pulse, which was normal. Then he took my blood pressure, which was not only a huge amount higher than it had ever been before (or since), but was furthermore unrelated to my pulse.

Make of that what you will. As a healer I was already familiar with the concept that it is possible (but not desirable) to take on the symptoms of someone I am working with. What really shook me was my lack of awareness. This particular client had not been on my mind since I'd seen them. I'd had no awareness of carrying them around, yet it seemed that I was doing so in an alarmingly physical way. The fact that that somebody working on my physical body could all but tell me the name of this client struck me as an incredibly important supervision issue. Presumably if I can be affected by a client in this way, then other counsellors (doctors? masseurs? homeopaths? acupuncturists?) can too.

My understanding of how I had come to be carrying my client's physical symptoms and what I could do about it came about through suggestions offered by the osteopath who'd identified them, conversations with healers, supervision, and my supervisor's inspired referral of me to a Ch'i Kung teacher. My understanding of how energy works suggested that I had resonated with my client's ch'i, her energy, in very much the way that one drum will spontaneously resonate and sound if another drum is played nearby. I don't have the space in this paper to go into the theory of this, but I can recommend Barbara Brennan's *Hands of Light* (Bantam) as an accessible introduction for those whose grasp of physics is practically nil; Richard Gerber's *Vibrational Medicine* (Bear & Co) for those whose grasp is a little stronger, and *The Dancing Wu Li Masters* by Gary Zukav (William Morrow) for those whose interest in, and grasp of, physics are stronger still.

I used to, when trying to massage someone's headache away, feel something travelling up my thumb and into my wrist, which eventually developed a click and ache. I learnt when I joined my group of healers, how to cleanse my energy system of unwanted energy. I also developed the habit of routinely grounding, protecting and energising myself. I suspect that as a person-centred counsellor in an on-going relationship with clients, and one in which I am emotionally present and seeking to empathise, my need to take these precautions is even greater.

Some traditions use fire to cleanse, others use running water, earth, smoke, air. Now, at the suggestion of the osteopath, I swim on days that I see clients and supervisees, to clear myself in moving water. I also burn cedar essential oil in my workroom. Native American shamans burn what they call juniper (but is our cedar), and other dried plants in order to cleanse the energy of their working space. Burning cedar oil is more discreet, less smoky, and doesn't smell illegal!

Energy follows our intention, and moves with our breath and so we can intentionally expel unwanted energy as we breathe out. When I do this I experience something like a shiver, but without the coldness. I presume that when these shivers of energy are moving downwards, I am successfully discharging energy back into the earth. I mentally move it out through my bare feet just to make sure. I do this because I believe that there is an ecology of energy just as there is an ecology of the earth, and do not want to be an energetic litter lout. As I understand it, the earth recycles unwanted energy in much the same way that it absorbs and balances surplus electrical charge from the power grid or from thunderstorms or recycles biodegradable waste.

We breathe in; we breathe out. We absorb energy; we release energy. We expand and connect; we contract and separate. Our physical, emotional, and spiritual aliveness is dependant on this rhythm, this pulsation. My Oxford English Dictionary defines psyche as soul; spirit; mind. It tells me that it is from the Greek word for soul, and also means breath, life. The ancient Greeks did not separate life, breath and spirit, nor do Tibetan, Chinese and Indian healing practices (to name but a few). I believe that our healing practice, therapy (from the Greek therapeia — healing), is greatly enriched by mindfulness of the unity of life, breath and spirit.

All my photographs were still packed away after moving house when I was asked for one for this book, so my partner took this.

POEMS

11

MEG HILL

The Cave

The womb, darkness and unknowing —
Fear and pain and terror —
How? Why? Where?
A shaft of light on water
Gives hope.
The gift, a candle —
Respite, help a way to freedom
And the green world above.
Do not look back, but know
What is there, and rejoice
In the world of life.

A poem written in a workshop with Maria Bowen — on intuition

'You and I, in the light —
The shadows come and go between us and around,
Liquid and flashing —
Our hearts and hands are open.
The Earth rolls on.'

This is the editor's personal choice out of a few photographs that Meg sent with the instruction, 'Choose any one you like!'

A Phenomenology of Motherhood: The Early Years

12

Jo Cohen Hamilton

Preamble

In this chapter I present a look at how being and becoming a mother throughout the first four years of motherhood has influenced my work as a person-centered counselor and counselor educator, has tested my beliefs in person-centered principles, and has challenged and expanded my self-concept development. Bringing my whole self into therapeutic relationships means bringing my new motherhood in juxtaposition to my work. Being genuine involves empathic acceptance of and trust in others and myself. In allowing myself to be known, I have grown in transparency, empathy and acceptance. This transition into motherhood has brought rich rewards and unexpected discoveries, and I would hardly propose that the path has been easy, nor always pleasant.

Bruno Bettelheim (1987) proposed that empathy involves a transformation of the client's experience into self-knowing on the part of the therapist. An empathic reflection thus conveys a mutuality of human experience. He states:

> Freud spoke of the sympathy that exists between the unconscious of
> one person and that of another, suggesting that we can understand
> another person's unconscious only through our own. One cannot
> adequately explain what is involved in love, anger, jealousy, or anxiety,
> nor can words really convey what one feels in depression or elation.
> But if one has experienced these states of being one knows what another
> person is likely to be feeling. When we feel empathically with another
> person, we get very close to him; we can understand him much better
> than if we had to rely only on what he can tell us.
> ... [We] must rely on what their words suggest to our own unconscious,
> responding to symbols, suggestions, and metaphors (p. 89).

True empathy is not a process observed from outside oneself, but is a person-to-person, in-the-moment event. The more I permit others' lives to touch my own reason and emotion, the broader my entire organismic experience becomes. As my self and organismic experiences grow more congruent, my capacity for empathic acceptance of persons' individualized actualization tendencies is released. Further, an openness to all of my experiences (self-actualization tendency) deepens my connection to the common, universal understandings of humanity (the fundamental actualization tendency). In *Person-Centered Therapy: A Revolutionary Paradigm*, Bozarth (1998) concludes that 'The core condition is us' (p. 177). He states

> The core motivational condition, from a holistic view of the theory,
> is that the individual has a directional and formative tendency towards
> the fulfillment of inner potential. Being in touch with . . . [one's]
> organism is naturalistic and universal (p. 178).

The bridge to self-actualization in 'traditional' person-centered therapy can be found in the therapists' trust in self-actualization as expressed through the core conditions.

In the paragraphs below, I have changed the names and have significantly altered the identities of clients to protect their confidentiality and anonymity. Although the circumstances and events have, I believe, been altered beyond personal recognition, the descriptions given have preserved the essence of therapeutic relationships that took place. The substance for this work was created by virtue of my family. I have used fictitious names for some family members. Respect for privacy and protecting confidences was a central guiding value in my writing about both clients and family. I invite you to glimpse my life's journey as a new mother. Thank you for reading.

The birth

I had just experienced the miracle of birth of my first-born daughter — Elizabeth. I gazed in awe. Several months before, we had concluded that her name would be Elizabeth, after Ellis, my father's father. We had considered Esther, Emily, and Elissa, and other names for other letters. My mother's mother, Pauline, a beloved woman with caring consideration and unconditional love for her grandchildren, was thoughtfully considered. But it was decided that Elizabeth would be named after Floryne's husband, Ellis. The spirits of ancestors and old friends were among us. My husband — much more here-and-now, and practical, couldn't but help respect, appreciate, and even join in the journey.

Elizabeth. Her forest of black cropped hair stood straight up, capping her rosy cherubic face. Her entire just-born body was covered with a yellowish-white cream-cheesy film. Underneath she was reddish pink and wrinkly. Later, upon closer examination, I could see in her the cheeks of my mother's mother and the eyes of my husband. Her past, present and future spoke volumes as I held her in my arms. There was so much history, so much possibility. And here we were now with one another. Elizabeth was a marvel and a wonder. She hypnotized me with her total complexity and utter simplicity. I was stunned by the immense profundity of her being. Then I thought, 'She must be shocked to be out in this world.' (Could

Leboyer's birth trauma warnings be right?) Well, I would do my best to make her feel right about being here. Though I wasn't sure precisely how, I trusted that empathic positive regard was going to be sufficient. But, I needed to learn how to swaddle her, to feed her, to bathe her, to hold her. Nurturing her and trusting in myself to do so were essential. Could I do it?

Settling into life as a 'brand new' mother

Understanding what it means to be a mother would take time. I read profusely about infant care and development, and then about toddlerhood, including sleep and toilet teaching. I read and listened to developmental research; to advice in magazines, journals and texts; to works of fiction and non-fiction; to television, movies and any medium available (including passers nearby, parents of all generations, and with anyone who seemed interested in 'most every context I visited). Parents commiserate with one another, sharing their discoveries. Laurie said, 'When I can be empathic it almost always makes things better,' while Jan remarked, 'I don't know if this will help you, but I used lollies to get them to potty on their own.' Both helped!

Bettleheim (1987) captured my phenomenological credo on parental advice-seeking when he stated:

> Subconsciously we are leery of child-rearing advice even as we seek it. Deep down, we know quite well that . . . the problem . . . contains much that is unique to the parent and child involved . . . and even when the problem we are facing is a common one, each of us is a unique individual' (p. 19).

I wanted still, at times with frustration and near desperation, to decipher how to be a good parent. In my reading I have kept in mind Sir Francis Bacon's (1561–1626) consideration that 'Some books are to be tasted, others swallowed, and some too few to be chewed and digested'. Although I have found no certain recipe on how to raise a child, many authors brought important perspectives. Dreikers (1964), Gordon (1970), Ellis (1977, 1966), Faber and Mazlish (1980), and Rogers and Freiberg (1994, 1969) all offered useful insights on how to raise children with respect. The larger discovery would now have to build on our lives.

Bettleheim (1987) also helped me to clarify my longing to appreciate the individual nature of each of my children. 'Thinking in terms of the norm in relation to our child belittles his singular importance to us, and that of our relationship, because it implies that we are comparing him to strangers' (p. 35). Even if compared to non-strangers, the singularity of my children's identity was compromised, whether friend, relative or stranger serves as the comparison. How could I, as a new parent seeking to do my best to facilitate my children's development, avoid anchoring to norms, and also relate to them with personal intimacy? I would prefer to be less of a novice at deeply trusting myself.[1]

Despite greater comfort (in the sense of familiarity) rearing a second child, the addition of Lilly into our home presented me with the question of how to relate uniquely and intimately with two children. We prepared for Lilly coming into the world with considerably less focus than had been placed on Elizabeth's arrival. We were consumed with the care of an infant all the while Lilly was in the womb. My husband's thoughts at the time went something like 'how in the world are we going to *do* this all over again?' As for me, I wondered 'Is it possible to love another baby with as much love as I feel for Elizabeth? Will my affections be divided? Impartial? Will I be able to rise to the occasion of appreciating their uniqueness?'

I was surprised at how loving I felt toward both of my daughters as individuals. I am still challenged to be sufficiently present for both of them. Sometimes they battle so strenuously for my favor that I am literally seated in the middle of them as they stretch my arms in two separate directions. In these moments I feel as though there simply is not enough of me. I have expressed understanding of being wanted by both of them. Sometimes they don't seem particularly impressed by that understanding, and are even irritated by it. Further empathizing with their irritation has resulted in even further irritation. Usually empathy helps. I have learned that when the goal of empathy is to change their behavior because it annoys or dissatisfies me, it is less likely to be helpful. Empathy helps most when it is given out of love (unconditional acceptance and appreciation of an individual) and respect being genuinely interested in an individual's self-expression) rather than the desire to change or control.

Identity transformation through the looking-glass

Each to each a looking-glass, reflects the other that doth pass. Charles Horton Cooley (1864 – 1929).

People around me felt invited to ask about the pregnancy and then the baby. My status was that of a pregnant woman who would be giving birth, and then what? A change was presenting itself, necessarily. In becoming a parent, I felt grief at the loss of my familiar life — not at first — but when the awesomeness gave way to sleeplessness and exhaustion. Most parents with whom I have spoken have felt this. I was happy in my career, loved my partner, and was enjoying our time together. And then, in a single breath, so much changed.

Walking the steps, the parking lot, the classroom, the hallways — voices asked earnestly, 'How are you?' 'How's the baby?' 'How do you like being a mother?' 'Are you getting any sleep?' 'Girl or boy?' 'How many pounds and ounces?' The familiar and less known along every path I crossed offered 'Congratulations,' and then, incredulously, 'You're back already!' The experience of a shifting identity, incorporating, assimilating and accommodating my new self-perception and the perception of me by others, was not an entirely stabilizing process. Despite years of fantasizing being a mother, my rather single-minded professional identity was unprepared for the continuing redefinition of who I was in not only my own eyes, but in the eyes of others. Motherhood was easier as a fantasy.

I stretched the limits. The counseling group room at my workplace became the place where Elizabeth stayed once a week for the first academic semester of her life. I needed to create opportunities to have her near me, even if I was working. Her baby-sitter tended to her, and any chance I could I spent time with her. A few minutes here, a half-hour there. I was aware of the imposition on the workplace. I was certain that although she could not make out the words I was saying, she could hear my voice in the next room. I was concerned that she might feel the anxiety of hearing but not seeing me, but she was not responding with cries, and usually seemed happy to see me. Elizabeth spent the first year of her life joining me at work on Tuesdays, and spending the hours away from me with my husband's family.

The day before Elizabeth's first birthday my second daughter Lilly was born. The emotional strain of wanting to be with both girls was great. I wanted to hear them babble, see them cut teeth, soothe them when they were unhappy, and make them feel secure and able to depend upon me. Most of the working parents whom I knew labored to convince themselves that the full-time rearing of their children by people other than themselves was nothing to feel guilty about. A friend who was a stay-at-home mom marveled at my 'having it all'. Day care providers assured me that it would be O.K. Lots of people and advice-giving literature encouraged me to part quickly and guiltlessly lest my child inherit my separation anxiety. 'Don't let them sense that it's not O.K.' 'Once you decide to leave your child in the care of another, communicate the trust that you have decided to place in them.' 'Walk away confidently and don't look back!'

What could I do? I could not afford to seriously consider a leave without pay lest I be willing to change my way of life dramatically. My career identity was not keen on the prospect of its demise, even if temporarily. Part-time work was not an option at the university. In retrospect, I might have been able to manage a leave without pay, taking on part-time employment elsewhere. As it was, I accepted the purpose of day care. I believed that Elizabeth and Lilly would learn a lot, and would probably benefit from the social interaction. We debated over different arrangements — someone in our home, our children in a private home, all of the various available centers.

I knew that most caregivers were naturally patient and kind, or were trained to be, but I was certain that my children could not form the depth of attachment toward a caregiver whose affections were divided among six. Still, we chose a day care center because it was located at my workplace, it had a good reputation, and there seemed to be less risk than to trust a single stranger. When I dropped the girls off, I wanted to respond to their beckoning me not to leave. Sometimes I did. I hugged them once, twice, and again. I hung around until I had to go, or be late for work. I am lucky to have family who generously and lovingly provide day care for the girls once or twice a week. After two years of two three-day-a-week day care center experiences, the girls are now in a caregiver's home. Working parents try all sorts of arrangements. I felt envy toward those who managed to feel satisfied with their day care situations. Then I learned that some of them envied mine!

How much being out of control of child rearing must a full-time working parent endure? They use a walker despite your warnings right out of the latest pediatric update. They watch too much television and are sitting too close. I was once certain that they would not ever (or at least rarely) eat candy. Now I wasn't certain of anything. I resisted giving up my right to make daily, moment-to-moment decisions about what my children would experience. My lifelong motherhood fantasies had not included moments of disassociation, self-abandonment, depression, or hypocrisy.

One Tuesday morning, Elizabeth took 20 minutes to get dressed because although she agreed to get dressed, she refused to dress herself, and refused to be dressed. She then had a ten-minute tantrum because breakfast didn't include candy. We finally sat at the table for breakfast. I never actually sat centered on the kitchen chair because, after toasting a piece of raisin bread, Lilly's order changed to not-toasted and the juice in both of their cups needed to be poured back into the container and replaced with strawberry milk in the elephant cups. At times I tolerate demands that I experience as ridiculous. I have wanted my own personal tantrum. I suppose that is how they must feel about my demands. They are seeking self-confidence and self-control alongside me.

When I hear stories of an adult abandoning, inflicting pain upon, or even killing their infants and children, my immediate reaction is to feel horrified. Most parents and many counselors would be unable to look such an individual in the eye and communicate acceptance. I have spoken with jail and prison psychologists who have described their work as lonely because people wonder aloud to them, 'How can you talk to people like *that*?' I understand through experience the enormous frustration and anxiety that goes along with the day-to-day task of being empathic with demanding and needy children. I also have some vicarious knowledge of the impetuous actions of people on drugs (e.g., crack, alcohol, amphetamines), particularly those abused as children, and those with deep feelings of rage and a history of antisocial actions, who are the most likely to inflict pain on their children.

Fortunately, for most people, the pain of being without their children overshadows the struggle to be with them.

Child-centered, career-driven partners try to 'have it all'

There were moments when the approach-approach conflict of working and mothering felt almost unbearable. Being sensitive to the pull I felt to be with Elizabeth, and also the experience of being pulled to continue being the also passionately connected worker/career woman I was, and was becoming — practically contorted me. I sat with my clients in the day, suffering through the sleepless nights and the relentless identity upheaval that wanting to work and also be a full-time mother presented. The desire to maintain my growing professional status, and my sheer joy of mothering clashed interminably. As a mother, various responsibilities pertained to me, and one of them was to be physically and emotionally present with Elizabeth, and then also Lilly. Even in the womb it had become important to eat better, lay low on the caffeine, not drink alcohol and use drugs, get more sleep, not inhale gas fumes from the filling station, walk extra carefully on the ice, and so on.

I remember colic as that sleepless stage when my husband and I quarreled to win the race of who is most tired and who needs more sleep. 'I'm so tired.' 'I'm even tireder.' 'Well, I'm even more tired.' Mustering up a chuckle, I secretly loathed what I expected to follow and almost always did. 'Do you mind if I go take a little nap?' My husband's one-hour naps always seemed to take two hours. Mine seemed even longer to him. I could barely tolerate hearing myself (and him) trying to get free from parenting. My appreciation for the havoc that uninvited colic could wreak, grew.

Neither of us wanted to slow down — career identity success. We both desperately needed to sleep, to slow down, to take time for ourselves, for our new parenthood, and for one another. Two years later, when I was not promoted at work, a friend of mine reasoned, 'Maybe they're saying "Relax a little. You're a new mother now and you don't have to work so hard."' Despite physical and emotional exhaustion, Ed and I were both resolved to move forward with our careers. We both felt frustrated and sometimes discouraged that the sacrifices to our family life seemed to be insufficiently financially or emotionally remunerated.

When opportunities arose for more work, we sometimes supported each other in accepting the challenge, but we often have resented each other's lack of parenting priority with expectations that the other would do more. Surely it would get easier if one of us submitted our ambitions. We have both felt stress over how to not compromise our ambitions (and recreations) while not sacrificing a priceless relationship with our children. How could we do it all? We would have to learn to grow together with our children. How?

Our conversations shortened as our exhaustion grew. Our schedules were overbooked. As the children developed, their demands for attention seemed to increase in predictable synchrony with the moment my husband and I were about to speak to one another. We have tried lots of things. I suggested, and still would prefer, a less argumentative conversational style. I believe my children (Elizabeth especially) are less likely to interrupt when our conversation is polite and respectful. Part of my belief derives from observation, although it is certainly influenced by my own comfort with a less argumentative style of conversation. Sometimes my husband and I speak half-spoken sentences, and then conclude when the interruption ends, that it wasn't important. At times we have simply avoided initiating meaningful conversation with one another. It simply was not worth the frustration of a probable interruption.

Considering our children to be old enough now to respect us and to tolerate our needs, we announce that 'It is important for mommy and daddy to talk to one another.' We quite recently presented a 'united front' in warning one of them that if she interrupted us again there would be no ball game. I can appreciate how people on the outside looking in might think we had little regard for our child the way we hushed her. I trust that I have given my children ample opportunity to speak and be listened to, and that if their parental unit is to survive, we must be accorded the respect as a couple to have a relationship apart from them. Which is more of a guarantee?

Family preservation: defining the boundaries of empathy's 'as-if' condition
When clients shared pain, I relegated pure empathic listening to a secondary status beneath my infant Elizabeth's (and developing child's) well-being. I allowed myself to get close to painful experiences of others, but refused to carry the pain into my home. Developing an as-if stance was actually facilitated by my insistence on not absorbing the pain into me. I would not risk carrying a client's pain home to my newly forming family. I was reflecting rather than absorbing their affect. The caveat, however, is that it is not possible to reflect what one has not absorbed. These seemingly orthogonal dimensions are *both* essential for empathy to occur. The as-if condition is present the instant the client's meaning is experienced. Empathy relies on this condition, and exists in toto when the client perceives its presence.

Clients

How important are my clients in my life?
In pregnancy I suffered a client's admonition. How unfair that it was the baby and not he being born to me; and who would naturally elicit more of my care and attention. We examined, sometimes gruelingly, the meaning of our relationship, the value of us both to one another, and the meaning that the baby would have in that. Resentment was shared, and all the while, it was not entirely clear to me just what the baby *would* mean to me, and I had difficulty making it clear, perhaps afraid that the truth might hurt too much.

My client shed a flood of tears from the pains of past losses. Another loss was imminent. His partly healed abandonment wounds felt so present, unable to be submerged in the face of my imminent motherhood. My pregnancy threatened our relationship. It raised questions about my loyalty and degree of care for my client. Over time, my trustworthiness grew to quell the doubts. I kept in contact, and soon returned to work for sessions. I even brought my daughter in for a couple of visits. I continued to show that I cared. It was a new birth for our relationship, a re birth of survival from pain, and a message to me that others would sometimes know more than I about what it would mean for me to be a mother.

Help; I'm projecting and I can't shut up!
I am about to share an error in therapy that my history cannot escape. Many readers have worked with clients who have struggled with infertility. One of the several clients I have worked with on this issue scheduled counseling at a time when I was beyond my own infertility experience and awaiting my child's birth. If her presenting problem had been known before the scheduling, perhaps I could have prepared myself. The circumstance presented a hard lesson for me.

I discussed with her my own experience with infertility, suggesting through words and my obviously pregnant belly that there was hope. As I spoke, I thought to myself, 'be quiet, this is not about you,' and 'this is not helpful, so please stop talking.' But, after years of wanting, my delighted, proud, and relieved-to-be-pregnant self insisted on being heard. I had experienced all of the frustration that she had felt, and I just wanted to make it better. I knew I was in error, and in a feeble attempt to rescue myself, ended my tale-telling with some mutterings about how one never knows what will be. We agreed to meet the following Monday. She never showed. I do not know the outcome for this woman. Perhaps she eventually got pregnant. If she did, maybe she even believes I helped to give her some hope, although I imagine I created more frustration, anger, and resentment, than hope.

A self-centered client confrontation

My client pronounced that he had the right to be drunk on the highway at 1:00 in the morning. If he killed someone while he was drunk, it was their fault for being so stupid as to drive while drunk drivers were on the road. Was he serious? As mother of an infant and toddler, who spent sleepless nights wondering if a hospital visit for a fever might save a child's life, the client's words drew an instantaneous surge of protectiveness over the safety of my infants. The primitive, nurturing, gut-felt shift toward their protection drove me away from the client before me. A 1:00 a.m. visit to the hospital for a fever could result in my child's death, and he would be responsible.

I confronted my client with my fantasy. 'What if I have to drive my child to the hospital . . . ?' Of course he agreed with me that it was ridiculous to think that I had no right to be on the road.

Some sessions later, after thinking it over and over, alone and in consultation, I was able to help him with glimpses of himself, though we were a long way from his feeling a sense of control over his alcohol abuse. I believe I am closer to understanding my client in retrospect. His irritation with and disregard for others expressed his largely masked (deeper) struggle to actualize his brilliance, while also longing to simply fit in. He felt weighed down by taking himself too seriously, and then drank himself into triviality. He was both touched and amused that others offered him support despite his obvious 'fuck-ups'. In believing that he had been given too many chances, he felt both entitled and undeserving. An Adlerian would probably say that he had a superiority complex. He lacked responsibility towards and felt superior over others. He expressed this through an alcohol abusive lifestyle. Both were covers for deeper insecurity. I don't pretend that I could reach this client today, but I'd like to think that I'd be a bit closer than telling him that he had no right to be on the road drunk at 1:00 in the morning so that my children were safe. I hope that if there is a next time I will get closer to the client's reality.

A distracted empathic stance with a client who I imagined would be 'a very nice daughter'

I was only partly present for my client as I wondered what I would do if *my* daughter got her nose pierced, and then more significantly, if my daughter used crack as my client did. The returning thought led me to think of Rogers' (1989) position that 'I endeavor to voice any *persisting* feelings which I am experiencing toward an individual or toward the group in any significant or continuing relationship' (Rogers, In Kirschenbaum and Henderson, 1989, p. 347).

I was wrestling with the meaning of this guide to congruence. I was fairly clear that it did not mean I ought to share my recurrent thoughts if they seemed to have much more to do with me than with my client. I also realized that I would not be happy if one of my daughters used crack. I wondered if I would be the sort of mother who would raise a child who could become addicted to crack, what sort of mother that was, and if I had a choice. I listened to my client describe her frustrations with being addicted to crack. I understood her belief that if she disclosed the addiction to her parents, they would probably respond with initial disbelief. They would be ashamed of her, might never trust her again, and would most certainly cut off her ties with her closest friends. Her dilemma: maintaining a false identity by concealing the truth to her parents, or risking their loss of love and the loss of her friends.

I wondered if her parents were so unforgiving, while I privately sided with them in their cutting her off from crack-addicted friends. I likewise understood her friends' importance to her and appreciated their value despite their own personal struggles. I silently mused that in the past I might have tended to side with my client in an adolescent rebellion against parental authority. My client wanted her parents to know and to help her, but she was afraid. She convinced me (and herself) that her parents were to some degree aware that 'something is wrong'. I distracted myself with thinking that given my line of work I would probably recognize a drug problem and say something about it. I managed to keep the voices in my head *relatively* quiet. I had to remind myself, 'she's not talking about me, she's talking about them.' Sometimes my own circumstances occupied me even further, as with 'hopefully, if I am flexible and teach them that I truly accept them, they won't need to use crack, and if they do, they will be able to come to me to solicit my help in getting clean.' On more than a few occasions I got lost and had to refocus to listen. I did not moralize or judge, but I cared for the client as though she was my own daughter. When she deliberated over how she might tell her parents what was going on without suffering them having a stroke, I offered her the option of my being a mediator in the disclosure if she decided to tell them. Although she did not take me up on the offer, we continued the therapy for several more sessions. I later learned that she was working a rehabilitation program.

Understanding a parent's point of view facilitates resolution
My client had betrayed his parents' trust. He valued their opinion of him, and wished he could turn back time. He had gone hunting without a license, convincing his friend to join him by touting his great skill as a hunter. He had hunted the area since age nine. However, an unpredictable freak circumstance led to his accidentally shooting his friend. The friend was injured to the degree that they needed to seek outside aid, and that is how he was found out.

My client was a charming and sincere young man who deeply regretted his actions, although he seemed more focused on his own predicament than on the well-being of his friend. At first, his parents' disappointment in him, though unsettling, seemed understandable. But, after admitting guilt, feeling shame and remorse, asking for forgiveness, and vowing never to act so irresponsibly again, he wanted their faith in him restored. He described his relationship with his parents. They seemed like the type of parents that I would like to be. They were supportive, encouraging, trusting, and loving. They created numerous opportunities for him to enjoy life, and he had flourished in his schooling and social life under their care. This was the first time he had deeply let them down, and he felt needy of their forgiveness, especially that of his mother. He felt troubled by not fully understanding why she was having such a difficult time.

My client's distress echoed the helplessness that I have also felt wanting to be treated with the trust and respect that I knew I deserved, but that I had betrayed. But now I also had the experience of feeling mistrusting as a mother. I disclosed my own impatience and irritation waiting for my parents to renew their trust in me after I erred. Then I shared that I thought I might understand, even though I was a relatively new mother, what his mother might be going through. Even though my children were very young, I sometimes took longer to forgive them when I felt disappointed or angry with them than I would have liked.

I recalled a recent episode. My two-year-old daughter destroyed an important computer disk of mine despite the rule that she was not to touch my work desk. I felt angry with her much longer than I wanted to. For two days, every time we came within five feet of my desk I reminded her not to touch it. In the afternoon of the second day we were playing near my desk. It was probably the first time we were within the danger zone that I hadn't mentioned the incident. She asked, 'Are you still angry at me mommy?' and I replied, 'I'm less angry than I was but I'm still upset with you. I love you, but I am not happy that you destroyed my things. That disk that you broke had some very important work of mommy's on it and now I can't use it at all. I have to do all that work over again. So please don't touch *anything* on my desk again unless I say you can. O.K.?' Later that day she again pled forgiveness. 'Are you still angry at me mommy?' I said, 'Honey, I know you don't want mommy to be angry anymore but it upsets me when I think about all that work being ruined. I'm sure I won't be angry too much longer, and I'm sure you're tired of hearing mommy tell you not to touch her things, but I just really want you to understand that you are not to touch the things on my desk. O.K.?' And then later that day, 'Mommy, I didn't touch your desk all day. Are you happy with me?' 'I'm very happy about that sweetheart.'

I suggested to my client that maybe his mother just needed some time to let go. My client's entire body relaxed, and a soft smile came over his face. He recognized my story as his truth and said, 'Yeah, that's exactly what my mother said. She said that trusting me again would take some time. He had heard his mother say that, but he had not really understood it until that moment when he looked at it through my eyes. Perhaps the less intense emotional relationship that he had with me, compared with his mother, permitted him to understand a mother's lament without wanting it to be untrue. Despite unrest with his current status, he was comforted in knowing that it would just take some time. My goal was not to comfort my client. I simply expressed an experience of my own that seemed to earnestly capture the once elusive meaning of his mother's remarks. I saw my client, in passing, on a few occasions after that. He always acknowledged me with a warm, secure smile.

Children (adults too) crave acceptance. They do not distinguish between being disapproved of for their acts and being disapproved of as a person. It may soften the judgment to say 'I accept *you*, but do not accept *your behavior*,' but the judgment is felt nonetheless. Parents who want to offer their children unconditional love are in the precarious position of needing to teach their children socially acceptable behavior. Many therapists argue that you can fully accept a person but not their behavior. I disagree. I believe that if disapproval of behavior was acknowledged to be conditional acceptance of a person, a lot less confronting of client behavior would occur. Still, as a parent of a three and four-year-old I find myself using the word 'Don't'— and directing a lot of behaviour — a lot more than I would prefer.

Confronting incongruence

How in the world can I live the core conditions with my children when I define and control so much of their experience? Creating rules and balancing the rules with flexibility has been work. Clarifying the nature of a rule I ask myself, 'What is the purpose and to whose benefit is the rule made?' Clarifying the boundaries of the rule I ask, 'Under what conditions is it bendable or breakable?' Clarifying the rights of family members to make and break a rule I ask, 'How many and what types of choices are good for my child to make?' I am reluctant to make too many rules, and to be inflexible about the rules established, because I want to cherish my time with my children rather than spend it matching wills.

I met with a client who was examining some hard choices regarding the boundaries to set and the responsibilities to be taken for his young adult daughter. The frustrated father insisted that taking responsibility for his daughter must stop. He thought that despite all his best efforts to prevent her from prostituting herself, she needed to experience the natural consequences of her actions. He would no longer bail her out of jail after a raid. He would no longer give her lectures about the dangers of STDs and try to line up other jobs for her. Then, with added irritation, he told me that after leaving the session he had to deliver his daughter's unpaid fines to the courthouse so that she could be released from jail.

My client had worked with me in therapy for quite some time. We had been through his separation from an abusing wife, and had unearthed memories of his abusive childhood. We had shared dozens of hours together. He knew I had two young children (we worked together during and after my second pregnancy), and sometimes requested parenting advice. At times we discussed developmental issues of concern to him. He was a well-read and intelligent parent who wanted to do what was best for his daughter, but who could not seem to stop her from hurting herself and those around her.

When my client announced his afternoon agenda, despite his vehement refusal to take responsibility for his daughter just moments before, I felt personally challenged to address the contradiction. My own anxieties about contradictory rules motivated me to have him resolve the contradiction. I communicated my uncertainty about what was best, but in feeling anxious about the contradiction, implied that a resolution should be sought.

Rather than functioning as a therapist, I became a member of a two-person parent support group whose members were debating (because I wanted to) how to resolve dilemmas of inconsistent parenting. I commiserated over the excruciating task of deciphering whether maintaining the rule or breaking it would best protect his daughter's welfare. He had long since convinced me that there was no easy solution. He stood between the proverbial rock and hard place. We had been through it several times before. It was the first time that I had ever confronted my client's incongruence, and he appeared uneasy with it.

Session after session I accepted my client's struggle to have some hope amid the growing futility. When I challenged my client's inconsistency I was not passing judgment; however, considering my more usual non-directive stance, and his apparent tension, he probably perceived it as a judgment. Prior to my personal quest for congruent communication as a mother, I probably would have focused on his irritation with having to take care of his daughter's business rather than on his contradiction. I do not know what my client decided to do, but shortly thereafter, his daughter moved out of state with her aunt, much to my client's satisfaction. I rarely confront clients because I believe that doing so is usually counter-therapeutic. Is it possible for a confrontation to be empathic? Yes. Is it possible for a confrontation to express unconditional positive regard? No. Is an empathic confrontation ever helpful? Probably. Is it usually helpful? Maybe, maybe not. It depends at least on the context of the relationship and the intended and perceived unconditionality of the offering.

Clients and Students

A lesson in trusting self-actualization

I was ashamed to speak the feelings and thoughts that surfaced in me a few months after Lilly's birth. It was extraordinary that so many of the women students and clients I encountered during this time were lesbians. The question of my own daughters' future sexuality was virtually unavoidable. My unconditional acceptance of my lesbian friends, colleagues, clients, and students felt so transparently real to me. I now questioned whether it was a pretense. I found myself preoccupied with the notion that one or both of my daughters might possibly be or become a lesbian. Trying not to think about it didn't help, and I felt puzzled and disturbed over the distraction. I had truly believed I accepted homosexuality. I now found myself preferring that my daughters be 'straight'.

I considered all of the gay men and women whom I cared for deeply. At first I dismissed the possibility that I did not truly accept them. But I ruled it imperative for me to look deeper; to confront my resistance; and to move toward acceptance of whatever I might find. Worrying about my daughters' sexual identity implied my conditional regard for homosexuals. I discovered that my prejudice had two primary sources: moral and social condemnation; and personal exclusion. First, I have learned so many moral, social prohibitions against homosexuality throughout my lifetime. No one in my family, so far as I recall, ever explicitly said homosexuality was wrong. However, the message got through in so many places along the way. Homosexuals were so often condemned to moral repugnance that not to have developed some modicum of aversion would have meant I was a social isolate. How could I have avoided so pervasive an indoctrination? Feeling somewhat less responsible for my learning, my guilt lessened, while feelings of anger, hurt, and resentment for the pain that a gay person endures grew.

Regarding the second source of discomfort, that of personal exclusion, I realized that I perceived myself to be distanced and excluded from the homosexual world by virtue of my heterosexuality. I felt some resentment toward homosexuals for excluding me from their lives. My perception that I was being excluded clearly derived in part from my own projections. I did not consider myself a genuine ally. While I understood that gay people tend to be leery of heterosexuals' sincere acceptance of them (see e.g., Davies, 1998), I misinterpreted their socializing with other gays to suggest not merely an exclusion of me, but a rejection of me. I harbored ill-will over feeling mistrusted and left out. I can appreciate from my own experience a person seeking like companions. Still, I have long believed that a greater peace is achieved when people are willing to live acceptingly with each others' differences. Indeed, 'We are all much more simply human than otherwise' (Sullivan, 1947, p. 16.)

The very best mother that I can be for my children is one who accepts them unconditionally, who offers understanding, and who genuinely supports their self-actualizing tendencies. My greatest gift to my children is supporting them in being and becoming themselves.

Accepting mortality

I fear dying like I never did before becoming a mother. I worry about aging, smoking, stress, chest pains that I hope are 'merely' stress, and whether my husband can pull off being a parent without me. At first my death anxieties revolved around my children's safety. As they grew less fragile, I worried about them living their life without me, knowing that no one could completely fill the void. I became grief-struck at the thought that I would not be able to parent them and watch them grow. I felt devastated contemplating what my life might be like if one of them should die. I could barely fathom the loss of spirit seized from me.

I have done some things to ameliorate my anxiety. First, I spend time with my children, even though to them (and me) it never feels like enough. Second, in an attempt to assure that a part of me is carried with them, I read a couple of story books on audiotape for them to listen to in case of my death. I would like to say that I have been taking better care of my body, but I still smoke, rarely get sufficient exercise, and get too little sleep. I do allow myself to feel afraid of death now, and that helps. It is no surprise that in accepting my fear, I feel less afraid.

Many parents think about providing for their children in the event of their death. People write wills, select guardians, and so forth. My husband's point of view is that the most important thing that should happen if and when we die is that our children are deeply loved and accepted for who they are.

Afterword

I have heard and read many parents' exaltations on the worth of motherhood being captured in those priceless moments when a child looks into your eyes and says 'I love you mommy.' Elizabeth has an extraordinary way of reaching me to let me know that she loves and feels loved by me. Every so often, usually just before going to bed at night or just waking up in the morning, she holds my face in her hands, stares deeply into my face and eyes, and then gasps a long deep breath. I see how utterly full of love she feels and I feel so fulfilled in knowing that I am a part of that creation. Lilly, on the other hand, is much more inclined to express her affection with a delightfully spoken declaration. A few months ago, as Elizabeth, Lilly and I were sitting together playing games and reading stories, Lilly turned her attention to me, cocked her face in front of mine, gently patted me on the back and said sweetly, 'You're a good little mommy.' My daughters are so precious to me. They have brought immeasurable joy into my world, and every day they teach me a little more to trust myself.

Notes

1. I am grateful to my dear friend Patricia Kay Berenbrok for suggesting and loaning me a copy of Bruno Bettleheim's *A Good Enough Parent* and marvelling in my 'having it all'. Also to Paula Jo Bickham for letting me know how her post-ADPCA (Association for the Development of the Person-Centered Approach) visit to the home of a 14-month-old and two-month-old was much more than she imagined she'd be paying for.

With thanks to my mother Adele Cohen, who contributed moral and editorial support throughout the entire manuscript preparation, who grew boundfully with me in its creation and re-creation, making its present form possible.

References

Bettelheim, B. (1987) *A Good Enough Parent*. New York: Vintage/Random House.

Davies, D. (1998) The six necessary and sufficient conditions applied to working with lesbian, gay, and bisexual clients. *The Person-Centered Journal*, 5 (2), pp. 111–24.

Dreikurs, R., with Foltz, V. (1964) *Children: The Challenge*. New York: Hawthorn Dutton.

Ellis, A., with Moseley, S., and Wolfe, J. L. (1977) *How to Raise an Emotionally Healthy, Happy Child*. Hollywood, CA: Wilshire Book Co. (Original work published in1966.)

Faber, A., and Mazlish, E. (1980) *How to Talk so Kids Will Listen and Listen so Kids Will Talk*. New York: Avon.

Gordon, T. (1970) *PET Parent Effectiveness Training: The Tested New Way to Raise Responsible Children*. New York: Peter H. Wyden, Inc.

Rogers, C. R. (1989) Can I be a facilitative person in a group. In H. Kirschenbaum and V. Land Henderson (ed.), *The Carl Rogers Reader (pp. 339–57)*. New York: Houghton Mifflin.

Rogers, C. R., and Freiberg, H. J. (1994) *Freedom to Learn*, 3rd ed. New York: Merrill/MacMillan. (Original work published in 1969.)

Sullivan, H. S. (1947) *Conceptions of Modern Psychiatry.* Washington, DC: William Alanson White Psychiatric Foundation.

I think I have the perfect photo — it's a picture of me holding my infant daughter standing in front of a chalkboard! (Much of the text in my chapter focuses on the difficulty I experienced balancing work and parenting.)

Beyond the Labels: A Personal Perspective on the Person-Centred Approach in Retirement

13

Anne Newell

Since giving up my job in July 1996 I have not been in any regular employment. I have, nevertheless acquired a number of labels, *retired, unemployed, care assistant, supervisor, trainer, interviewer, parish councillor, volunteer,* none of which seem to have any relevance to who I *am,* or the process I am going through. I am currently giving myself permission and space to find out how I want to live my life and how I can best contribute to the society in which I live. It is a challenging time and particularly so as I do not choose to identify myself with the labels we all so readily seem to pin on people. How does one respond to the familiar question 'What do you do'? How will people rate me now that I don't have a job? More importantly, how do I rate myself without one? Where does all this fit in with the person-centred approach?

After the Person-Centred Forum in Greece in 1995, I found it increasingly difficult to settle back into my work as Team Manager with Social Services. The job had changed significantly during the four years since the Community Care Act was introduced and my stress levels were high, I could see no way forward. By November, I realised that I needed to take time to listen to myself, as I was becoming depressed. The next few months were a time of fruitful inactivity, when I became aware that I needed to give up my job and with the support of my doctor, my counsellor, my colleagues and friends, I took early retirement the following July.

Clearly, this was not done lightly, and I experienced a great deal of fear about the future. How would I manage financially? What work alternatives were there? What did I want to do? I had fantasised about myself in different kinds of work, ranging from overseas development work, management training and consultancy, to working in a tea shop. Really, it felt that the world was my oyster at one moment and the next, I was full of doubt as to who would employ me. My energy levels were not what they had been, and my stamina was poor. I was not lacking in possibilities, but did not feel inspired to do any of them. I signed on as unemployed and found that I was entitled to government retraining. I took this opportunity to become computer literate. I built up my résumé and explored a number of realistic avenues of employment, without success. I discovered that I did not want to return to counselling or do anything I had done before. What was more important I did not actually have to work to survive financially. It took me some time for this to sink in.

It is 27 years since I saw the film interview of Carl Rogers with Gloria and 'the earth moved'. It had such an impact on me! It was certainly a major turning point in my life. I was at that time working as a counsellor at the University of East Anglia (UEA) and was about to become the mother of twins. I was fortunate that shortly afterwards, Brian Thorne came to UEA as Director of Student Counselling, and I was able to follow through my interest in PCA whilst working closely with him over the next ten years. Although my introduction to PCA was as a counsellor, it soon became apparent that this was not just a way of working. Being authentic was not just something one was with one's clients. Nor were empathy and acceptance limited to a working relationship. These were all part of a way of being which affected all relationships and every aspect of my life, however imperfectly I lived it. It was not that I sought to be a counsellor with everyone — heaven forbid! It was more that as I became more aware of and accepting of myself, I could risk being more open with others and was more accepting of them and able to give them space and to take space for myself. This has not been easy, it has meant the break-up of my marriage and years of bringing up my children as a single parent. It has meant sometimes working against the grain in institutions where people were used to imposing their values on others, and of recognising too, that I was in danger of imposing my values on them, in my zeal for PCA. It requires that I be scrupulous about myself, aware and acknowledging to myself what I am thinking and feeling and taking responsibility for how I behave, all the time. In 1982 I left UEA to take up a post with Social Services developing services for the mentally ill in North-East Norfolk. Initially, I was very much on my own as far as PCA was concerned, and worked hard at introducing this approach to working with mentally ill people, within the hospital and within the community services that I set up. Particularly successful were the interdisciplinary training courses in 'Listening and Responding', which introduced the basic core conditions of PCA to a large number of practitioners, many of whom took this further. Later, in 1988, I became Team Manager of Mental Health Services in the Northern District and continued to develop and run services from a person-centred base, often in direct conflict with the authoritarian approaches of health service colleagues and of some of my Social Services colleagues. By 1996 I was exhausted!

So what now? I had hopes of using my skills and past experience to advantage, and I felt that I should be doing something 'worthwhile'. But no one seemed to want training in interpersonal skills and I didn't want to join a high-powered management training group as I didn't feel comfortable with pressure and high expectation. I tried to get back to basics, but after one session as a care assistant in a nursing home, Matron let me go. I was relieved! An attempt to get work with the

Mental Health Review Tribunal drew a blank, there were no vacancies. Currently, I have one person for supervision once a month and I do interviews for a national dating agency, which in the last year has produced one interviewee. Whatever alternative avenue of work I explored came to a dead end, even the local tea shop was fully staffed. What will happen to my credibility if I am no longer working, particularly as I have been used to a professional status? Signing on as unemployed felt disempowering and being retired sounds so old! It was time to apply the core conditions to myself, to really listen deeply to what was going on, to be really aware of myself, to really value myself as a unique being and to stop investing in outcomes. If I can truly value myself just enjoying life in the moment, without being a *contributor,* then how will my life be? I was afraid of being too self-indulgent, unwanted, boring, but I had to test it out. So there has been a conscious decision to do what I enjoy doing, to delight in life around me, and to join with other people in doing so. Rather than looking for what to do next, to allow the space for life to evolve, and at the moment this is in a very low-key way, compared to my previous working life. Something really exciting seems to be taking place though, right here in my own village and I feel an integral part of it. A new sense of community is developing (hopefully a caring one) and because I am not distracted by work outside, I have the time and the energy to participate fully.

I live in a small village on the North Norfolk coast where the original farming community has been replaced by newcomers over the past 20 years or so. Several of the houses are holiday homes. The pub and village shop, both giving a focus to the community have long since disappeared, and the village school attracts pupils from a wide area. Whereas in the past, most of the population worked for the local landowner, were related by marriage and had gone to school together, most of us newcomers had had no previous connection, and once here, it was difficult to connect, as there was no common meeting place, and so many of us were absorbed in our own lives. Four years ago, an art gallery and tea shop opened, providing the much needed focus for spontaneous contact. The rector is often to be found there, much more in touch with the people than his predecessor. There are others too, mostly artists, who meet there regularly. Also over this period, several energetic people retired and have more time to spend locally, and a new head teacher has taken on the school, who wants to encourage more interaction between the school and the community.

Last year, a number of us joined together to plan a village festival to raise funds for the local church and for the school. Most of the village participated and we enjoyed a weekend of festivities, with local artists showing their work and various musical events, including a musical, 'Captain Noah and His Floating Zoo', performed by the school children. It was a huge success, but the most important outcome for all of us was that it brought us together as a community for the first time. Now people stop and talk to each other and there seems to be much more interaction. We are planning another festival for this year.

Now that I have the time, I am becoming increasingly involved in village activities. For a number of years I have been a member of the Parish Council, but last year I became Chair. For two summers I have helped out at the children's music camp run by an inspiring musician living in the village. In September, I joined her choir, which attracts people from a number of the surrounding villages and we have sung in Faure's 'Requiem', Handel's 'Messiah' and on Good Friday, Bach's 'St. John Passion'. For the past two terms, I have been a volunteer at the school, helping the six to seven-year-olds with their reading and sometimes joining in their maths lesson. There is a happy, creative atmosphere in the school and I get so much pleasure from being there. Over the past year too, I have been participating in a Julian Group, which meets monthly for silent prayer. This has been a source of inspiration for me, and brings me in contact with others in the village who want to share on a more spiritual level. From this we have become aware of the need for many of us to share and support each other, and we have now started a monthly group which is open to people outside the village as well.

All this takes place within a relatively narrow focus and it would be easy to just bury myself in this very beautiful part of rural England. It is my connectedness to the person-centred network, that somehow stops this from happening, and helps me to see myself in a wider context, which is very important to me. It is about the relationship and significance of one individual to the whole, not just me, but all of us, who meet, correspond and interconnect all over the world. I can bring my personal experience into this wider community and be heard, and in doing so, I may encounter others who are experiencing similar things and then, through sharing, a new perspective emerges. In January when some of us met in Sedona, it was by one person sharing her fears of retirement, living without the labels as she put it, that made me start to look at what I was doing and feeling about this very thing. I saw myself then as making a definite contribution within the community in which I live, by my way of being and relating to others, which is essentially, person-centred. Not that I alone am creating this new-found sense of community there, but that I am nevertheless affecting its development. In being part of the person-centred community as well, life in my village ceases to be something that happens in isolation, but is part of the worldwide picture, and takes on an entirely different meaning for me. By speaking out about where I am, I no longer fear that I am slipping off the edge into oblivion, but I feel visible and an active participant in life around me.

I went through all my photographs and finally came up with this one. It was taken just before the PC Forum in Greece and was at a time when I was particularly happy and relaxed, enjoying being a woman! It was also the beginning of the changes that led to me giving up work.

Conversation with Ruth Sanford at the 5th Person-Centred International Forum, at Terschelling, 1992

14

Ruth Sanford

(This transcript has been edited from the original only for clarity.)
This conversation was intended to address the question 'What was it like to work closely with Carl Rogers?' and to celebrate not only his life, but the effect it had on those who knew him.

When I thought of this conversation, I had in my mind a picture of a cozy room with a carpet on the floor and a nice little intimate group. Well, here we are. [The audience consisted of about 70–100 people distributed along some 30 meters of the pews of a lovely old stone church.] I don't know exactly what you're expecting. I do know that my thought in thinking about this is that this is a celebration of life, a celebration of Carl's life and how that has become a part of all of our lives in one way or another and this is the fifth anniversary of Carl's death. It seemed appropriate that we would be gathering here and remembering the time he walked with us. But I think also I would like this to be a celebration of our lives and a celebration of the richness that Carl left with us from being in our midst and what we heard about the way of being that has brought us all to this place. I don't know exactly where to start and I don't know how well I can hear questions from people who are sitting, I understand, rather far back.

By the way, I am surprised at the number of people who have come out on this night when so many people have been soaked two or three times today and I hope everybody is warm enough and is not catching cold. I am surprised indeed that so many people persevered this long but I'm happy that you're here and although I can't see you, I will be feeling your presence.

I would like also as I reminisce somewhat, I would like to have your questions about what you want to know. I would like also for you to be thinking of what you recall and would particularly like to share about the way in which you knew Carl because I think that most of the people, or many of you at least, have had experiences of working with Carl. There may be a few of you who have never met him. I hope you will ask the kind of questions that may help you to feel that you've come a little closer to knowing him.

Since I believe that life is a becoming — it never finishes and in that sense, all of my life I have been preparing for this moment. I welcome your questions and your comments as well as we can work it out. If you can't be heard from back there, then maybe if you have a question you would want to come up here. I don't know. I do want to have participation with other people — not just mine.

Where shall I start? Usually people say if they don't know Carl well or don't know me well, 'How did you start working with Carl? How did you get to know him?' It seems to me in a way there was a series of chance happenings that brought it about. I've heard it said that nothing in this world just happens; everything is brought about. So, I don't know what kind of a plan or the effect or influence there was. But I do know that I retired from my 25 years in education, counseling and administration and thought, 'Well, I'm going to have a nice relaxing time now. I'm going to take about a year and do nothing excepting to be with my family and maybe travel a little.' I was asked to stay on from September to January to find a replacement, so I did.

In January 1977 I decided that my first vacation would be to go to San Diego to a conference — The Association of Counseling and Development. When I got there I discovered that the keynote speaker at the banquet of all places, was Carl Rogers.

I heard him speak for the first time. He talked about something on becoming a psychologist or becoming Carl Rogers, but it seems that he must have hatched a title for his biography many years before it was written. I had hesitated to do much group work because I'd seen so many groups in which people were literally taken apart and never put back together again and I shied away from them. So, I listened very carefully to Carl talking about the work which they did in La Jolla and about the La Jolla program. I thought, 'Well, if this man named Carl is one who has originated these ideas in this plan for people, of coming together and learning how to facilitate the growth in one another, I think I can trust it and I would like to come out here in the summer,' which I did. But you know, I got on the plane and I thought, 'What am I doing this for? I'm feeling pretty good about my life the way it is and if I go out there I may get all mixed up.'

If I had not been on that plane, if I had been on the train, I think I would have gotten off. But I stayed and went to La Jolla that summer. That was the first time that I heard Carl speak and met him in person face-to-face. It was a bit later I went to Mills College workshop. The facilitator for each group was chosen by pulling a number out of a hat. The person delegated by our group chose Carl's number. I was with Carl for two weeks there. That was another chance.

Another one was that when I was leaving the workshop at Mills College, I realized I had forgotten to make a reservation on the plane. I wanted to go down to La Jolla to visit a friend. I called and found that they had one seat left on the plane and if I got down there in half an hour I could go on that plane. I threw everything into my suitcase. I rushed my cab down there, got on the plane and they closed the door. I went to sit down and who was sitting in it beside the only empty seat on the plane? It was Carl.

We were both worn out and we napped most of the way to San Diego. That was the beginning of our meeting. The beginning of our correspondence was when he wrote and asked if he could write about some of my experiences at Mills College in his book *On Personal Power* (Rogers, C.R., 1977, New York: Delacorte, p. 156). You'll find it in the chapter on how to build a community — how a workshop grew.

It seemed that a series of unusual juxtapositions of the incongruous, if you want to say so, brought us together and we started working together in 1977. It was 7/7/77 that I took a ride up to the Adirondack Mountains and I told Carl that I had some ideas about bringing more of the person-centered approach to the East Coast with local staff and he said, 'How are you going to choose your staff?' and I said, 'I don't know.' (This was a workshop in the Adirondacks.) 'The only way I know is to go ahead into the dining-room and to begin talking with people and tell them about the idea and if they get excited, I'll invite them to come to a first meeting to find out who is going to be the staff.' He laughed. He said, 'I guess that's about as good a way as any'.

That's how we started working together — which was really in that sense — in 1977. I think that's enough of the history of it because many people like to say, 'Well, how did you get started?'

The other part of it, which was the international work, was Carl's speaking about many invitations to go to South Africa. He had refused because he was afraid that he would be considered a guest of a white university. He wanted to have all peoples of South Africa represented if he went there for a series of workshops. Then he had a second or third invitation from Len Holdstock who was a former student in his classes in the States. He said he would like to go but at that point he didn't want to go alone.

One day I received a letter from Carl saying, 'I was thinking for a long time about going to South Africa and I don't want to go alone. I thought I would ask you to go but you have a family and you couldn't be away for five or six weeks at a time. I suppose you can't go but I was eating breakfast on the patio this morning and I said to myself, "The hell with holding back; I'll ask her!"'

I read the letter to my husband. (He had planned to be in Thailand for two years in the Peace Corps, so we had pretty much worked this kind of thing out.) I read the letter to my husband, Niel, and I said, 'What do you think about it? It's going to mean that I will be away from home for quite a long time. What do you think of the idea?' He said, 'Well, of course, you must go. You couldn't possibly miss this opportunity.' That was the beginning of our work together. It started in Johannesburg with Len Holdstock organizing the work that we did there which was very exciting to us. So that's how it began. That is usually the first question that people ask.

What are some of the things you would like to know? Do you have questions? (Silence.) Well then, I'll talk a little longer.

Some of the little anecdotes would be as interesting as anything. There's one that happened in Guadalajara, Mexico. We had a very big group. I've forgotten how many, but about 1700 people, I think, in an auditorium first. Then they said,

'We're going to break into small groups now. The groups will be on campus at the university.' Carl and I were told what group we were to go to. Our group turned out to be 200 — a small group of 200. (Laughter.)

This is one of the stories I like particularly about Carl's sense of humor. We were working with translators. One young woman who was Carl's translator was waiting to respond because he was talking too long a time without pausing. She said, 'I want to be able to catch up with you.' She started translating. Well, I don't know Spanish and I just sat there thinking, 'Hmm, it must take longer to say something in Spanish than it does in English.' Then she turned to Carl and she said, 'How was that?' And Carl said, 'That was just fine. I liked *your* speech too.' (Laughter.) I realized then why it would take longer to say it in Spanish.

A very poignant one which I think is a very intimate comment about Carl and others he was meeting. I don't know how many thousands were there but it was in a ballroom. I remember looking out on a sea of faces. The only thing I could think of was this was a ballroom and here were literally thousands of people and all I could think of was I would rather be dancing. So I said that and I felt more quiet with that size of an audience of which Carl and I were cofaculty. The thing that touched me very deeply about Carl, which he said a lot, for all the people who admired him and worked with him and, as he said, 'sometimes stood in awe of him' which made him very uncomfortable, he had a hard time believing that people who came close to him or who came up to speak to him in large groups and so on were really doing it because they cared about him and not just because he was a prominent person or something of the sort.

When he was introduced the whole audience stood and applauded for, I don't know, maybe two or three minutes until he begged them to sit down. Then he put his hand over the microphone and in a very soft voice he whispered to me, 'I think at last I must accept that I am loved.' That always brings tears to my eyes when I recall that.

Of course everybody who knows Carl, that is most of you, some of you have known him very well indeed and have known him longer than I knew him, but I think the thing that happened with me and that's the most I can tell about is that, at the beginning, on the way to South Africa that first time, I was plagued with a sense of awe too. I felt often like looking over my shoulder and saying, 'Who, me?' I couldn't believe that I was there or why Carl had asked me but as we traveled together and as we started working in South Africa together, sometimes with very large groups, I began to realize that Carl was the same whether he was with one person or two people or fifteen or two hundred or a thousand. He was the same person and he was the same person who wrote as he wrote, so that it was simply getting to know a little more closely the person who was there before you and to trust that that was who he was, exactly who he was.

I think his quietness, his acceptance of people, excepting when he was driving the car in La Jolla, then he had anything but unconditional positive regard. He used to say, 'Now these people are not significant others in my life.' (Laughter.) So that was a real treat. He was openly what he was and he would talk to the drivers as we passed them sometimes. He would talk to them inside the car but very explicitly sometimes. I enjoyed that part of it too.

One of the things which was probably more important in all the years that we did work together very closely, happened by chance again and I keep saying this — by chance. I don't know what it was by, but it seemed like chance. Carl had developed macular degeneration so that his central vision was not at all good and he could no longer read papers. I told him I thought it was great that he wasn't working with papers anymore, not that he couldn't, because I think Carl was at his absolute worst when he was reading a paper. He was at his best when he was just being himself and talking with people.

We went to Johannesburg and we found that we were in this big auditorium with several hundred people, fixed seats like an amphitheater. We were on a raised stage with lights shining on our faces and it was being video'd and we said, 'Well, how are we going to do this? How are we going to get communication back and forth with an audience like this? How are we going to prevent it from becoming a very stiff lecture kind of thing?' We had never worked together like this before.

We walked out onto that platform and quietly we said, 'The only thing I think that we can do is for us first to introduce ourselves, to tell what resources we brought to South Africa, to tell that we've come here to learn and to be with people and learn from them as well as they learn from us. We hoped that our being there would help in someway in communicating across lines of difference. We knew that we could not resolve the conflicts but we hoped that we would be able to set up in some way a communication that would help people to reach their hands across their chasms of difference and be able to see each other as living human beings with the same kinds of feelings.

We spoke to the group, the audience, that way. We said that we would like to tell them about resources that we thought we were bringing. We would like to tell them about the person-centered approach and how we felt that that would help in communications and then we wanted to hear from everyone what they had come there for, what questions they had, what they would like to tell us. As these were reported to us, I wrote them down and organized them into questions.

Then Carl and I started dialoguing. Carl would say, 'I'll take this question,' and he would start answering it. If I thought of something else or I disagreed or whatever, and we did disagree, I would add my comments. We got into trouble sometimes for disagreeing, especially in Moscow and I'll tell you about that. If we disagreed or however we wanted to do it, we began dialoguing afterward and it seemed to go very well. We then began answering the comments and questions that had been asked and the audience got involved. There were microphones so that we were able to talk back and forth and we found that it was possible to carry on conversation even with several hundred people.

Carl made a suggestion which I wrote later in *Beginning of a Dialogue in South Africa*. Carl said, 'I hardly dare suggest this, but I would like it very much if we could have a small group, a small intensive group here for a couple of hours. People would volunteer and I would want it to be mixed, representing all the peoples who are here. I realize it may be in the interest of some people to do that.' And so I met with all the people who said they would like to become a part of that group, would be willing to, and after some talk and assuring that no one would jeopardize him or herself, a group of people (11 or 12 besides Carl and me) formed this kind of encounter group. I don't like that word. I don't like the 'encounter' part. I like it to be an intensive group or simply a group, but it was that format. We found that one Black man said that this is the first time that he had ever talked to a White person excepting to say, 'Yes, boss.'

Some others were very verbal and it was a real revelation that in two hours that group could get down to some very deep, deep differences, that they could address them in that group. I'd like to say that the only facilitation I think that Carl and I did there was to listen to people and when we got to someone who was wanting to speak and couldn't because others were speaking, that we would try to make room for that person. I believe I've recorded that correctly and that's the way I remember it and it can be read in a paper called 'The Beginning of a Dialogue in South Africa', which was published in *The Counseling Psychologist* a few years later. I was deeply touched by that.

Some White persons in that group said that they had never met in this way another Black person. They had met them mostly as servants. I would like to go into more detail but I think that gives something of the picture of it.

Of course, Carl did a therapy session, a short one, at the same time. That is one of the times when he took 'an intuitive leap' as he said when he was interviewing the young woman. He took an intuitive leap and said that he felt somehow that she was afraid of moving into the dark ahead of her in the future. He thought if she could just take that little girl that was living inside her, that little girl who had been afraid before, if she'd just take her with her and love her, that she wouldn't be so lonely when she went out into the new part of her life. I think that was one of the early times when Carl associated that kind of deep empathy with the term intuition, which sometimes is considered now a fourth condition, which I see as a deepening of deep listening or deep empathy, becoming so much a part of the other person's world that you feel that you're really there with that person, but you know that you're not that person. Am I getting some of the things you wanted to hear? Can I get some response?

Question: How do you work with conflict?

Ruth: I think that it was pretty much the group that I had just spoken about was a group in deep conflict, and the most in working with that group which either one of us did, was to try to make it a safe place for any person, no matter how frightened or how threatened he/she felt — feel that it was safe and that we cared and we wanted to hear. I think that's what Carl conveyed, is what I tried to convey along with him.

In the Soviet Union, it was a completely different kind of situation. In the Soviet Union in 1986 we had thought that in the Soviet Union people would be rather hesitant to speak or to express differences in a group like that. Somehow a repressed society is what we had in mind. We thought that they might be rather phlegmatic people. You see that just shows you can't second-guess people because you're usually wrong if you try to do that.

We got into that group and there were about twice as many people as we wanted in the group. They'd been invited from many different parts of the Soviet Union, many parts of the City of Moscow. We found that as soon as we got together there was a whole big question, 'Who is going to be allowed to stay and who will have to leave?' That was the point at which I felt that I would like to keep the group rather small, like about 30 or 35, and if everybody stayed, it would be over 40 people. By the time you added the translators and us, we would have 45 or more people and I was hoping that we could keep it a little smaller, but Carl with his big heart said, 'Well, all right, let everybody stay.'

Right away what was assumed from that beginning group was that Carl and I were in conflict because I said I'd rather have it smaller and Carl said, 'Let them stay.' They thought later that we had cooked up that difference between us in order to get them started when in reality we did nothing to get them started, because from the beginning they felt that some people were being excluded, and others were being included who weren't on the original list. They began shouting at one another and were really sharp and vicious in their attacks on one another. The main thing that Carl and I did was to try to slow them down and say, 'I want to hear you. I can't hear you when several people are speaking at once. I can't hear you when two people are shouting and I want to hear. I care and I want to hear.'

Gradually through that day there was a little bit of listening but people came to us, 'What are you doing here? You're not doing anything. If you don't stop this chaos here, we're going to be doing this for the next several days and we'll never get anywhere.' It went on in that way. That night we suggested that people sit quietly for five minutes before they left for the night and not talk with one another on the way out. The next morning when people came back, there was a different spirit.

That kind of thing was repeated in different words at various times in that session and I would say again that how did Carl deal with conflict in that situation? How did he deal with it? It was mainly by letting people know that we cared about them; we cared about what they had to say; that we really wanted to hear them and by giving time (and someone said later 'modeling' it — I didn't think of it as modeling; I thought of it as really being there and being present with my whole self as I can be) and I know that was Carl always in a group. So, how to deal with conflict?

I would say that was the main way and we never thought that it was going to resolve all those conflicts. Shirley Shochot was with us in Cape Town when it almost came to blows between two members of the group who were in deep conflict. Shirley stood up and happened to be between them and they continued talking rather than coming to blows. There were young radical students who were volunteering to fight for the differences they had. We had officials who were there from the government who came to take notes and learn how to resolve conflict and who were given first-name buttons and gradually became a part of the group.

A young woman from the University of The Western Cape (this was on our second visit) screamed at one of the officials at one point and said, 'I can't be in the same room with you. I can't stand it! I can't be in this room with you!' Again, the facilitation I think that we used there, all of us who were working to bring some kind of understanding of conflict, was to try to help people to hear one another. All ages and personal interests were represented in that room. It is easier to remember the part that I took part in than the parts specifically that somebody else took part in, but I know this was true of the way Carl worked too, and that was to say when two people were talking past each other like this (moves her hands past each other in opposite directions) and missing, not responding to one another, that one of us would ask, 'Did you hear what E was saying?' And the speaker would say, 'Yes, I heard her,' but he would go on talking about this other thing.

And then I would say, 'E, would you repeat what you said?' She would repeat it and then one of us would ask the man who had been confronting her, 'Did you hear what she said? Would you say it back to her?' until gradually the practice of listening seemed to take hold and it seemed to me that when people can listen to one another and hear them as other human beings and see them as a person who is real there and not as a color or as a badge or as a decision, that then the conflict begins to change. It doesn't go away then. It's not healed, but it's possible then for communication to take place. It's possible then for them to talk with one another and to be with one another without these strong feelings that shout the other out.

I think the thing that moved me very deeply in that intensive workshop was that those two people came together at the end when the young professor and a white young woman, said to the other (the man said to E), 'Can you be in the same room with me now?' And she was so choked up with feeling and with tears that she said, 'I can't answer now.' But later on I understand they really worked together in a position of real conflict in which there was bloodshed and they were able to help the security police to hold their fire and to listen to the people. I don't know. This was reported to me. I wasn't there, but I understand that these two people who had not found it possible at first to be in the same room with one another did find a way later to make it possible publicly to save lives by having the security police even, listen to them enough that they would hold their fire.

I don't know whether that answers your question or not. I think it was Carl's way of being and listening and no matter when he almost gave up hope sometimes that he said, 'Sometimes I give up hope and I think, is it worth it? Is it worth the struggle? But I always come out to the other side and know that it is worth it.' When you see in a group split asunder like that with people suffering because they've been oppressed, and people feeling guilty because they have oppressed or been part of a group that has, and you see those people coming together and being able to tell each other how they really feel — 'I feel uncomfortable in your presence and I don't want to feel that uncomfortable, but I do.'

I remember one woman saying to a woman from Soweto, 'I don't want to feel this way. I hate feeling this way but I sometimes wish all the Black people would go away because they complicate my life so much.' She was in tears because she felt that way. To see as people sat there, day after day, and listened to one another and felt the pain in one another that they began to realize, 'I can't resolve this conflict now but I've got to start,' and I think that's all that we hoped to do at that time. And certainly that was the way that Carl worked. I know that there are people here who could say more about that probably, in ways that you worked with him and I would like to hear about that. I would like somebody else to come up here and tell how it was to work with Carl. Will you do that? Is there someone who's willing to do that?

Julius Huizinga: One thing I find very difficult that someone says to you, 'You are not able to understand' and I often think of an article that Carl wrote about this South African experience. He wrote about his experiences. It was in the *Person-Centered Review.*

(Someone in the audience asks him to repeat his question.)

Julius: I said I am very disappointed about one article I read of Carl's. And that was an article in which he writes about his experiences in an encounter group in South Africa. And that was an article in the *Person-Centered Review*. He described a very nasty encounter where someone said, 'It's very nice that you come here and listen to us, Carl Rogers. But you will never understand what's happening here.' I would not be able to stand such a reaction, I would find it very difficult. And I would like to know how Carl reacted.

Ruth: I heard in a later session that that happened a little differently. That was that I think Carl was really in tears at that point. I know I was in tears too, because a woman from Soweto was telling about the sacrifice that she made to come there, that it very well could be that when she went back to her home, she'd find her home burnt down or she would find her family had been attacked, or at least her home ruined or something of the sort, because she had come in to be at this meeting with White people in Johannesburg. And she had felt so deeply that she got up to leave the room. Carl felt that he was in the presence of something that was much bigger than he could take in. I said, 'I can reach my hand across this chasm but I can't reach you because I have never been there. I can't imagine how that would be.' I think that's a real limit of empathy and I think it exists quite often and it was clearly acknowledged and I think this expresses what you are asking about Carl. I think he went as far as he could go. He had been saying, 'Yes, I can't really understand what it is to be you. I am trying as much as I can to understand how it would feel but I can't always do that.'

I think what was important there was that he cared that much that he would try as hard as he could try, to be there with that person, and that person felt that and it was not all that was needed but it was enough to make that person feel, 'I'm cared about here and I'm being listened to and there's hope.'

Ruth: At this point I did not hear the question, how did Carl respond to his client's apparent lack of respect for him? I have since responded more directly to the question by letter. Carl was staying so empathically close to the client that he did not respond to the personal criticism of the client. But members of the audience expressed anger at what they considered disrespect for Carl. Because Carl was able to stay so close, the client was able to face his own fears. He said later the experience with Carl changed his life.

Is that responding to you?

Julius: Yes, thank you.

Ruth: Shirley, I think you were trying to say something.

Shirley: I think I would like to add to what you were saying about that particular incident. That happened on the second visit that you and Carl came to Johannesburg in 1986 which I had organized, in which you and Carl trained I believe it was 40 Black and White men and women to facilitate dialogue in small groups. This particular incident was one of the most deeply shocking incidents for each and every one of the 40 and perhaps particularly for two people in that group. I think the fear that the audience experienced of the state of that woman was more than any of us had ever encountered in our life. The way in which I recall it was that Carl sat close to her. He did that often and would go closer to someone that was talking in order to be able to hear him correctly. He, on a couple of occasions, got up and sat on the floor at the feet of whoever was speaking.

When he got up to listen to this woman speaking, as she was talking about being a sellout and what could happen to her, Carl simply sat and the tears just rolled down his cheek.

Some months later, a piece of research was done on the work which Carl and Ruth did in South Africa, and the way in which it was researched was each person was interviewed who had been a part of that group. Every single person when they were asked what was the greatest impact of being in that group, each person mentioned that it was Carl's, not his ability to do anything, but his deep, deep caring. He was unchanged. He just sat there, tears streaming down his face, not doing anything. But that in itself was healing. Many, many people said that image stayed with them.

Young Woman: I read somewhere that for Carl religion was a taboo and I would like some comments, if it is possible, from you on that topic. I am surprised there was a taboo around that.

Ruth: Carl was definitely a very spiritual person but he was not a part of organized religion. I don't mean that he was against religion or religions. I understand this somewhat because I think we both got an overdose of very strict religion, known in the United States as Methodism, or something similar to it which is very narrow and circumscribes a great deal of life. I think it was that that Carl reacted against. In fact I know it was, because we shared that. It was not that he was against religion, it was that he was against religions that told others how they should be. As long as a person practiced it himself or herself, that was fine, but he was not wanting to be part of an organization that imposed that kind of observance or belief on someone else.

Is that responding?

Young Woman: It's difficult. There was a kind of taboo.

Ruth: I don't know. I just know that a religion that required a great deal of circumscribing people's lives was painful to Carl. But I think it went beyond religion. Other parts of life too in which people did the same kind of thing and tried to impose their will on other people and have power over, Carl would have resisted that too, and in that sense that was taboo too in his way of thinking and being.

It doesn't feel right yet? You want to pursue that further?

Ed Bodfish: Carl liked Buber and he liked a lot of spiritual questions in a number of fields.

Ruth: That's right.

Nat Raskin: I can maybe add a little to that. I would guess that some of you know and others of you don't know that Carl actually intended to have a career in theology and he started out at the University of Wisconsin, majoring in agriculture but decided, I think, as a result of going to China with a delegation of young Christians, he came back and decided to major in history at the University of Wisconsin preparatory to becoming a graduate student in theology, which he did. He went to the Union Theological Seminary in New York and actually one summer he worked in a church, I imagine something like this in Vermont as an Assistant Pastor or something like that.

Ruth: Summer Pastor.

Nat Raskin: So, yes, I guess he had the full responsibility. Whatever attitudes he developed about it came out of really close experience. He decided after being a student at Union Theological Seminary to move across the street, to cross Broadway to Teachers College and become a graduate student in clinical psychology, which he did, but I agree that he was basically a very spiritual person. But I think that he also went through some different phases about that.

Ruth: I think part of that at Union Theological Seminary was that at that point he had a hard time intellectually accepting that theology, even the most liberal theology, but I never knew of his saying that he would stand in the way of somebody else doing it.

Nat Raskin: I certainly agree with that. One thing somewhat related to this thing — I remember when I was a graduate student living in Ohio State and we were both very young. I was 19. He was 38. He had a very scientific attitude and I remember him being just very apolitical. He wasn't interested in politics or in trying to change the world or anything like that.

I saw him change over many years in that he became extremely caring, extremely concerned about people who were deprived or poor or discriminated against. He really warmed up as a person.

Ruth: I think there was some question about someone saying to him that this is political. He had taken a political stand. Carl said, 'I don't get involved in politics.' But then he wrote *On Personal Power* and what is that but politics? He even wrote *The Politics of Administration* and *The Politics of Education* later on. The field kept broadening. At first it was client-centered therapy and then it was person-centered approach. The very last part of his work involved not only politics but it involved working with people who were responsible, even, on a second-to-the-top level of diplomacy. If we had gone back to the Soviet Union another time when Carl was living, which we planned to do, the design was that we would meet with some of the diplomatic corps of both countries and try to work with them in bringing about some kind of communication different from the diplomatic communication of, you know, bargaining. Trying to listen to one another.

We did have in South Africa, I think there were two people there who were from Parliament, one person was definitely a member of Parliament and other very political figures. We had a great deal of people who were very much interested in politics.

Ruth (aside): What was 'S'?

Shirley Shochot: ANC.

Ruth: So we had people who had a lot of interest in politics. Even after he broke his hip that last week before he died, Carl said it would be healed in time so that he could go back to South Africa. The intent was to move farther over into the political field and try to help introduce communication among people who had some clout politically, which of course did not work out. He died in the interim.

Nat Raskin: This makes me think of something else. It's true if you wanted to try to better things by working, trying to influence people with power. On the other hand, it really made no difference to him what position or status a person had. This was true from the beginning of my association with him before I began doing graduate work with him at Ohio State. I wrote to him from New York City where I was an undergraduate student. He wrote back a very personal, interested kind of letter, encouraging me to come out to Ohio State. I remember an incident after I had left Ohio State — I had, like many of the other students there, made a verbatim typescript of a complete therapy case. And here I left Columbus, Ohio, I was working for the Army of the United States in West Virginia, and I got a letter from him enclosing this live interviewed case that I had done many months before, and Carl wrote that he had intended for a long time to go over this case and he sent back the most detailed kind of reaction to my responses. I remember one where he wrote, 'terrible', where I had been particularly nonempathic. This is my experience over the 47 years that I knew him, that he was always personally interested, personally reaching out. He wrote me many, many letters of appreciation. He himself was such a considerate person.

Man: Why did Carl not apparently pay any attention to the body as is done in bioenergetics?

Ruth: I think he did. The thing which I always felt from Carl talking about the therapist and the client or, which I like better and he did — the therapist and the other — was that if you are being as completely present as is humanly possible to be with the other person, if you have set aside your own needs for the moment, for 'that present time', and are really entering into the other person's life and experience in a very deep and empathic way, you're really prizing that other person and entering into his/her experience. You are aware not just of what is going on with their body or what's going on with their eyes or what's going on in their voice but you are totally with that person, which certainly includes the body, but not trying to read body language and interpret it and say, 'What does that mean?' It all became a very subtle part of a very living relationship and at its best he was really able to enter into that person's experience and the person felt it and sensed it. I don't know whether that's answering your question.

I don't think he did try to interpret body language. He never tried to interpret dreams. He never tried to interpret or to try to manipulate it to try to get the client to a certain place. Someone asked him in an interview in Moscow, 'Did you ask that question in order to get this person to another place and awareness?' He said, 'I didn't intend to get that person anywhere. I was trying to understand where the person was.' I think that's the best response I can give to your question.

Mieke van Schaik-Verlee: I should like to add one little thing because I met Carl a few times and the first time I was very nervous, like I am now, and my husband and I, we told him we were in a school based on the ideas of Carl Rogers and my husband wrote a book about it and he was devoted to Carl, then Carl said, 'I hope to exchange my ideas and my basic feelings.' That was exactly what I heard that you said. He didn't label. He didn't want to be in any association that was revolutionary, that was not liberal, that told things to people. He said, 'I hope you change in your own way.'

We told our director when we came home. Our administrative director didn't understand, because he said, 'You were disappointed, weren't you?'

Ruth: Thank you.

Grace Chickadonz: I'm interested in you, Ruth, in your life and I wondered if you would share with us some of the ways in which your life was touched or changed by experiences that you shared with Carl.

Ruth: It's undertaking a good deal to say that. I'll try and touch on some of the things briefly. As I said, I intended to retire and was going to take it easy. I found that there was a kind of explosion in my life after my first work with Carl. It was the kind of explosion that kept saying to me all the way along, 'Well, I really don't know my potential yet.' It just kept expanding and expanding and I found myself doing things that I never had any idea I could do, because Carl would simply say to me, 'Would you do that with me?' or suggest that I do it, not making a demand but saying, 'No, let's do this or would you like to do that?' and I found myself doing it, things I had no idea before that I could do. So that is one very big impact, and I just finished a paper in which I ended that way 'and I *still* don't know what my potential is'.

I think it's that whole sense of expanding and becoming that became so real in working with Carl because that was always the direction, it was always the motion. In writing a chapter with him, a chapter on 'Client-Centered Psychotherapy' for the *Comprehensive Textbook of Psychiatry* (it was the first one that we did together), I tried very hard respecting Carl's writing because after all it was his article and we were writing a revision of it, so I was trying very hard to stay in Carl's style and to do whatever work I was doing in revision in that light. I was having a very hard time and so I said, 'I'm getting too bogged down here. I'm stalled. I'm not getting anywhere,' so I put that aside and I started out and I did it my way. When I saw Carl next, we had time to sit down and talk. I showed him the two versions and I said, 'I would like for you to read them now. This is a revision of your chapter. I would like you to read those, if you will, and tell me which one you prefer.' Now here is the measure of the man. He read it over and he said, 'I think yours is accurate. I think it says what I would want to say. It is fresh. It is fresher and therefore I choose it.' To me that was almost unbelievable. I was expecting he would say, 'Well, take this little part here and put it in there and so on.' But I had no idea he was going to say that. But that was a kind of trust. He had trusted me to revise it, but he trusted me. I was thinking he trusted me to move a few things around or introduce a couple of ideas maybe, but I did not take in that he really trusted me to do it until he said, 'I choose this one' — a person with Carl's stature and his position and all of that, it seemed to me that that was a real measure of his openness and willingness to accept it.

There's another one — I was having a very, very difficult time with a relationship which had ended, or not ended but I felt I was disappointed. It wasn't working out the way I had hoped and I talked with him about it. His response to me has stayed with me since then and I think it's always with me when I find that I have a feeling of difference with another person who matters to me, who is really important in my life. He said, 'First of all, you are grieving a death. You are grieving a loss. I can hear it. You feel that you have lost this valuable relationship. I would hope that first you would let yourself grieve and then I would hope that you would be able to accept that relationship for exactly what it is and enjoy that.' That was saying it may work out differently from the way I expect. I may find myself disappointed or feel abandoned or cut loose or whatever, but if I can really accept that other person, although I can't yet see her/his point of view because I'm too blinded by my own loss. If I can accept that for the time being and then let that relationship grow in its own way, it will be different probably from what I wanted, but it can still be a good or rich relationship. Or I can decide I don't want to invest anymore in it because it's not that significant. But that meant a great deal in my life and it taught me a great deal about my relationships with people.

Also, we had a lot fun together too. It wasn't all work. Carl had said to me that he thought he never really learned to play, and I love to dance and certain kinds of play I like very much, and I think he enjoyed that and sometimes he said, 'I think that you're teaching me how to play.' I think, as Nat was saying earlier, more and more he was able to be demonstrative in his feelings, more and more he was able to lay aside his discipline. He was the most disciplined person I ever knew. He could be the most empathic and open and outgoing but in his work, he was absolutely disciplined. He would get up in the morning, see the eight o'clock news which was short but contained all the essentials, have breakfast, go to the desk and probably worked with Valerie who came every day, was his secretary, until noon. At 12:30 he had lunch, took a half-hour nap and then whatever. He told me that in earlier years he would get up at 4:00 in the morning and do his serious work and writing until breakfast time and then go on with his full day's work. He did that year after year. That is why he was able to do as much work with people as he did and still write as prolifically as he wrote, the volumes and volumes of articles and books that he wrote. I think it was because of his discipline.

That discipline also had another side, was very controlled and didn't always show at the time, and it could mean that he didn't always show his feelings a lot of the time, and I think he had difficulty for a number of years. People sometimes accused him of being angry or not being able to express his anger. I think he had difficulty for many years expressing anger, expressing warm feelings for people unless he knew them in a family or in a very intimate way; I think he relaxed that more as he went along. He said it was easier for him, to hug somebody for example. It was easier to accept that kind of body contact. So I think that's another part of Carl, that he was very disciplined, had a great deal of control over his own feelings. That's why it was so significant when he cried.

I'd like to say in the time I knew Carl, there were three times that he cried because of the great sadness or the great loss of his own. He cried when trying to empathize with, getting into the experience or the pain or the despair of another person more easily than his own. On one occasion I said to him, 'Carl, you're feeling very, very sad about something. Is it something you'd like to talk about?' He said, 'No. I think I must be slightly depressed. I feel like crying and I don't want to.' And he didn't. But I think there were times when he felt very sad and some disappointment in a relationship of his own and at that point he sometimes did cry for himself and for his loss. But I think three times in the time I knew him.

I guess it's important to have noticed those things.

And he could get angry and he did get angry. We sometimes got angry with one another and I'm glad we could because if I hadn't dared get angry with Carl and he hadn't dared get angry with me, I would have felt that our relationship was a shallow one.

So I appreciated that, although I didn't appreciate it always, at the time. It didn't happen very often but it did happen. So Carl was able to be angry.

There are two things that come to my mind if I can keep one in mind while talking about the other one. The one — maybe someone who knows me pretty well will remind me — about cutting the tree and I want to get back to that. But I want to tell you a little incident which says something more about Carl. It says something about me, and it says something about Carl. We were in an intensive group in Tbilisi, in the Soviet Union in 1986. I noticed on the second day of that group that people were switching in a kind of rhythm which I often see happening in a group. That sometimes we [people] get very intellectual, very theoretical, and other times we get very emotional and very deep into their own personal selves. It goes in a kind of rhythm like the waves of the ocean and you learn to expect and to appreciate that. But on this occasion in this group which had been going very well and I felt very much a part of it, I suddenly noticed that every time there was a theoretical or an intellectual question, it was directed at Carl and I began to feel invisible and I didn't like it. I felt myself withdrawing because I didn't feel included. I was withdrawing myself. I was not really present. At the end of that day I said something to Carl, 'I felt I was invisible today. I wasn't there. I felt uncomfortable . . .'

He said, 'Well, I would hope that you can tell the group that.' So the next morning I went to the group and I said, 'I feel very much a part of this group for the most part, and I felt very close to many of you, but yesterday I felt invisible. I felt that every time there was an academic or intellectual question, you addressed it to Carl, and I don't know why that was. I wondered if it was because this is in Georgia, the Soviet Union, and that it is your expectation that only men should respond to intellectual or academic theoretical questions, or whether it's because Carl is a renowned psychologist and you recognize him for that and so you assume that he is the person to whom you should direct your questions and if that's the case, that's all right? Or is it because you think that only a man thinks?'

And I said, 'I have worked too long to appreciate my intellect that I'm going to put it aside now. You don't have to say anything to me. You don't have to explain or apologize or anything but I just had to say that, and now that I've said it, I can *be* with you.'

The amazing thing that happened was for the first time in the Soviet Union, we spent most of the rest of the day discussing men and women issues, where it had been said there was no man-woman issue because women had equal rights. But we got into some very deep things that day and Carl loved to tell that story. So, there Carl opened the door. He said, 'I hope you will say that in the group,' which was encouraging. When I was able to do that, it opened the door for the whole group. I learned from that, that when I could truly be myself, even though it is a negative or confronted feeling, that it can be very helpful to the group, and it turned out to be.

The director of the institute said at the end of that day's discussion, 'I want to tell my staff and I want to tell my wife, who is present, that from now on I am going to think much more carefully about valuing a woman in the same way that I value a man whether it's on my staff or in my family, and I intend to follow up on that and I want everyone to hear it because I want to follow that through.' That to me was a tremendous experience, and the fact that Carl encouraged me to do it. I don't know whether I would have done it on my own or not. I can never tell that but the way it worked was fine and helpful.

Another story that Carl liked had to do with not expressing anger. After one of our workshops in the east, Carl had come home with me. I have a huge tree in my garden in my back ard that has five big branches just like fingers of a hand. I feel it's a protecting hand for me. Even in a hurricane, I trust it. I came home from a workshop. Carl came back with me. He was in the house. I saw sawdust on the driveway and I couldn't understand why. Then I looked up. I saw that my neighbor, in my absence, had had a tree surgeon come and cut off the limbs of that tree exactly at the fence, at the line. So here was the tree, shorn on this side and tall all the way around. I went over to see my neighbor. I was furious and I went over to see the neighbor to speak with him about it. He wasn't at home which was pretty bad. I had to hold onto that for quite a while.

When I was telling about that in South Africa in Cape Town one time, I was saying that I finally went back and saw the neighbor and said to the neighbor, 'Don't you ever touch my tree again! If I'm here, let me know, and I'll have it done, but don't you ever touch that tree again!' And he said, 'I'm sorry you're unhappy about it.' I said, 'Unhappy — nothing! I'm furious! I don't want that to happen again. I'll take care of the tree, if you let me know if it troubles you.'

Well, I told that story and a psychologist in the audience in Cape Town said to me, 'Well, don't you think it would have been a little better if you had put a cushion in there and told him first something that you liked about it?' (Laughter.) I said, 'I did not want to put a cushion in there at that point.'

Carl loved to tell that story too and he said the message he got was, 'Don't mess around with Ruth's trees!' (Laughter.)

So, we had fun together too.

The last week we spent together was halfway between my birthday and his birthday. I had celebrated one birthday with him, but he never celebrated a birthday with me. When I went out there, we were finishing some project that we were working on. He said, 'I have a birthday gift for us.' The birthday gift was that he had planned and paid for, and given to both of us as a birthday gift, a three-day trip to Las Vegas. (Laughter.) Las Vegas is a gambling center of the United States. He said, 'I thought we should go somewhere and do something we had never done before.' I was really taken aback. I was surprised that he had chosen to do that. But we went, and we had a great time. We went to three nightclub shows in three days, and Carl enjoyed them all. I enjoyed them too. We played the slot machines. We started with quarters. We decided then we'd graduate to a dollar. The first dollar I put in, I got 25 back. That was a real come on. Immediately Carl reached in his pocket and got the dollars out. He said, 'Here, you take them.' (Laughter.) We agreed to stop when we were even, or when we had spent no more than ten dollars, and we finally did. It was really a fun time and something different.

We came back on a Wednesday and on the Friday night, after we had been working — we were planning another trip to South Africa — we finished our work and that night, as we did very often, we put on some of the records from the musicals that we liked like Camelot, My Fair Lady and so on. We were dancing in the living-room. It was free-form dancing, we each did our own thing, but we danced to the music, and it was fun doing that. The next morning about four o'clock I heard a call from Carl's room, and I went rushing in. He said, 'Ruth, something has happened. I don't know, but I got up to go to the bathroom, and I lost my balance, and I sat down hard, and my right hip hurts. I don't think it's broken, but I think we better get some help.'

So, I called the hospital, and they sent an ambulance. We went to the hospital and found that the hip was broken, and he had to go into surgery that day, which he did. He came through the surgery fine. I talked with him afterwards and stayed until about midnight that night, wanting to stay in the hospital room and watch, because he had had an anesthetic and general anesthesia, and his heart was not strong, and I was concerned. But he said, 'No, go back and get rest and I'll see you in the morning.' He was as bright and cheerful as ever and was planning. He said, 'They tell me I can go to South Africa in six weeks, but I can't cross my legs. I'll have to watch that hip, but I'm going to South Africa.' The last thing he said was, 'You go home, and you go back and rest, and I'll see you in the morning.'

At four o'clock in the morning I got a call saying that Carl had cardiac arrest and gone into a coma. He never regained consciousness. He died three days later, still in the coma.

I have this pleasure and this satisfaction, even in the depth of that grief, that he had his wish that he didn't have to live long and be a burden to other people and to suffer. So far as we know, and I don't know if we can know that, so far as we know, he was in so deep a coma that they say he was brain dead, and that he did not suffer, did not know what was going on. At any rate, it was only three days and he got his wish. He got his wish to die young. We were dancing the night before. He got that wish; he got the wish that he didn't have to suffer, he didn't have to be a burden on his family or to others for a long period of time. To me, it was enough to temper the sorrow of his leaving in the form we knew him. I don't know, maybe that's a good place to stop unless you have something you wish to add.

Julius Huizinga: I'd like to thank you for sharing that with us. To me, it's a very good time to stop. Thank you very much.

* A photograph of Ruth Sanford appears on page 83 at the end of Chapter 7.

PC Therapy – A Short Story

15

Sarah Ingle

The CD-ROM arrived in a brown padded envelope which plopped through my letter box one morning. It had a label on it saying 'PC Therapy World' and inside was a disk entitled *Do-It-Yourself Therapy — the Person-Centred Approach brought to your home computer.*

I wanted to start on it right away but I wasn't dressed yet and though I've been on my own now for almost three years, I find it best to stick to my old habits, so it's always chores before pleasure. I do like to keep the house looking clean and tidy.

'Remember one day the Queen might call,' was what Mother used to say.

Not that she ever has, of course. But then no one calls on me. Not now. I used to keep the place pristine for George. George, my husband. I kept house to keep him. Silly, wasn't I. He walked out one day and never came back. Went off with the tarty daughter from two doors down. Not a word from him since. No money. No address for an emergency. What if something should happen to me? Would he care? He'd never know. I doubt there's anyone in the world who cares about me. Except for my cat of course, dear Barnaby. He's my friend. Mother used to be quite rude about him, said he had an ugly face! Stupid woman! No wonder she always complained about being lonely.

I haven't had my computer long. I watched some programme on TV about how easy it all was, and then a leaflet came through the door with a special deal from a local computer firm. They offered everything the TV said they should: setting it up for you, home support, all the right hardware. See, I know the technical terms. Anyway. I rang them up immediately and ordered one before I could talk myself out of it. What a treat! I'd never have done that if George was still here. It would have been weeks of buying magazines, deciding on the right model, then traipsing round the shops comparing prices, then finding the one you want is out of stock. We did that when I needed a new cooker. I'd have rather struggled on with the old one.

The very next day after I'd placed my order there was a ring at my door and on the step stood a cute young man with black curly hair falling over his ears — he needed a haircut, truth be told. He had with him three huge boxes — my new computer. Now I wasn't sure about letting him in the house, you can't be too careful these days can you, but he had a sweet smile so I stood back politely and said 'Come in.'

He carried everything into the dining-room for me and set it all up. I don't eat in there any more so the table's free. I made him a cup of tea for his trouble. Steve he said his name was. He was very good. He showed me how to get on-line and how to use the World-Wide Web, though of course I knew a bit about that having seen it on the TV. He told me about email and newsgroups. It's all very clever — contact with the world without having to go out. Suits me fine.

I was sorry to see Steve go. He was so kind. I wanted to give him a little kiss.

Well, I got 'surfing' as they say, and I found a web-site dedicated to *Therapy and Mental Well-Being*, which led with a number of clicks to an offer of a CD-ROM introducing a therapy that could bring 'healing through self-understanding' leading to 'more positive self-regard'.

I have to admit I was feeling a bit down that day. I've found it so hard to go out after all the George nonsense. I couldn't bear the thought of people looking at me and talking.

'There goes Catherine. Look at her, all wrinkles and flab. No wonder George went off with Susie, she with the page-three figure and the dyed red hair.'

It was so stupid of me not to know what was going on. He used to go out most nights but he said he was going to see his friends in the pub. Turned out there was only one friend, and they didn't visit the pub either, but her flat, spending most of the time in her bed, no doubt. What a fool he made of me.

Chores done, I sat down with the CD at my computer and tried to unpick the cellophane cover. Doesn't that stuff drive you mad! I had to go and get a pair of scissors and stab the plastic then tear it off with my fingernails. Then I put the CD in and watched the *Welcome* screen appear.

'Enter the name you wish to be known by,' it said.

I typed in 'Catherine'. George used to call me Cathy but Mother always called me Catherine. She'd say, 'That's your name. Don't let anyone change it for you.' But I let George change it. I let George do whatever he wanted.

You'll never guess what happened next. The computer spoke to me! It said, 'Hello, Catherine!' in a sincere American accent. No-one had said that to me for ages. That Steve who came kept calling me Mrs Marlow, and the man at the newsagent's calls me 'number fifty-four'.

'Come to pay your bill, number fifty-four?' he goes, as I walk in. 'That'll be £3.45.'

I try to make myself go down each week but if I'm feeling bad I leave it. Sometimes I see one of my neighbours when I'm out, but I don't talk to them any more. Not since George left.

The next task on the computer was to select the voice that I liked best. There were lots to choose from — *New York educated, Texan drawl, Welsh sing-song, Londoner, Mid-Atlantic*. I finally settled on *Edinburgh burr, female*.

'Hello, Catherine,' I heard and it sounded so like Grandma it made me want to cry.

The next screen had two big pictures to click on — icons they're called — one labelled *Your Therapist* and the other, *Your Journey*. The voice spoke again.

'Welcome to the world of Person-Centred Therapy. Explore each section at will. There are no boundaries, no forbidden areas. Do not rush through the screens and only spend one hour a day in the program or you will have to start again. There are no points to be scored, no prizes to be won, but you will find your own rewards as you progress. Keep in close contact with your therapist at all times.'

I clicked on the *Therapist* button. There was a trickle of pan-pipe music and the screen changed to a darkened room with an easy chair in the centre. In the chair sat a tall woman, her hands folded in her lap, her head inclined to one side. She had piercing blue eyes, the colour of a summer sky, and she seemed to be gazing straight at me. Very thoughtful, she seemed, and caring too. I'm still not sure if she was real or not. She seemed real to me. Margaret was her name, at least that's what I called her. It was a bit strange talking to her at first, but she always listened to whatever I had to say.

'I'm here whenever you need me,' she told me. 'Just click on the therapist button at any time and I will speak to you. I am always here for you.'

'Er, all right,' I said, 'Thank you.'

'You're welcome.'

That didn't sound right in a Scottish accent, but I knew she meant well.

I went back to the main screen and clicked on *Your Journey*. The next screen was covered in little icons, each labelled with a subject like 'your childhood', 'your first kiss', 'your church', 'your wedding', 'your best friend', 'your boss' 'your dreams', 'your husband', 'your children', 'your parents'. There were some blank icons as well so you could fill in your own topics.

'Don't worry about the path you take on your journey,' Margaret's voice came through the speakers. 'Some days you may just want to sit quietly with me, sometimes you may want to use these icons to look at different parts of your life. Whenever you want to, you can press *Escape* and you will exit the program.'

Well, where should I start? I wasn't going to look at the 'parents' area. I don't want to end up like Mother, so I clicked on the *Wedding* icon instead. I was looking for clues, you see. Why did George just up and go like that? What was he like back then? Why did he marry me in the first place? It was hard work. I typed in every detail I could remember, the Vicar, the music, the flowers, my dress. Then some photographs came up on screen. It was very odd, they looked just like mine. There was Mother worrying about her hat blowing off and George with his arm round my waist. We looked very happy together. We were happy together. Then the computer bleeped and my hour was up and the program closed automatically. It shook me up a bit. I had to have a cup of tea and a little cry.

I was hooked though and I did my hour every day. One morning I clicked on the *Childhood* icon. The button dissolved and a new image gradually filled the computer screen, lots of different colours slowly merging into a complete picture. It was a garden with a narrow paved path leading invitingly into the distance, a mass of foliage and flowers filling the screen on either side. I pressed the 'up' arrow key, and a small child appeared on the path and started to wander away, looking around her as she went. There were flower-beds filled to overflowing with colourful blooms, peonies, carnations, pinks, lily-of-the-valley; they had no sense of season, all blooming at the same time. There were even some snowdrops, hiding beneath the leaves of a pale orange lily. At the far end of the path was a sunny patch of yellow — a grassy bank strewn with yellow primroses and a great bank of crocuses. The child went straight to the crocuses and bent down to examine their petals. I zoomed in with the magnification button, and saw tears trickling down the child's cheek. Then I noticed the crocus petals had all been damaged; pecked by birds, or eaten by slugs. Their perfection was long gone. Poor little girl. I wanted to comfort her and as I reached out to her with my heart, I found I had stepped into the garden.

Scary it was. This garden was all too familiar. I wanted to get out, but I couldn't press the *Escape* button now, could I? There was a sweet scent in the air, which I traced to a tiny patch of violets hiding beneath some ivy. I picked one of them and breathed in the fragrant scent. It reminded me of Grandma. As I sniffed, the violet started to grow until I had to hold it with both arms, and then gently place it on end so it was standing on the path beside me, the petals opened invitingly.

'Step inside,' said a voice.

I giggled, this was silly. I looked around to check I wasn't going to be seen, then dived head-first into the violet. It was soft and slippery inside as I slid downwards, arms outstretched over my head. Round and round I went down the stem, landing face first in a soft pile of rose-petals. Laughing and tossing my head to shake the petals out of my hair, I stepped out into a new world.

The air was clean and the colours looked as fresh as springtime. I shook the stem of a giant bluebell and little drops of water showered down, like gentle rain. Then I stroked the petal of a golden buttercup and rays of bright light shone through the waterdrops creating a rainbow over my head. I sat down on a mushroom stool to savour the beauty. It felt so safe.

Then I noticed the steady beating of a clock — tick, tock, tick, and saw a dandelion clock beside me, its dainty white seedheads being blown away one by one. Time was marching even here. I had the feeling there was some adventure awaiting me, but at that moment the computer beeped and the program exited to the *Therapist* screen.

'How are you, Catherine?' came the voice.

'Oh, Margaret, that was lovely. I didn't want it to end.'

'Don't worry. You can go straight back there next time.'

'Thank you,' I said. 'Goodbye.'

'Goodbye, Catherine.'

That afternoon there was a ring at my door-bell. When I looked out I could see a tall man with a thatch of greying hair and crinkly blue eyes. He was wearing one of those leather-patched corduroy jackets so I decided he was unlikely to be up to any mischief and answered the door. He said he was an antiques dealer who had been visiting next-door and had seen what he thought was a Meissen vase through my lounge window. Was I interested in a valuation? Well, as I've never liked that vase, it's one George brought back from some business trip, I thought, 'Why not?' and invited the man in. John, his name was. He told me when he was drinking his cup of tea. Told me what a lonely life he led, travelling from town to town, but what good company I was and how kind. Well, that was rather sweet, wasn't it? So when he asked if I had any other items to sell, I told him to come back the next time he was in the area. I thought it would be worth looking out some more of George's mementoes, especially as John had given me so much money for the vase, which I knew was an imitation. He promised to return soon.

I went back to my safe computer world the next day. There was a meadow in front of me filled with long grass and wild flowers with butterflies dipping into each secret store. A small stream ran beside the meadow, willow trees lining its bank. To the far right was a dense wood, beyond which I could just see some caves. I didn't like the look of them. Nasty creatures lurk in caves in my experience.

I started to walk across the meadow then noticed the undergrowth wiggling as something came towards me. I fixed a smile to my face as whatever the creature was drew nearer, then out of the waving grass padded a large stripy cat. It was Barnaby.

'Hello,' I said. 'What are you doing here? Are you going to help me?'

He miaowed, rubbing his back against my legs, then turned back the way he had come, so I followed. We crossed the meadow and reached the dark wood, full of tall conifers which cut out all the light beneath their needle-filled branches. I didn't want to enter, but Barnaby set off purposefully, glancing back to encourage me. I didn't want to lose him, so I took a deep breath and continued.

After a number of twists and turns we came to a large pool of dark water, surrounded by overhanging willow trees, their leaves dipping into the water, making it even gloomier. The sun was out overhead, but there was no sparkling reflection in the water. I wanted to move on and find somewhere less oppressive to rest, but Barnaby stopped, and started to wash his face, stilling his paw now and then as his attention was caught by a movement in the water. Suddenly he leapt forward and thrust his paw into the pool. The ripples spread but no further than a yard or two before being turned back on themselves. Barnaby caught nothing and sheepishly resumed his wash as I watched the broken surface seal over. It was a bit disturbing.

Suddenly a great plume of water shot in the air and showered down all over me. I slipped and fell, sliding into the pool. Terrified, I sank into the filthy water and could feel weeds wrapping themselves round my legs, pulling me further down. I was desperate to breathe but then there was a blinding flash of pain in the top of my head and the whirr of what could have been a drill about to penetrate my skull. The pain was so sharp, my legs jerked up free of the reeds and I managed to struggle to the surface. I could see Barnaby on the edge and swam ferociously towards him and clambered out as fast as I could. I was shaking and crying, though when I put my hand to my head, I couldn't feel any blood or cut. Barnaby led me away from the pool, through the trees to a grassy clearing where I sat down to recover. Barnaby settled into my lap, licking my nose and purring and as I stroked him I started to calm down. The program exited and I went to make myself a drink. I needed comforting. That was a really scary session.

I was about to collapse in front of the TV for the evening, when the door-bell went again. It was John. He said he'd had an unexpected call out this way and thought he'd drop by. Truth to tell, I was pleased to have his company and I managed to stretch my supper to feed two with a bit of extra pasta. We had a good laugh about the polite way to eat spaghetti and he showed me how to twiddle it round my fork, leaning over my plate. Then he started to gobble up the other end of the strand I was eating and suddenly he was kissing me. It was gorgeous, like ribbons of golden syrup interweaving inside me. Like I said, I was in need of comforting, and well, before I could even clear away the plates, we were in bed together — my marriage bed, that cold, lonely, empty space on the right filled with a living, warm and, dare I say, very sexy man. It was lovely. John had to leave that night, but he promised to be back soon.

There's nothing like a bit of loving to give you a boost, so I decided to be brave and went back into the *Therapy* program the very next day. Barnaby was waiting for me, sitting neatly upright with his tail curled round his legs, ears pricked expectantly.

'All right,' I said. 'We'll do it. We'll go and look at those caves, even though they do scare me, because I know there's something there I have to face.'

Barnaby led me along the grassy path, his tail erect. I could hear the scuttlings of small creatures in the dried needles on the forest floor, but there was no birdsong or any other sign of life. We approached the caves and I could hear a rumbling from one of them. The hairs on my arms stood to attention and my heart started to pound. I wanted to stop, to survey the situation and plan my next action, but Barnaby kept going, nose raised and twitching as though in pursuit of boil-in-the-bag haddock. He walked steadily to the mouth of the cave, then disappeared inside. I froze. No way was I going to go in. I tried to call him back, but my mouth was dry. I didn't know what to do so I pressed the *Therapist* button.

'Hello, Catherine,' came Margaret's voice, though the speakers were crackling, so she sounded a bit distant. 'How are you?'

'I'm scared,' I said. 'I don't want to go on. But I can't leave Barnaby in the cave on his own. What am I going to do?'

'What do you want to do?'

'I don't know,' I snapped. 'What do you suggest?'

There was a pause.

'You have to make your own decisions, Catherine. Only you know what's best for you.'

'Oh, you're no help,' I said and turned the computer off.

I was worried about Barnaby and I had to search the house until I found him, curled up in a sunny spot beside my wardrobe, legs twitching as he dreamed. I let a few days go by while I decided what to do. So long as the real Barnaby was safe it didn't matter if I didn't visit the computer world. I missed John. It would have been helpful to talk to him, but the phone number he had left me didn't work. I must have written it down wrong.

I almost ran to the door when the bell finally went again. But it wasn't John. This time it was a shorter man, thick set with lots of rings on his fingers. Made me think of the Beatles and that funny film, *Help!* wasn't it called? Anyway, this man was a rep for a company selling gutters and fascia boards, whatever they might be. I showed him round and then he asked me for a drink of water. We got chatting and I found he knew all about the film, and we had a laugh, and before I knew it, well, we were in bed together. It was all right, this time, not as sweet as John, but good company all the same. He said he'd be back as well, but I didn't encourage him.

I'm not sure how word got round, but I had a steady stream of callers after that, all sorts of products being offered to me: kitchen cabinets, double-glazing, paving for the driveway, dusters and tea towels — that was a beautiful young man, garage-doors, new bedroom furniture. I didn't have time for the computer.

Then one day, Barnaby went missing. He always wants his breakfast first thing in the morning, patting my cheek with his paw to get me out of bed, but he was nowhere to be seen. I hunted high and low, but he was in none of his usual haunts and none of the more obscure places I could think of either. I was sick with worry, and, silly as it sounds, the one last place I could think of looking was in the cave in the *Therapy* program. So I sat down in my negligee, and went into the program. I went straight to the mouth of the cave and I called him.

'Barnaby,' a bit squeaky at first, because I was sure I could hear heavy breathing from inside, but then louder, as I was desperate to find him. 'Barnaby!'

There was a rustling sound, like scales being rubbed along a wall, then the stomp of something heavy walking towards me. I put my hand to my mouth to stop myself screaming and my other arm round my waist to try to stop my shivering. Then in the mouth of the cave there appeared a dragon, at least ten feet tall, with fierce nostrils and blazing eyes. Its feet had long pointed talons and as it unfurled its wings it raised one leg, as though to pounce on me. Then I saw that out of the dragon's mouth there hung a stripy tail.

'NO!' I shouted. 'How dare you! Give me back my cat.'

I rushed at the monster, and yanked the tail so hard that Barnaby flew out and landed in my arms. The dragon roared in fury, a spurt of red fire flashing from its nostrils. I turned to run, when a bell sounded. My door-bell. Barnaby jumped out of my arms and I rushed to the front door. On the step were two men, clean-cut and dressed in suits. I was so pleased to see them, though I had never had two together before. They were staring at me and then I remembered that I was still in my nightie and I was aware that something wasn't quite right. One of them swallowed, he was a bit pink in the cheeks.

'Er, Madam,' he began, staring at a spot just above my head, 'have you ever thought about Jesus and what he has done for you?'

Then I started to laugh, and then I couldn't stop laughing. And then I got hysterical and they had to call an ambulance and that's why I'm here talking to you.

The photograph shows me relaxing in the garden of an English country pub when I was in the company of my family, my favourite people, beside a game of cricket, my favourite game.

Middle Age: What Is It? When Is It?

16

Suzanne M. Spector

The recent birth of a healthy baby to a sixty-three-year-old woman calls into question any notion we may have had of a fixed sequential script with clear chronological markers for various activities during the life course. This sixty-three-year-old woman is just two years short of what we used to think of as the outer limit of middle age — that significant yet arbitrary milestone of retirement at age sixty-five. This paper explores some of the historical, social, biological and psychological factors relevant to a newer multidirectional, multidimensional understanding of midlife. Middle age is viewed neither simply as the end of youth, nor as a time for stocking up on assets of health, money, and relationship in preparation for old age. Rather, it is a fluid, creative phase within the lifespan.

The focus in this chapter will include factors impacting women's experience of middle age more than men's experience for several reasons: first, women's lives have changed more dramatically than men's in the last thirty years; second, the original definitions of adult development need to be amplified because they were based only on men; and, third, the author's own research has been on mid-life women. Although often treated as a homogeneous group by researchers in the past, in the last decade or two, women have exploded the traditional markers of age, marital, and parenting status. The basis of this paper is research mostly on American culture, and of primarily middle class women within that culture.

As originally conceived by Erik Erikson, adult development was formulated as a unidirectional, irreversible stage theory, like child development. Levinson built on Erikson's theory, conceptualizing the mid-life crisis of anguish over inadequacy of achievement and concern with mortality. Both theories were based on the experience of men. In fact, Levinson's sample consisted of only forty-four men between the ages of thirty-five and forty-five. Adult female identity, if

---

This chapter is adapted from a paper presented at the Fourth International Conference on Client-Centered and Experiential Psychotherapy, Lisbon, Portugal, July 1977.

acknowledged at all as being different from men's development, was totally defined by childbearing and rearing. Consequently, a woman's life was considered over at forty or so, when the task of rearing young children had ended. Menopause and the empty nest became milestones to be dreaded for they signalled the end of women's uselfulness.

Studying middle-aged men and women in the late 1960s, Neugarten was one of the first researchers to debunk the myth of the empty nest, finding instead that the generation of women who had stayed home to raise children were enthusiastic, even elated, at the opportunity to create a new chapter in their lives when their children left home. Many went back to school and started new careers. She also made an important contribution by noting that psychological themes of identity and intimacy, of commitment and freedom, of purpose and goal setting, assessment and reformulation, of self-judgement and self-acceptance, occur and reoccur throughout life, not passed through once like steps on a staircase.

The ideology of the women's movement of the 1970s profoundly affected our conception of middle age. Called away from the home and family into the workplace, women's experience became much more diversified. As premarital sex and cohabitation became the norm, the pressures for early marriage diminished for both women and men. As social values shifted, more women not only delayed, but even declined marriage altogether. Changing economic conditions supported the feminist dictum, making middle-class women's move into the workplace, not only a matter of choice, but often necessity. Extended education in preparation for career also contributed to a delay in the timing of traditional markers such as marriage.

Modern medicine not only gave us birth control, but also the promise of fertility technology to facilitate childbirth regardless of the biological clock. However, this promise is not always fulfilled. Many of the pregnant women we see on the street today may have grey hair, but many other women who delayed childbearing to pursue careers have encountered despair when they discovered that they or their partners are no longer fertile.

The medical establishment also took over menopause, treating it as a disease, with hormone replacement therapy proferred as the magical treatment to promote youth and alleviate the effects of aging. Although estrogen is the most widely prescribed drug in the United States today, 85% of American women are not buying it. They have found that when they are physically active and healthy, as well as emotionally and intellectually involved in work and important relationships, menopause is not a difficult marker of middle age — even without drugs.

Current conceptions of adult development have moved away from one-dimensional conceptions of middle age for both men and women as a period of despair at worst, or, at best, preparation for old age. With an increased lifespan, protracted young adulthood, and prolonged education, the markers for adulthood are occurring later than they did before. Fifty-year-olds now face issues of middle age which forty-year-olds faced a generation ago. The mid-life crisis may still occur for some — now females as well as males — whose sense of identity is primarily rooted in career. Even when that script of mid-life crisis does unfold, it is likely to occur a decade or two later. However, instead of a negative characterization of middle age, today's view incorporates a recognition of the opportunities for growth and change throughout the life-cycle. This is particularly evident in the fluidity and variety of possibilities that the current generation of baby boomers is exploring. As a major American news magazine summed it up, 'middle age is starting later, going longer and looking better than ever before'.

In America, many women and men in their thirties and forties do not feel that they are middle-aged at all because they have not been married long, bought a house, or begun a family. Others who did marry young, do not feel that they are settled into middle age because they are separated or divorced, changing jobs, and or back in school. As a consequence of all these factors, we may now meet a divorced forty-five-year-old single parent who is leading a life style that looks much the same as that of a twenty-five-year-old — wearing the same clothes, working out at the same gym, living in the same apartment complex, attending the same singles events. Both the forty-five-year-old and the twenty-five-year-old are looking for a good relationship and a better job.

In addition, how is a forty-five-year-old supposed to feel middle-aged when her parents are looking and acting youthful instead of elderly? No longer are the middle-aged and elderly out of place in the college classroom. In fact, the biggest growth area in education is in the age group of adult learners. Remarriage after the death of a spouse, moves to new environs, and new careers are also characteristics of active, healthy, competent adults who may still be labelled senior citizens. While enjoying their discounts at the movies and airlines, they define the upper boundary of middle age by what it is not — the real or imagined senility, decrepitude and incompetence attached to the stigma of old age. If old age is defined as the last fifteen years of life, the boundary of middle age often extends into the late seventies. My ninety-two-year-old mother has only started identifying herself as a 'little old lady' in the last few years.

With this fluidity in the rhythm of life events and lack of normative timing, how does middle age play out in people's lives? Neugarten described how people assess their own well-being in terms of being on time or not for life events, but they make these judgements of life satisfaction within the context of their particular cohort rather than the larger culture. When I was researching mid-life maternity, I interviewed a woman who had lost her peer group when she had an unplanned pregnancy at age forty-six. Helena was looking forward to her freedom as her three children began to leave the nest. At lunch one day when she told her friends she thought she was starting menopause, they suggested she might be pregnant. She chuckled as she described how she and her husband found themselves running for their reading glasses to read the home pregnancy test. They were shocked by the result. After much anguish, she decided to have the baby. Her husband had never had children before and agreed with her decision. Three years later they were struggling. Although she had physical and economic resources to handle another round of parenthood, her strong Italian family values precluded her turning over child care to others and neither her husband nor her friends were supporting her commitment to a child-centered life. When I met her, she was having difficulty finding a social peer group because she and her husband were significantly older than the other parents of young children they encountered and the change in their lifestyle was putting a strain on their marriage.

On the other hand, many of the women I interviewed found their middle-aged parenting completely age-appropriate and some had peer group support. Carol was a product of the feminist revolution, who was passionate about her career as a documentary film maker. She never intended to get married or have children. Invited to participate in a prestigious artists' retreat, she observed that the women artists who had children were more interesting and less self-absorbed than those who were childless. She decided that she wanted children but she wasn't so sure about marriage. After their first child was born, she and her partner decided to marry. She was thirty-eight. Now forty-four and the mother of two, ages six and three, she and her husband juggle parenthood and careers. She jokes that his office and his life is neater than hers because he has a staff and a wife. She is not expected to be home all the time, but finding childcare substitutes is her responsibility. Although she often finds it exhausting, both physically and psychologically, she says, 'I love my kids. I'd only be half a person without them.' In Soho, the artists' neighborhood in New York where they live and work, most of the mothers in her son's first-grade class in public school are her age and have careers.

Both Helena and Carol were able to cut back somewhat from full-time to part-time work in which they have some flexibility about time for family responsibilities. Carol has to work for economic as well as intellectual and psychological reasons and is clearly stressed but satisfied, while Helena, who has more financial resources than most mid-life mothers, is having a harder time because she is out of sync with her peer group and previous marital lifestyle. But, she is determined to 'have it all', and is struggling to make it work

Recently a controversy erupted in the American media over the publication of a book by sociologist Arlie Hochschild entitled *The Time Bind: When Work Becomes Home and Home Becomes Work.* Based on one midwestern Fortune 500 company which she studied from 1990 to 1993, she claims that women are enjoying work so much and finding family life so stressful, that they are choosing to work more, even when family friendly policies are offered. In short, she claims that the workplace has become the haven, with a calmer pace, less demands, more affirmation and a sense of community, while time at home has become a frantic attempt to cope with an inexorable time bind that does not serve the needs and the pace of the children. Psychologists and educators have leaped into the fray claiming that quality time is a myth and that children are suffering from their assembly line lives.

In the media, much less attention has been given to the contrary, more extensive, research results which find women and men highly satisfied, despite stresses, with their lives as working parents. In 1996, Rosalind Barnett, a psychologist and senior Radcliffe scholar, and Caryl Rivers, a journalist, published *She Works/He Works,:*

How Two-Income Families are Happier, Healthier, and Better Off in which they described the results of their four-year, $1,000,000 study of a random sample of two-earner couples in the Boston area. They found that the dual-career family creates economic stability and a close-knit, cooperative family atmosphere. In the study, both women and men reported warm close relationships with their children and high levels of satisfaction with their lives, despite the stress. The authors contend that careers outside the home have paid off for women in heightened self-esteem, improved physical health, and a reduction in the high depression rates characteristic of homemakers in the 1950s. They also debunk the old belief that men derive their identities from the workplace rather than the home. Barnett and Rivers claim that a strong connection to their families is central to men's identities and that, with dual careers and shared parenting, more fathers are enjoying close relationships with their children than ever before. Although this study is completely consistent with several other very large national surveys that demonstrate how well two-career families and family friendly-work policies can function, it did not get a fraction of the attention from the media as the Hochschild book. The media tends to continue bashing both women who make work a priority in addition to their families, and men who make families a priority in addition to their work. For example, no media attention was given to a survey of more than 6000 employees at DuPont which showed that nearly half the women and almost as many men had traded career advancement to remain in jobs that gave them more family time. And little attention is given by the American media to reports of other countries where family time is more highly valued. The attention to the Hochschild study is of particular concern because it undermines the efficacy of existing family-friendly policies rather than promoting them.

Barnett and Rivers' study supports my qualitative findings that mid-life maternity not only works, but often works better than parenthood undertaken earlier in the life-cycle when there may be more physical stamina, but less psychological maturity and economic resources. Most women I interviewed were in their forties and fifties and were working, but had modified their work schedules, sometimes even changing careers, to accomodate child rearing. My sample included not only partnered middle-aged mothers who were making their lives work, but single mothers as well. Although marriage and maternity have traditionally been quite intertwined, today, by choice or by circumstance, they are seen by an increasing number of women as separate endeavors. Some women give up the heterosexual nuclear family dream, recognizing that it is a cultural prescription that no longer fits. Then they create alternative relational networks — both heterosexual and homosexual — that support motherhood without marriage. While single parenting may be a clear decision to fulfill the dream of maternity without a partner, more often it is the ultimate resolution of a failed marriage.

My studies have also included interviews of mid-life women who had made the decision to be childfree and who were happy with their lives. Biologists who claim that the maternal urge is universal, do so from a patriarchal framework in which a woman's destiny is defined by her ability to bear children. In this postmodern age the importance of social and psychological factors are acknowledged as equally significant determinants of our behavior and even of our construction of reality. In this context we can truly hear the voices of those many women who have had the courage to say that they simply never felt the maternal urge. Some of the women I interviewed in Japan, Europe, and the United States described their mothers' lives as diminished by entrapment in childrearing and unsatisfying marriages. Clearly, their mothers' unhappiness had a powerful psychological influence, consciously or unconsciously, on their own decisions not to have children. But this was not the case in all of the stories.

Women in their forties today, part of the baby-boom generation, heard the call to self-expression in the world as they entered puberty. Some followed a direct path to career success without any pull toward marriage or family. Others felt oriented toward children but never felt an urge to have children of their own. Patricia, one of the women I interviewed, was absolutely convinced that she could not have achieved career success, a solid marriage and happiness if she had been restricted in her choices by having children. She said, 'Maybe there's something lacking in me. If so, I'm very, very grateful for it. I would have felt unfulfilled as a woman if I had had children because I would have missed so much. I used to feel selfish but now I believe I've made a contribution to our overpopulated world by not having babies.' Women — single and coupled — who made a conscious choice not to have children, find challenge, fulfillment, and satisfaction from a variety of pursuits: developing themselves, making a contribution to the world, maintaining loving relationships, pursuing careers, becoming financially secure and independent, maintaining a healthy body, and deepening their spiritual connection. These were the same pursuits that I found women deriving satisfaction from in an earlier study I did of single women in their fifties, most of whom had completed major parenting at an earlier age.

What is the psychological impact of this proliferation of time schedules and life choices for middle-aged women and men? One of the biggest source of problems is the gap between this new, open, external reality and internalized standards and prescriptions. Our first models of adulthood are our parents and it is still difficult to deviate from their pattern. One of my thirty-something daughters who is unpartnered, childless, and in career flux, is astounded when she realizes that at her age, I was long married, raising three children, and deeply and passionately into a career. I remind her that a decade later, I burned out, gave it all up, and went inward in search of self and spirit, a place that she is in right now. I trust that she will find and create meaningful connection and purpose in her life, as I did, but she struggles with feeling that she has travelled a different course, but has nothing to show for it.

As person-centered therapists, our task has always been to help our clients find their internal locus of evaluation. Without clear external markers this task is more imperative than ever. While choice may not be unlimited, this end of the twentieth century certainly offers the middle-aged a wider array of choices than ever before. And given all this choice, we must help our clients set realistic expectations for themselves as they explore the myriad and sometimes conflicting paths to self-fulfillment.

References

Barnett, R.C. and Rivers, C. (1996) *She works/He works: How Two-income Families are Happier, Healthier, and Better Off.* San Francisco: HarperSanFrancisco.

Erikson, E. H. (1963) *Childhood and Society.* (2nd ed.) New York: Norton.

Hochschild, A. R. (1997) *The Time Bind: When Work Becomes Home and Home Becomes Work.* New York: Metropolitan Books Henry Holt & Co.

Levinson, D. J. (1980) Toward a conception of the adult life course. In N.J. Smelser and E. H. Erikson (Eds.). *Themes of Work and Love in Adulthood.* Cambridge: Harvard University Press.

Neugarten, B. L. (Ed.) (1968) *Middle age and aging: A reader in social psychology.* Chicago: University of Chicago Press.

Neugarten, B. L. (1979) Time, age, and the life cycle. *American Journal of Psychiatry,* 136, 887–894.

Irene Fairhurst writes, I like this photograph of Suzanne because it shows her relaxing and enjoying herself, reminds me of how much fun she is as well as being intelligent and knowledgeable.

The Person-Centered Approach: Solution to Gender Splitting

17

Peggy Natiello

My long journey into gender-related conditions of worth became dominant when I was eight, and my adored twelve-year old-brother, Jimmy, died. There were four siblings, but he was the first child and only son. As I watched my emotionally fragile mother fall to pieces, and my powerful, stoical father struggle with unspeakable anguish, I decided I had better try to fill Jimmy's shoes. That was quite an undertaking as he was a gifted child with musical and academic skills that far exceeded mine. I began in the most obvious place — taking over his chores. I learned quickly that the tasks that had been his suddenly exhibited flashing 'No trespassing' signs when I approached them. I was 'too small' to mow the lawn or drag the ash cans from the furnace room to the garage; 'too delicate' to knock the Japanese beetles off the rose bushes; 'too vulnerable' to walk alone to the playground or swimming pool; 'too sensitive' to bear the harshness my Dad voiced when Jim's work wasn't perfect or on time. It was eminently clear that there were different standards for me, and that, hard as I tried, I was not allowed to take up his work.

Gender-related conditions of worth

Many years passed before I realized that these standards were gender-related and had a significant effect on the way I valued myself in my early life. I began to judge myself in accordance with the approval or disapproval my behavior evoked from others, and much of that was an outgrowth of my being female. I did not know it at that time, but these experiences constituted my first awareness of the 'conditions of worth' (Rogers, 1959) that influenced my early life.

Because my father had always been encouraging and challenging to his four children, I continued my efforts at self-expansion. With Jim gone, my Dad continued to talk consistently to his daughters about the boundless opportunities in life, never hinting at any limitations. I forged ahead accepting his words as the absolute truth. 'You can do and be anything you choose,' he would say. As I experimented with new behaviors that had heretofore belonged to Jimmy's world, lots of obstacles were placed in my path — many of them by my father himself. One early evening I slipped away from my parents' dinner party, and went to the creek to play Tarzan. There had been a fierce rainstorm in the afternoon, and, in my new white playsuit with the blue rickrack, I swung across the water on the thick tree vines and skidded triumphantly into muddy landings on the far bank. Upon my arrival home, I was spanked in front of the dinner guests. I knew that the problem was not the mud, but rather the physical risk I had taken. The Wyomissing Creek was not a place for girls alone; I had entered forbidden territory. Some weeks later, carrying Jim's bow and arrow, I hunted snakes with neighborhood boys who had been his friends. I was 'grounded' by my parents for this new breach of boundaries.

Upon reflection, I know that my parents wanted their daughters to have opportunities equal to Jim's. Their overprotectiveness was a response to the prevailing, gender-biased view that females are more vulnerable and less competent than males. My mother and father were completely unaware that they were reinforcing conditions of worth distinctly related to our being female. Although conditions of worth are viewed as being transmitted primarily by parents, it is important to remember that they also reflect the introjected values, biases, and social conditioning of the world we live in. There is ample research that documents the differences in the way almost all parents handle male and female children from the moment of birth. These differences reflect the cultural expectations of normative gender development, as well as the vulnerability of the subordinate gender, and are, for the most part, performed without awareness.

By the time I reached the age of twelve, I was ordered to give up my adventurous, solitary horseback rides through the green, empty meadows near Fry's stables. It was not acceptable for a girl to be out in those fields by herself. As the warnings heated up, it became difficult not to feel afraid. My increasing trepidation grew stronger as I grew older, and threatened my sense of adventure. My father continued to push me out with one hand and pull me back with the other. I was confused by the conflicting messages I was receiving, and becoming increasingly convinced that I was not competent to engage the world as freely as Jim had.

Conditions of worth intensify

My sense of obligation to follow Jim's academic lead pleased my father immensely, but my mother seemed completely disinterested in that aspect of my life. She wanted me to be kind, gentle, responsive, caring, and socially acceptable — the characteristics that distinguish a 'good girl'. Accomplishments in school met with no enthusiasm from peers, either. The considerable influence I had with them came from the same nurturing qualities and strong empathic skills I developed to assuage my mother's grief and continuing fragility.

The conflicting messages — coming now from many directions — intensified as the need for peer approval and popularity took center stage. I became aware of more serious limitations on my behavior; most of them quite blatantly connected to my gender and my budding sexuality. One part of me sought out the more normative feminine behaviors that won approval from my peer group. Another part, however, rebelled fiercely against the boundaries placed around me and the submissiveness I was encouraged to develop. By the age of sixteen I began to manifest signs of anorexia, a condition associated with the cultural fear of femininity, the need to control one's life, the suppression of secondary female sexual characteristics. The relentless process of internalizing others' ideas of what would make me loveable and capable was well underway. My need for positive regard from others — a need that Rogers (1959) said is universal — was in conflict with my own organismic needs and my inherent potential for growth. I was edging ever further from my spontaneous self.

As a disciplinary measure in response to my rebelliousness, my parents sent me to a rigid Roman Catholic high school in the nearby city. I was miserable, angry, and non-communicative. I wanted to get away from home for awhile, and managed to secure a summer job as a stable girl on a ranch in Montana. It was no surprise when I was forbidden to accept it. 'That is not a healthy environment for a young girl. There is a lot of drinking among the cowboys and guests, and no supervision.' Angry and devastated, I continued to hear messages that I could not take care of myself, and that I had better be careful, tone down, get into line. The attitudes and behaviors I had worked so hard to offer my parents as compensation for Jim's absence were getting me in trouble. I was losing my pride, and cringing under others' judgments. I became quieter, shyer, and increasingly unassertive. Although I didn't realize it, much of my life was being ruled by internalized conditions of worth, and I was increasingly less able to live in a state of congruence or authenticity.

Conditions of worth carry over into adulthood

Much later, as an adult with five children and all the attendant responsibilities, my faith in my intellectual abilities and in my rights and privileges as an independent person wavered dangerously. The conditions of worth around conforming or not conforming to normative gender expectations had slowly eroded my vitality, confidence and self-esteem. I dug deeply into myself to uncover enough determination to pursue a masters and then a doctoral degree while raising the children. It was with great personal turmoil that I made those decisions which seriously conflicted with the norms of middle-class motherhood. Would my children, whom I loved and enjoyed, suffer? Could I do more than I was already doing? Was I capable of rigorous academic work at this point in my life? My answers and the incredible juggling that went with them, brought down lots of criticism, much of it from some other women in the family and the community. I was viewed as an inadequate, uncommitted mother when I accepted a position as professor in the evening division of the Masters program from which I had graduated. Most people completely overlooked the full-time and loving parenting I continued to provide along with my other responsibilities.

These last events took place in the late '60s, and, in concert with the mood of the country, I was becoming increasingly politicized. My consciousness around sexism, racism, classism and other cultural inequities was raised. The women's movement validated my anger about rigid gender-defined limits to my growth as a person. Still, I was divided within myself, much as I had been for most of my life. My anger and attempts at activism were difficult to balance with the nurturing mothering role that still remained of the utmost importance. My sometimes-radical stance around sexism, which I now recognized as the deep-seated reality that leads to gender-related conditions of worth, generated social criticism, isolation, and some upheaval at home. My voice alternated between muteness and fury. In the face of social disapproval and fear of failing as a woman and mother, I could not figure out how to integrate the conflicting aspects of self.

I discovered the root cause of my internal division, when I engaged in a study of the literature being rediscovered or produced during the Feminist Movement. The writings of Betty Freidan (1963), Simone de Beauvoir (1953), Nancy Chodorow (1978), Nancy Cott (1977), Margaret Mead (1955), Jean Baker Miller (1976), Roger Gould (1978), and many others began to throw light on my dis-ease and self-estrangement. I understood that my own struggle was undoubtedly replicated in many women and men, living half-lives in a sexist culture.

Conditions of worth and gender splitting

The meanings of my childhood experiences helped me to understand my adult feelings even more clearly when I read of Rogers' conditions of worth, and saw their connection with Daniel Levinson's (1996) concept of *gender splitting*.

> [Gender splitting] refers not simply to gender differences but to a splitting asunder — the creation of a rigid division between male and female, masculine and feminine, in human life. Gender splitting has been pervasive in virtually every society we know about in the history of the human species, although there are wide variations in its patterning. What is regarded as 'feminine' in contrast to 'masculine' has varied among societies, classes, and historical periods, but the splitting operates at many levels: culture, social institutions, everyday social life, the individual psyche. It creates antithetical divisions between women and men, between social worlds, between the masculine and feminine within the self. It also creates inequalities that limit adult development of women as well as men (p. 38).

The gender splitting that Levinson defines is still alive and well. It leads to disparate expectations for men and women, and affects their way of functioning in the world. Women's primary responsibilities in the domestic sphere (despite increasing entry into the institutional world) require nurturance, deep emotional connection, and a willingness to put aside one's own needs, particularly in the rearing of children. Men's primary responsibilities lie in the more public domain, and encourage competitiveness, aggressiveness, and splitting-off of deep emotions in order to 'make it' in the men's world (Levant and Pollack, 1995). Women's charge leads them in the direction of growing *interrelatedness* (Gilligan, 1982), while men's gender expectations go in the direction of increasing *autonomy* (Levant and Pollack, 1995).

These cultural mandates damage those of us who *do not* conform to the norms of maleness and femaleness as well as those who do. The conditions of worth that result from gender splitting create deep fissures in the personal psyches and relationships of men and women, and prevent both from being whole, self-aware and congruent. In one sense, my determination to claim aspects of myself that are generally defined as 'masculine' resulted in fuller development of self. The downside of that determination was that I had no model for integrating what seemed like separate sides of myself. My social conditioning about how to be female led to serious internal conflict and questions about where I fit in the world.

Healing through the person-centered approach

My salvation from the conflicts and self-doubts caused by gender splitting came in the form of the person-centered approach, and in opportunities to study and work with Carl Rogers and like-minded colleagues. As I struggled to incorporate the facilitative conditions of empathy, positive regard and congruence into my life, I found the search for congruence to be the most exhilarating, challenging and, ultimately, healing for the gender-related rift within myself:

> Congruence is the state of realness and authenticity that exists in persons who have deeply explored the experience of self and accepted the truths they find in their exploration. Once those truths are accepted, the desire and ability to be emotionally and intellectually authentic in relationships is generally trustworthy and even compelling (Natiello, 1987, p. 206).

The state of congruence contradicts the messages I first received, as a girl taking over my brother's chores, about being careful, adaptable, sweet, nice, submissive; and later as a woman required to take care of others' physical and emotional needs, and even be responsible for their happiness. It celebrates the *full* self — gender expectations aside — and encourages all of us to reclaim disowned aspects of our wholeness. My experience in training other women teaches me that I am not alone in viewing the search for congruence as the most important part of the person-centered journey. The opportunity for women to be real, whole, and personally powerful has traditionally been discouraged in the culture of sexism, and the exuberance with which some women finally speak in their own voice is glorious to hear, though sometimes startling.

Men's path into congruence takes a different route. They also have to struggle to be real and whole, but their struggle seems more focused on making deeper contact with feelings, developing their capacity for empathy and nurturing — attitudes that are not considered 'manly' in a sexist society. Their efforts to reclaim the empathic, emotional, receptive aspects of self — values that I sometimes rebelled against as contributing to the passivity and submissiveness encouraged in women — have helped me to appreciate and reintegrate my more feminine side. Our birthright entitles each one of us to an endless range of behaviors, attitudes and feelings, and the conditioning that demands *successful* men and women to conform to certain normative development violates our capacity for wholeness.

In their discussion of congruence in relationships with clients, Mearns and Thorne pose the challenge to counselors, 'Can I dare to be me?' (1988, p. 75). They follow that 'dare' with a number of specific questions that reveal challenges most person-centered practitioners face in striving for congruence. I want to consider some of those questions, and a few of my own, in terms of gender splitting, and briefly review the diverse obstacles confronted by women and by men in *all* relationships as a result of their social conditioning.

Challenges to women

Let us begin with the questions that seem most challenging to women. Do I dare to:

- *Show my anger when strongly felt?* Jean Baker-Miller (1991) says that in an androcentric culture, women's anger is repressed, denied, and 'virtually always seen as pathological' (p.182). Fears of retaliation or of not being acceptable impede most of my female clients from showing, *or even feeling,* their anger.
- *Shout when something is seething within me?* Women don't *shout!* This behavior is alien and frightening to most women who have conformed to gender expectations, and hazardous to those women who have not.
- *Be forceful as well as gentle?* Forceful is generally a difficult behavior for women who are encouraged to be passive. Women are more often taught to get what they want indirectly or through forms of manipulation — coaxing, teasing, seducing, or cajoling. Women who choose forcefulness are often labelled 'bitchy, power-hungry, harsh'.
- *Admit my distraction when challenged about it?* Women are expected to give undivided attention to others, and find it difficult to admit any deviation from that norm. Women learn that others' needs supersede their own.
- *Let go of my caretaking skills, my need to make things better?* Women often want to help, fix, soothe rather than allow a client, group, student, child to dwell in their pain. It is incredibly difficult for women to release themselves from the caretaking role and trust that clients can take care of themselves.
- *Take the risk of owning my personal power — my full self?* Most women are taught to beware of being *too* much. The consistently expressed fear and recurring experience that I hear from women is that, if they allow themselves full and empowered presence, they will be too much, and expect to be abandoned by those whose acceptance they need and want. Often that has been the reality for my clients who have empowered themselves.

Challenges to men

Some of Mearns' and Thorne's questions that I believe pose particular gender-related challenges to men in attempting to grow into the condition of congruence follow below:

- *Can I feel the feelings that are in me?* The social construction of men's roles does *not* include the valuing of feelings. Men's acquaintance with, and vocabulary around, feelings require hard work, and rejection of their normative gender expectations.
- *Hear another's feelings without trying to change or take them away?* In my practice of therapy, and in my personal life, I see how difficult it is for men to simply allow another to have feelings, especially in a primary relationship. Many women tell me it is impossible to share sad or conflicted feelings with their male partners because the response is likely to be, 'What do you want me to do about it?' or 'What did I do wrong?'
- *Admit my distraction and confusion when it persists or is challenged?* Competence and expertness are expected from men. It is difficult and generally out of character for them to admit this kind of vulnerability.
- *Can I trust that others will be able to solve their own problems and let go of being responsible?* Men and women have different ways of caretaking. Men are socialized to solve problems. In the person-centered approach to relationships, all persons must be trusted and allowed to solve their *own* problems.
- *Put words to my affection when it is there?* Emotional stoicism, rather than expressiveness, is the normative male style in relationships (Levant and Pollack, 1995). In addition, fears of sexual harassment charges are placing new constraints on men's expressiveness.
- *Be spontaneous even though I don't know where that will lead?* Focus, certainty, and expertness, rather than spontaneity, are considered successful attitudes for men.
- *Be gentle as well as forceful.* Gentleness is not viewed as integral to the male role, especially the professional role. Forcefulness is more likely to be affirmed. Men who are consistently gentle are often not taken seriously.
- *Step out from behind my professional facade?* Image and the mandate to maintain a competent facade, are particularly strong for men.

These questions indicate conflict with normative gender expectations that men and women often confront in striving for congruence — full awareness and unconditional acceptance of attitudes heretofore repressed or denied to experience — and a willingness to be fully and transparently present in relationships. The conviction that gender splitting is very much a part of women's lives is validated consistently in my therapeutic work with other women, in training person-centered facilitators, and in the resistance I continue to meet in my efforts to further integrate myself. My commitment to raise four sons with fewer gender limitations, as well as continuing work with many male clients, inform me that social expectations have barely changed at all for men. Those women and men who succeed in expanding beyond their gender expectations are often penalized or rejected. Those who over-conform live half-lives and sacrifice their vitality and freedom.

Conclusion

There is no simple answer to the gender dilemma, although the issues have changed somewhat since the late '60s. Opportunities for expanding interests and behaviors are more available, and yet strong taboos to stepping away from traditional gender norms still prevail. Indeed, Daniel Levinson (1996) says, 'the level and intensity of gender conflict has risen since 1980'. Many men and women are resisting the need for more changes as those already instituted threaten the fabric of institutional, domestic, and interpersonal life (Faludi, 1991; Levinson, 1996; Kaminer, 1990). The changes can be so painful and overwhelming, that it is tempting to slip back into denial, to say we have accomplished enough, or to blame the other gender group for all the upheaval, problems and change.

My experience, however, negates those solutions completely. I would not change the course of my own development that included taking on some of the male expectations when I was a child. I met resistance from outside, confusion and conflict from within, but I believe I profited by expanding my vision of what and who I could be in the world. It has been difficult to heal the internal rift, but it would have been far more formidable to try in later life to develop aspects of myself that I repressed in reaction to gender-related conditions of worth while growing up.

I certainly wanted our five children to be as free from gender expectations as possible, although the culture they live in made that almost impossible. I saw the price for over-conforming and for under-conforming that each of them paid at one time or another. Just as in my own life, I was aware of their confusion when they expanded themselves beyond behaviors that characterized a 'successful man or woman'. And yet I see the enrichment for our sons in their unusual nurturing capacity as parents, their commitment to social justice often to the detriment of financial success, their ability to take care of their basic needs, their competence in the domestic sphere. I remember our sixth-grade daughter cycling around town to gather signatures for a petition she composed, asking that the girls be allowed to use the basketball court at least two of the five days it was taken by boys. She argued the request with the principal and won the right for her female classmates. More important, perhaps, she had the joy of feeling her own agency and empowerment. Now, I respect her assertiveness (compromised a bit during seven years of child-rearing at home), her proven ability to be successful in the world of work, her refusal to be a victim, as well as her extraordinary gifts as a mother. These young adults are integrated human beings, and I believe change in gender splitting may be hastened some because of their consciousness and way of using themselves in the world.

That, perhaps, is the answer, along with a willingness to confront ourselves and a gender-based society that continues to place serious limits on our development as whole persons.

References

de Beauvoir, S. (1953) *The Second Sex*. Edited and translated by H.M. Parshley. New York: Alfred Knopf.

Chodorow, N. (1978) *The Reproduction of Mothering.* Berkeley: University of California Press

Cott, N. (1977) *The Bonds of Womanhood.* New Haven: Yale University Press.

Faludi, S. (1991) *Backlash.* New York: Crown.

Freidan, B. (1963) *The Feminine Mystique.* New York: Dell.

Gilligan, C. (1982) *In a Different Voice.* Cambridge, MA: Harvard University Press.

Gould R. (1974) Measuring Masculinity by the Size of a Paycheck. in J.Pleck and J.Sawyer (eds) *Men and Masculinity,* (pp. 96–100). Englewood Cliffs, NJ: Prentice Hall.

Gould, R. (1980) *Transformations: Growth and Change in Adult Life.* New York: Simon and Schuster.

Kaminer, W. (1990) *A Fearful Freedom: Women's Flight from Equality.* Reading, MA: Addison-Wesley.

Levant, R. and Pollack, W. (1995) *Toward a New Psychology of Men.* New York: Harper Collins.

Levinson, D. (1996) *The Seasons of a Woman's Life.* New York: Alfred Knopf.

Mead, M. (1955) *Male and Female.* New York: New American Library.

Mearns, D. and Thorne, B. (1988) *Person-centered Counselling in Action.* London: Sage Publications.

Miller, J. B. (1976) *Toward a New Psychology of Women.* Boston: Beacon Press.

Miller, J. B. (1991) The construction of anger in women and men. In *Women's Growth in Connection* (pp. 181–196). New York: The Guiford Press.

Natiello, P. (1987) The Person-centered Approach: From Theory to Practice, in *Person centered Review.* California: Sage Publications, Inc.

Rogers, C. R. (1959) A Theory of Therapy, Personality, and Interpersonal Relationships, in S. Koch, (ed.), *Psychology: A Study of Science, Vol.III,* New York and London: McGraw-Hill, pp.184–256.

Taken at a family farewell for our youngest son, enroute from Vermont to two years Peace Corps service in Mongolia. A mixed experience indeed — the joy of reunion and the sadness of goodbyes.

A Woman's Place

18

Lesley Rose

Introduction

The aim of this chapter is to trace a very personal, subjective journey made by the writer over a number of years. It is an essay which will endeavour to show the effects, both disadvantageous and beneficial, of differing therapeutic orientations on a woman who is also a Jew. It is, therefore, particularly relevant for me to compare the attitudes to women of two men, Sigmund Freud and Carl Rogers, whose thinking has had a tremendous impact both on current therapy and on my own process in particular. I wish to discuss their contrasting ideas and I shall conjecture that while Freud did not consider himself an observant Jew (Klein, 1981, p. 45), the deleterious stance towards women adopted by Orthodox Judaism (which I intend to demonstrate) may to some extent have influenced Freud's own outlook on '*a woman's place*' in the world.

Freud and female sexuality

Freud is often praised for the breadth of his achievement: here I would wish to focus on his view of women and their sexuality. To Freud, it was quite clear that women are not the equal of men. Central to his thinking was the concept of the castration complex and of penis envy. According to Brown (1961):

> The girl becomes interested in her clitoris as the biological equivalent of the boy's penis but since this organ appears obviously inferior to the masculine one, she develops an envious desire to be like the boy. This is described by Freud as '*penis envy*' (p. 24, my emphasis).

I shall not here attempt to deal with the unfounded assumption in this passage that when girls, of whatever age, discover they possess a clitoris, they have a simultaneous knowledge of the existence of the penis, regardless of whether or not they have any cognizance of the male anatomy. I shall restrict myself merely to the fact that girls are not seen as sexual beings in their own right, equal to but different from boys; instead they are seen as '*inferior*' to boys. A girl does not just realise that she '*lacks a penis*', she has to accept that her sexual organs, in particular the clitoris, are inferior, and '*this realisation has a permanent effect on the development of her character*' (Hollitscher, 1947, p. 32). At this stage in my reading, I wondered if perhaps Freud had been misunderstood and that if I turned to Freud himself, I would find a different, less unflattering picture of women.

In 1917 Freud published his *Introductory Lectures on Psychoanalysis*. Lecture 20 states:

> As regards little girls, we can say of them that they feel greatly at a disadvantage owing to their lack of a big, visible penis, that they envy boys for possessing one and that, in the main for this reason, they develop a wish to be a man (Freud, 1917: Penguin 1991, p. 360).

It would appear then that far from being misrepresented, Freud has been understood only too well. A few pages later he has more to say about women, this time discussing their '*seduction phantasies*' (to use his own term).

> Phantasies of being seduced are of particular interest because they so often are not phantasies but real memories (ibid, p. 417).

This seems promising but the sting is to come:

> Fortunately, they are not real as often as seemed at first to be shown by the findings of analysis . . . and if in the case of girls who produce such an event in the story of their childhood their father figures fairly regularly as the seducer, there can be no doubt either of the imaginary nature of the accusation, or of the motive that has led to it. A phantasy of being seduced where no seduction has occurred is usually employed by a child to screen the auto-erotic period of his sexual activity. He spares himself shame about masturbation by retrospectively phantasying a desired object into these earliest times (ibid).

Freud *does* continue: 'You must not suppose however that sexual abuse of a child by its nearest male relatives belongs entirely to the realm of phantasy', which indicates he does subscribe to the reality of the truth of the child's experience. However, he concludes the passage:

> Most analysts will have treated cases in which such events were real and could be unimpeachably established; *but even so they related to the later years of childhood and had been transposed into earlier times* (ibid, my emphasis).

Perhaps Freud's views changed with time. Fifteen years later in 1932 he reiterated and expanded on his original ideas (Freud, 1932). He prefaces his lecture *Femininity* with the reassurance:

> Today's lecture . . . brings forward nothing but observed facts almost without any speculative additions.(Freud, 1932: Penguin 1991, p.146).

Let us, then, turn to his facts:

> In the period in which the main interest was directed to discovering
> infantile sexual traumas, almost all my women patients told me that
> they had been seduced by their father. I was driven to recognise that
> these reports were untrue and so came to understand that hysterical
> symptoms are derived from phantasies and not from real occurrences
> (ibid. p.154).

It seems, then, that although '*almost all*' of the women who came to him revealed
that they had been sexually abused by their fathers, Freud chose not to believe
them. (And this is when he talks of '*observed facts*': along what byways might he
have wandered had he allowed himself to be a little less objective, a little more
'*speculative*'?)

He is now faced with a problem: if his patients are lying, what reason do they
have for so doing? However, his fertile mind soon spawns reasons for their '*hysterical
symptoms*'. He decides that if they are to turn *towards* their fathers (in their phantasies
of secret wishes of seduction), they must also turn *away from* their mothers.

In 1917 he had said that:

> A little girl looks on her mother as a person who interferes with her
> affectionate relation to her father and who occupies a position which
> she herself could very well fill (Freud, 1917: Penguin 1991, p. 243).

Now, in 1932, he decides that:

> Unless we can find something specific for girls, and is not present
> . . . in boys, we shall not have explained the termination of the
> attachment of girls to their mother . . . this specific factor . . . lies in
> the castration complex . . . that girls hold their mother responsible
> for their lack of a penis and do not forgive her for their being thus
> put at a disadvantage (Freud, 1932: Penguin 1991, p.158).

He concludes:

> The wish with which the girl turns to her father is, no doubt, originally
> the wish for the penis which her mother has refused her and which
> she now expects from her father (ibid, p.162).

For Freud, the girl's discovery of her castration is a turning point in her life (Freud,
1932). It commences with:

> . . . the sight of the genitals of the other sex. They feel seriously
> wronged . . . and fall a victim to 'envy for the penis', which will
> leave *ineradicable traces on their development and the formation of
> their character* (ibid, pp.158–9, my emphasis).

Previously we have seen that women appear to possess only negative qualities: they
are inferior, they are filled with envy. Freud has, however, by no means completed

his indictment. For him, women are destined never to reach the superior moral heights apportioned to men: the flaw is immutable. In order to appreciate more fully the ideas expressed by Freud it is necessary to look further into the Oedipus complex and the formation of the Superego.

Briefly: Freud believed that the young child wishes to possess physically the parent of the opposite sex. Since this is forbidden, the child feels he deserves punishment and the fitting punishment must be castration. The male child has evidence on which to base his deduction that castration occurs since he is aware that the female is not in possession of a penis: it must therefore have been removed. (Hollitscher, 1947, p. 35). According to Freud, it is this fear of castration that signifies the end of the Oedipus complex and leads to the formation of the Superego: 'The Superego is stunted in strength and growth if the surmounting of the Oedipus complex is only incompletely successful' (Freud 1932: Penguin 1991, p. 96).

The value for Freud of the Superego cannot be overestimated. The Superego can be defined as conscience, morality, the internalisation of the demands of Society. Introjected parental authority is succeeded by the individual's own sense of higher ideals (Hollitscher, 1947, p.74).

It is readily apparent, then, that the development of the Superego is crucial to the individual's full psychological growth and health. For the boy, as we have seen, the Oedipus complex is ended by castration fears which in turn promote the growth of the Superego, the moral sense. But what happens to the girl? Since she cannot fear castration because her penis is already forfeited, she is thereby precluded from attaining the Superego state:

> In the absence of fear of castration, the chief motive is removed
> which leads boys to surmount the Oedipus complex. Girls remain in
> it for an indeterminate length of time . . . in these circumstances, the
> formation of the Superego must suffer: it cannot attain the strength
> and independence which give it its cultural significance (Freud, 1932:
> Penguin 1991, p.163).

In order to underscore the moral inferiority of women, Freud left in his Lectures one or two further ruminations:

> We attribute a larger amount of narcissism to femininity . . . so that
> to be loved is a stronger need than to love. The effect of penis envy
> has a share, further, in the physical vanity of women, since they are
> bound to value their charms more highly as a late compensation for
> their original sexual inferiority. Shame has as its purpose concealment
> of genital deficiency (ibid, p. 166).

and,

> The difference in a mother's reactions to whether the birth of a son or
> daughter, shows that the old factor of lack of penis has even now not
> lost its strength . . . A mother is only brought unlimited satisfaction by
> her relation to a son . . . A mother can transfer to her son the ambition

which she has been obliged to suppress in herself (ibid, p.168).

Driving a final nail in the coffin of women's morality, Freud remarks almost as an afterthought:

> The fact that women must be regarded as having little sense of justice is
> no doubt related to the predominance of envy in their mental life (ibid).

So there we are: Freud's opinion of women leaves nothing to the imagination mainly, I feel, because his own imagination, his own fantasies, have been given free rein. His *knowledge* of the incest wishes of children to parents came from his own self-analysis — especially with reference to dreams — (Jones, 1953: Penguin 1993, p. 280) and the arrogance of a man who uses himself as a paradigm from which to extrapolate all human behaviour in this negative way has had incalculable effects on generations of women.

Personal relationships with women

The foregoing are Freud's theoretical concepts derived from his clinical practice and one is left to wonder whether they were in any way modified by his attitudes to the women he knew on a personal level, in particular his immediate family.

Jones (ibid. p. 46) relates an incident which happened when Freud was quite young. It seems that Freud's mother, who was musical, arranged for his younger sister to practise the piano. One can well imagine that Freud, attempting to study, was very much disturbed by the fumblings of an eight-year-old and would have found this hard to endure. What is perhaps a little more surprising is that he not only '*insisted*' that the piano be removed, but that his will triumphed.

His mother's capitulation seems to have nurtured Freud's viewpoint that the affairs of women were subordinate to those of men, and especially that the wishes of those women who were nearest to him were less worthy of consideration than his own. By the time he was ready to marry Martha Bernays these early seeds of egotism had fully ripened.

Jones describes Martha as being five years younger than Freud, a girl who was:

> . . . very attached to her mother and much influenced by her, a matter
> that presently gave rise to great difficulties with her lover. Martha's
> mother . . . adhered to the strict rules of Orthodox Judaism and her
> children were brought up to do the same. This was in itself a serious
> source of friction since Freud would have no truck with it (ibid, p. 121).
> More serious were the stern demands he made on her. She had to
> change her fondness for being on good terms with everybody and
> always to take his side in his quarrel with her brother and mother. In
> fact she must recognise that she no longer belonged to them but only
> to him (ibid, p. 124–5).

She was not really his unless he could perceive his 'stamp' on her (ibid, p.126).

Wife or chattel? Even when she wanted to go skating, Martha had first to ask Freud for permission, and this was given only on condition that she skated alone, so that she should not be arm in arm with another man. (ibid p. 133). I find it unsurprising that Jones has no word to speak of similar permissions being sought by Freud and conditions dictated by Martha.

Perhaps his attitude to Martha, his assumption that his wishes should take precedence over hers and that she should be subservient to him, derived in part from the age in which he lived. I would also suspect that his thinking was inevitably coloured by the fact that he was a Jew and by his Orthodox Jewish background.

However, before considering to what extent Freud *was* influenced by his Jewish upbringing, it might be pertinent to look more closely at the status of women in Judaism and how their role was perceived.

Judaism and women

The roots of Judaism are planted firmly in the Bible and perhaps it is not coincidental that it is in the early chapters of Genesis that we have our first glimpse of Woman, Eve. We read the story of the creation of the whole world culminating in what is depicted as God's greatest achievement, Man (Old Testament, Genesis, Chapter 2). It seems almost as an afterthought, and only when the need became apparent, that God realised something was missing, that there was no one to be a suitable partner for Adam. And so Eve was created: but how? Was she, like Adam, formed from the dust of the ground, did God breathe life into her also so that she became a living soul? Was Woman thus the equal of Man?

The Jewish response to women contains for me two basic elements. The first is that women are seen as having secondary status to men, the second relates to woman as temptress, seducer, siren. Over the ages, concluding with the tenth or eleventh century, specific commentaries have been written on the Bible, searching for deeper meanings than the text itself allows (Pearl and Brookes, 1956, p. 62). I find it significant that one such *Midrash* states:'*On the day woman was created, Satan was created*'.

In the creation myth Eve does not exist in her own right, she is merely formed from one of Adam's ribs, one that presumably was of little consequence to him since we do not read of his suffering any loss. Here I feel is the first underlining of woman's inferiority, Eve quite obviously coming second to Adam.

I referred to two basic strands in Judaism with regard to women. The biblical message regarding the second follows swiftly on the first. When God questions whether Adam has disobeyed Him and eaten of the fruit of the Tree of Knowledge, what is Adam's reply? Does he freely own his evident guilt? I feel it took little courage to plead, '*The woman who Thou gavest to be with me gave me of the tree and I did eat*'. Here we have it. Only just created and Eve is already the temptress. Somehow, *eating* the fruit appears less important than being offered it. The implication is: it is all her fault, she made me disobey You, she is to blame.

I have dwelt at length on this well-known story because I believe its effects were far-reaching and profoundly damaging. In the space of two brief biblical chapters, the first woman bears the burden of inferiority and censure. It is little wonder that Judaism continued to cast her in this role.

As part of his daily morning prayers Freud's father would often have recited the benediction: '*Blessed art thou O Lord our God . . . who has not made me a woman*' (Singer's Prayer Book, 1890, p.6).

The rationale behind this particular blessing was that since women, because of their domestic duties, were exempted from commandments which had to be performed at a certain definite time (*Concise Jewish Encyclopaedia*, 1980, p. 373), men were merely thanking God for having the opportunity to fulfil His commandments. This could feel comfortable if women were to recite a similar blessing thanking God '. . . *who has not made me a man.*' However, no such benediction exists. It took another hundred years for a comparable prayer to appear in the liturgy and this reads: '*Blessed art thou O Lord our God . . . who has made me according to Thy Will.*' (*Singer's Prayer Book*, 1890, p. 6).

I can in no way read this as a '*parallel*' prayer (Greenberg, 1981, p.120). It appears rather to be a dutiful subservience than thankful gratitude.

On similar lines, the story of Moses recounting the ten commandments (Old Testament, Exodus, Chapter 20) is familiar to most Jews but what might be the cumulative effect of hearing so often: '*Thou shalt not covet thy neighbour's **house**, thou shalt not covet thy neighbour's **wife** . . . ' (my emphasis)*

Is it coincidence that reference is made to a wife *after* reference to a house, that a wife seems less important, has less status than a house? Or is it another subtle demonstration of the perceived inferiority of women?

Orthodox Jews of today have other ways of relegating women to second-class status and I will refer here only to those which have personal significance for myself. In the marriage service, for example, the bridegroom states:'*Behold thou art consecrated to me by this ring*' (*Singer's Prayer Book*, 1890, p. 298), but there is no opportunity for the bride to reply. In Jewish law, if the marriage fails, the man can divorce the woman but the woman has no similar right, *she* cannot divorce the man.

In communal prayer at the Synagogue, women are not allowed to sit with men. They are relegated to upstairs balconies or, worse, have to sit behind a '*mechitzah*', a special screen or partition, where they can see little of the proceedings.

At the age of thirteen, the Jewish boy reaches manhood within the Jewish community and a special ceremony is held in the Synagogue to mark this major event. For the girl of the same age, no such achievement in status is possible.

A quorum of ten is required for the commencement of many prayers. Only men are eligible, women lose identity and could as well be invisible.

Much of the foregoing leaves women negatively in the background. In one respect, however, they are — to my mind — negatively in the foreground. I refer to the institution of the '*Mikveh*', a type of ritual bath. The idea is of holiness and purification, and total immersion in water after each menstrual period is an obligation for Orthodox Jewish women. Because of menstruation women are seen as '*impure*' and the mikveh is regarded as a source of spiritual purification (*Concise Jewish Encyclopaedia*, 1980, p. 370). There are women who perceive the use of the mikveh as reinforcing '. . . *that deep inner contentment with a Jewish way of life.'* (Greenberg, 1981).It becomes a privilege rather than a burden. For myself, I see it as a denigration of what it is to be female. Whatever the intent and with whatever possible spiritual dimension, *'impure'* conjures a particular image.

Freud and Judaism

This, then, was the world inhabited by Freud's parents, one that was familiar, secure and doubtless unquestioned: after all, both Freud's grandfather and great-grandfather had been Rabbis and knowledge of Jewish tradition and rituals had certainly been handed down to Freud's father, Jakob (Jones, 1953: Penguin 1993 p. 47).

Sigmund Freud himself would have grown up in an Orthodox home, conversant with Jewish customs and festivals. Jones (ibid.) relates both that he had a knowledge of Hebrew and that Jakob gave him a bible on his thirty-fifth birthday with an inscription in Hebrew: presumably his knowledge of the language had developed sufficiently for him to understand his father's message. He liked telling Jewish jokes and anecdotes (Bettelheim, 1982: Penguin 1991, p.38), and his familiarity with the Jewish way of life is revealed even in his *Introductory Lectures on Psychoanalysis* where he refers to a dream related to him in which someone smoked a cigarette although it was a Saturday, the Sabbath, when smoking is forbidden. Not only the dreamer, but Freud too, knew enough about Judaism to be aware that *'a pious man . . . never could do anything sinful like that'* (Freud, 1917: Penguin, 1991 p. 221).

Perhaps Freud experienced the ambivalence felt by many Jews who try to shake off their Judaism and become assimilated in the prevailing culture. While he *'refused to observe the Jewish holidays that his father held sacred'* and *'took steps toward abandoning the Jewish culture of his home life as well as the traditions and customs of religion'* (Klein, 1981, p.45) he nevertheless *'had a clear consciousness of an inner identity as a Jew'* (ibid, p. 32).

The anti-Semitic atmosphere of Vienna in the 1890s prompted Freud to join the *B'nai B'rith (Sons of the Covenant)*, a Jewish brotherhood which stressed the values of unity and fellowship rather than the religion of Judaism. Klein (1981 p. 72) writes:'*Freud longed not just for friends but, by joining the B'nai B'rith, for Jewish friends: he had sought refuge specifically from anti-Semitic ostracism.'*

In his letters Freud himself wrote of the B'nai B'rith, *'At a time when no-one in Europe would listen to me and I had no pupils in Vienna, you offered me your sympathetic attention. You were my first audience'* (ibid, p. 74). These actions and words do not suggest a man who no longer feels himself to be a Jew, and who is no longer influenced by his Jewish heritage. As Klein (ibid) writes:

> In conjunction with the lectures on psychoanalytic topics, Freud's active interest in the expansion of the local B'nai B'rith indicates how highly he prized the Jewish society as a viable centre for intellectual discussion. Freud's association with the Brotherhood reflects an intense Jewish consciousness as well as a sympathetic attraction to other Jews (p. 87).

I would emphasise one further point connecting Freud's Judaism and his analytic ideas. We have seen that a central tenet of Freud's theory of personality development is the castration complex. It is perhaps impossible to say how much he may have been influenced in this by the fact that he himself would most certainly have been circumcised, as is the tradition for all Jewish males. Hollitscher (1947) believes that:

> Freud thought that the ancient custom of circumcision was a symbolic
> substitute for castration, and . . . expressed the son's subjection to
> the will of his father (p. 35).

This would indicate that at the very least, connections between circumcision and castration did exist in Freud's mind and influenced his thinking.

'When I was a child . . .'

My knowledge of and success with matters Jewish, when young, seemed to be not first a source of pleasure but of embarrassment to the adults around me. They did not deny my ability but I soon learned to hear the tinge of sadness in the praise and the sigh, voiced or otherwise, 'If only she were a boy!' I shouldered the imposed injurious constructs and did not realise that change was possible. I had been poisoned but was not even able to question whether an antidote existed.

But exist it *did*, and fell into my hands quite by chance when I was in the public library one day and was attracted to the title *On Personal Power* by a man called Carl Rogers. The author was unknown to me but the impact of the book will stay with me all my life. It seemed to give validation to all that I felt inside so that I *knew* I was right, and that 'they' had been wrong. If a book could be published which spoke of my innermost thoughts — although it was written by another — and appeared to be accepted by the world at large, maybe *I* could be accepted. The thinking may have been naïve but the ideas took root. I began to learn about the Person-Centred Approach.

Carl Rogers and the person-centred approach

For anyone accustomed to seeing themselves and to being seen as of secondary importance, the ideas of Carl Rogers provide a secure base for hope and change. It was in his book *On Personal Power* that I first learned of the **actualizing tendency:**

> There is in every organism, at whatever level, an underlying flow of
> movement toward constructive fulfilment of its inherent possibilities.
> There is a natural tendency toward complete development in man.
> The term that has most often been used for this is the actualizing
> tendency, and it is present in all living organisms. It is the foundation
> on which the person-centred approach is built (Rogers, 1977, p.7).

Rogers had become aware of this striving by everything to reach its full potential when he was quite young. As a boy, he had noticed how potatoes left in the dark cellar of his home had sprouted, and how the shoots had struggled palely and feebly, yet directly, towards the light (Rogers, 1980, p. 118). He had seen in a very practical way how the most ordinary of objects seeks to grow and realise its potential to become its full self.

Rogers' teenage years were spent on his father's farm: he kept chickens, reared lambs, pigs and calves. As a hobby, he bred moths, rearing the caterpillars, nurturing the cocoons (Rogers, 1961, p. 6). I would guess that from this, as well as from his later agricultural studies, he learned what kind of conditions must be provided in order to foster growth and development. Perhaps it is not, therefore, surprising that when it came to formulating theoretical concepts of human development, Rogers also thought in terms of core 'climatic' conditions. In 1957 he published *The Necessary and Sufficient Conditions of Therapeutic Personality Change*. One condition stated that the therapist has to experience *'unconditional positive regard'* for the client (Rogers, 1957: in Kirschenbaum and Henderson, 1989, p. 221).

For myself, unconditional positive regard is by far the most important of Rogers' conditions. One orientation sees me, the client, as inferior, the other wants me to be *'prized'*. (Rogers, 1986: in Kirschenbaum and Henderson, 1989, p. 136). For me a prize is certainly not to be taken for granted and belittled. It is a very special object, something worked for, achieved, valued and cherished, handled with care and pride. All these connotations combine to make me feel of special value.

In all his writings Rogers holds consistently to the views already expressed. In 1942 (Rogers, 1942: in Kirschenbaum and Henderson, 1989) he talked of how the therapist must accept non-judgementally both the 'positive' and the 'negative' sides of the client:

> The counsellor accepts and recognizes the positive feelings which are expressed in the same manner in which he has accepted and recognized the negative feelings. These positive feelings are not accepted with approbation or praise. Moralistic values do not enter into this type of therapy . . . It is this acceptance of both the mature and the immature impulses, of the aggressive and the social attitudes, of the guilt feelings and the positive expressions which gives the individual an opportunity for the first time in his life to understand himself as he is (pp. 72–73).

The important idea here, I feel, is that both negative and positive feelings are to be equally accepted, without the usual praise for *'the good'* and disapproval of *'the bad'*. This is truly what it means to be non-judgemental.

Nearly twenty years later, Rogers expands on his thoughts:

> I find that when I can accept another person, which means specifically accepting the feelings and attitudes and beliefs that he has as a real and vital part of him, then I am assisting him to become a person: and there seems to me great value in this . . . (Rogers, 1961, p. 21).
> By acceptance, I mean a warm regard for him as a person of unconditional self-worth — of value no matter what his condition, his behaviour, or his feelings . . . It means an acceptance of and

regard for his attitudes of the moment, no matter how negative or positive, no matter how much they may contradict other attitudes he has held in the past . . . (ibid, p.34).

When the therapist is experiencing a warm, positive and acceptant attitude toward what **is** in the client, this facilitates change . . . It means that he prizes the client in a total rather than a conditional way. By this I mean that he does not simply accept the client when he is behaving in certain ways, and disapproves of him when he behaves in other ways. It means an outgoing positive feeling without reservations, without evaluations (ibid, p.62).

Another two decades pass but Rogers' writings about acceptance do not deviate in any way from his former work. If anything, *A Way of Being* reinforces what we have already learned:

When I am not prized and appreciated, I not only *feel* very much diminished, but my behaviour is actually affected by my feelings. When I am prized, I blossom and expand . . . Thus, prizing or loving and being loved is experienced as very growth enhancing (Rogers, 1980, p. 23).

Attitudes to women

For Carl Rogers, the therapist's attitudes towards the client were of paramount importance. I have dwelt especially on non-judgemental positive regard because it is of particular significance for my own appreciation and understanding of the person-centred approach. However, I am aware that concentration on one particular aspect, even though it is especially relevant, may be seen as limiting the approach.

I have attempted to compare Freud's way of seeing a person with that of Rogers. Freud diminishes me as a woman; Rogers, in all his values, establishes me. I have searched through his writings to find any reference to women, that is, reference showing women in a *second-class* light. It should not surprise anyone, given the foregoing, that for Rogers women are not some separate sub-species. In fact, the only specific reference to women that I could find underlines his understanding and acknowledgement of women's position. In a special note at the beginning of *On Personal Power* he writes:

I am totally in sympathy with the view that women are subtly demeaned by the use of the masculine pronoun when speaking in general of a member of the human species (Rogers, 1977, p. ix).

These are not just words. He attempts to deal with the problem by deciding that in one chapter '. . . *all general references to members of our species*' will be put in feminine terms, in the next chapter, masculine.

Counsellor/client attitudes

Rogers knew that:

In any psychotherapy, the therapist is a highly important part of the human equation. What he does, the attitude he holds, his basic concept of his role, all influence therapy to a marked degree . . . the counsellor who is effective in client-centred therapy holds a coherent and developing set of attitudes deeply embedded in his personal organization, a system of attitudes which is implemented by techniques . . . and methods consistent with it (Rogers, 1951, p. 19).

Unlike Freud, Rogers believed that:

The therapist must lay aside his preoccupation with diagnosis and his diagnostic shrewdness, must discard his tendency to make professional evaluations, must cease his endeavours to formulate an accurate prognosis, must give up the temptation subtly to guide the individual, and must concentrate on one purpose only; that of providing deep understanding and acceptance of the attitudes consciously held at this moment by the client as he explores step by step into the dangerous areas which he has been denying to consciousness (ibid, p. 30).

In this passage Rogers talks of the therapist not allowing him- or herself to guide the individual, and we see the difference between directive and non-directive therapy:

The non-directive viewpoint places a high value on the right of every individual to be psychologically independent and to maintain his psychological integrity. The directive viewpoint places a high value upon social conformity and the right of the more able to direct the less able . . . Non-directive counselling is based on the assumption that the client has the right to select his own life goals, even though these may be at variance with the goals that the counsellor might choose for him (Rogers, 1942: in Kirschenbaum and Henderson, 1989, pp. 86–87).

The client *always* comes first. It is their world that is important and is to be understood; it is their own goals that they are to be helped to define more clearly; it is their view of themselves, and not that of the therapist, that is to be accepted.

The therapist perceives the client's self as the client has known it, and accepts it; he perceives the contradictory aspects which have been denied to awareness and accepts those too as being part of the client; and both of these acceptances have in them the same warmth and respect. Thus it is that the client, experiencing in another an acceptance of both these aspects of himself, can take toward himself the same attitude (Rogers, 1951, p. 41).

On the same theme Rogers talks of:

. . . the security which the client feels. This, very obviously, does not come from approval by the counsellor, but from something far deeper — a thoroughly consistent acceptance. It is this absolute assurance that there will be no evaluation, no interpretation, no probing, no **personal** reaction by the counsellor, that gradually permits the client to experience the relationship as one in which all defences can be dispensed with — a relationship in which the client feels 'I can be the real me, no pretences' (ibid, 208–9).

Conclusion

The theme of this chapter has been the effect on the writer of the work of both Sigmund Freud and Carl Rogers: where, for each of them, *is* a woman's place? The Freudian concept of myself as a person reduces my self-esteem and would leave me dependant on *'the expert'* who knows me better than I know myself. Rogers refers to Freud's mistrust of the basic nature of man, in that he saw the need for Superego control:

> To the end of his days, Freud still felt that if man's basic nature were released, nothing but destruction could be expected. The need for control of this beast within man was a matter of the greatest urgency (Rogers, 1977, p. 16).

Rogers sees not the beast in man but the organism striving as best it may to reach its full potential, whatever the circumstances. With Freud I am negated; with Rogers I am totally validated as a human being. I exist, therefore I am of worth. Knowing I can be accepted just as I am now creates a climate for my future growth and development. Rogers wrote:

> If I can help bring about a climate marked by genuineness, prizing, and understanding, then exciting things happen. Persons and groups in such a climate move away from rigidity and toward flexibility, away from static living toward process living, away from dependence toward autonomy, away from defensiveness toward self-acceptance, away from being predictable toward an unpredictable creativity. They exhibit living proof of an actualizing tendency (Rogers, 1980, pp. 43–44).

As a woman who is also a Jew, as a woman who is also a therapist, my place can only be within the person-centred approach. After all my journeyings, finally, I have come home.

References

Bettelheim, B. (1982) *Freud and Man's Soul*. London: Pelican, Penguin Books 1991.

The Bible (Old Testament). British and Foreign Bible Society, London 1953.

Brown, J.A.C. (1961) *Freud and the Post-Freudians*, London: Penguin Books.

Freud, S. (1917) *Introductory Lectures on Psychoanalysis*, translated by James Strachey. Ed: James Strachey and Angela Richards. London: Pelican 1973, Reprinted by Penguin Books 1991.

Freud, S. (1932) *New Introductory Lectures on Psychoanalysis*. translated by James

Strachey. Ed: James Strachey and Angela Richards. London: Pelican 1973, Reprinted by Penguin Books 1991.

Greenberg, B. (1981) *On Women and Judaism — A View From Tradition.* Philadelphia: The Jewish Publication Society of America.

Hollitscher, W. (1947) *Sigmund Freud: An Introduction.* London: Kegan Paul, Trench, Trubner & Co. Ltd.

Jones, E. (1953) *The Life and Work of Sigmund Freud.* Basic Books, 1961, reprinted by Penguin 1993.

Kirschenbaum H. and Henderson, V. (Eds.) (1989) *The Carl Rogers Reader.* Boston: Houghton Mifflin.

Klein, D.B. (1981) *Jewish Origins of the Psychoanalytic Movement.* University of Chicago: Wiley.

Pearl, Rev. Dr. C. and Brookes, Rev.R.S. (1956) *A Guide to Jewish Knowledge.* Jewish Chronicle Publications.

Rogers, C.R. (1942) *Counselling and Psychotherapy.* Boston: Houghton Mifflin.

Rogers, C.R. (1951) *Client-Centred Therapy.* London: Constable

Rogers, C.R. (1957) The Necessary and Sufficient Conditions of Therapeutic Personality Change. In *The Journal of Consulting Psychology. (21)*, 2. Also in *The Carl Rogers Reader.* Kirschenbaum H. and Henderson, V. (Eds.). Boston: Houghton Mifflin & Co. 1989.

Rogers, C.R. (1958) The Characteristics of a Helping Relationship. In *Personnel and Guidance Journal,(37),* American Association for Counseling and Development. Also in *The Carl Rogers Reader.* Kirschenbaum, H. and Henderson, V. (Eds.) Boston: Houghton Mifflin, 1989.

Rogers, C.R. (1961) *On Becoming a Person.* Boston: Houghton Mifflin.

Rogers, C.R. (1977) *On Personal Power: Inner Strength and its Revolutionary Impact.* London: Constable.

Rogers, C.R. (1980) *A Way of Being.* Boston: Houghton Mifflin

Rogers, C.R. (1986) A client-centered/person centered approach to therapy. In I. Kutash and A.Wolfe (Eds) *Psychotherapists' Casebook.* pp. 197–208. Jossey-Bass. Also in *The Carl Rogers Reader.* Kirschenbaum, H. and Henderson, V. (Eds.) Boston: Houghton Mifflin, 1989.

Roth, C. (1980) (Ed.) *The Concise Jewish Encyclopaedia.* A.P.Publishing Ltd.

Singer, Rev. S., (1890) Translator: *Authorised Daily Prayer Book of the United Hebrew Congregations of the British Empire.*

This photograph was taken at my workplace, so I feel I look presentable and it is the one I like best from by recent photos.

Exploring the 'We': Global, Relational and Personal Perspectives on Being in Relationships

19

Suzanne M. Spector

We're living in a time of such enormous social change that it's not surprising if we're experiencing confusion and difficulty in our own relationships as well as working with clients who are having relational difficulties. While recognizing that there are social and cultural differences and gender differences and individual personality differences, I'd like to start from the overriding perspective of global change which we're all experiencing. Every culture needs shared myths and stories — a cosmology that explains the universe and addresses such existential questions as how should we treat each other, deal with loss and death, etc. As we face the millennium and look backward, we're aware of the accelerated rate of change in modern life. The culture of ancient Egypt lasted for 1500 years, 45 generations of essentially one stable story. Now all cultures are going through such massive transformation, that their stories which give stability are breaking down.

Here's an example: a few weeks ago, I read an article in the New York Times about the impact of American TV on the culture of the South Pacific island nation of Fiji. In the traditional Fijian culture, anthropologists report, dinner guests are supposed to eat as much as possible. A robust, rounded body is the norm for both men and women. 'You've gained weight' is a traditional compliment and 'skinny legs' an insult. But all that may be changing since TV arrived by satellite in 1995. Unfortunately, what is shown on Fiji's one satellite channel are American soap operas. Dr Ann Becker of the Harvard Medical School Eating Disorders Center conducted a study of girls' body image and eating practices and found that young Fijian girls are developing eating disorders and dreaming of looking like American TV stars instead of like their mothers and aunts. The study began with interviews of 63 Fijian girls, average age 17 in 1995, one month after satellite signals began beaming 'Melrose Place', 'Beverly Hills 90210' and other American garbage to the island. Three years later, in 1998, a matched group of 65 girls were interviewed.

This paper was presented at the Centro Italiano Psychologica Centro, Rome, Italy, June, 1999.

15% of the students in the 1998 survey reported having induced vomiting, in comparison with 3% in 1995. And 29% scored highly on a test of eating disorder risk compared with 13% three years before. Girls who said they watched TV three nights a week or more were 50% more likely to describe themselves as 'too big or fat' and 30% were more likely to diet than girls who watched TV less frequently. Before 1995, there was little talk of dieting in Fiji, but by 1998, 69% of the girls said they had been on a diet at some time in their lives, suggesting more of them are dieting than even their American counterparts.

The anthropologists suggest these statistics reflect a more profound issue: 'The increase in eating disorders like bulimia may be a signal that the culture is changing so quickly that the Fijians are having trouble keeping up. Island teenagers are acutely aware that the traditional culture doesn't equip them to negotiate the kinds of conflicts presented by the 1990s global economy.' In other Pacific Island societies similar culture-shifts have been accompanied by an increase in psychological problems among adolescents. For example, researchers speculated that rapid social change played a role in the rash of adolescent suicides in Micronesia in the 1980s.

Rapid social change has not only hit the Pacific Islands. It's impacting all of us. As we face the millennium, at the personal and the relational and the global levels, we're all asking, 'What's happening? How do we cope? What should we believe in? How should we act?'

Person-centered futurist, Dr Maureen O'Hara, explains what's happening this way: We are in the midst of a transformation to a global, information-based society, with shifting boundaries, multiple realities and incredible complexity. The ancestral psyche that coped in more stable societies is no longer sufficient. We need a new, more fluid psyche to cope with this global reality. At the global level when the ancestral psyche and the new world clash, anxiety is created which can either wreak havoc or be transformed in positive ways.

When the anxiety is repressed, we see global neurosis characterized by more rules and controls to keep things as they are, fundamentalism; fortress tribalism; information protection; competition with those defined as outsiders in win/lose games; between them and us, with identity as a big issue — in short, what we're seeing in Yugoslavia today. If this anxiety were to be unleashed, we might experience chaos and violence, with no boundaries, no identity, no solidarity and a lose/lose game even greater than what is occuring in the hot spots of the world today.

On the other hand, when the anxiety is contained and transformed into higher levels of excitement and information, we will have a global psychic evolution with fluid boundaries, structures, and energies, characterized by creative pluralism, collaboration, diversity, and mutual recognition.

This view of what's happening at the cultural level is paralleled at the personal level. On the grand scale, when the mind-set of the past is confronted with the wealth of possibilities and options, the culture may become overwhelmed and take refuge in old patterns of fortress tribalism and division of the world into us and them. This is paralleled in our personal relationships when we experience disjunction and, not knowing what to do in a new situation, we retreat to old patterns which don't work. Our job as therapists and as human beings in relationships, is to transform these clashes and make them growth-enhancing. This emergent world requires a post-modern psychology, one that views identity as fluid and multiple, rather than fixed, that integrates the yin and the yang, that respects the non-rational, and is empathic. This psychology is not theory-centered anymore — it is person-centered and relationship-centered. In this post-modern psyche, anxiety is contained through relational connections.

Keeping in mind this cultural reality of change and its demands on us, may help us be compassionate with ourselves and each other. It is no wonder our relationships are problematic! They carry the burden of containing the anxiety caused by psychic and cultural changes. To transform this anxiety, we must stretch ourselves and try to become comfortable with ambiguity and differences. We must learn to tolerate in ourselves and others the reality that each of us is actually many different people inside one skin at any given moment. This multiple, fluid concept of identity is a long way from the traditional linear models of development toward a fixed adult self. Those of us who are women have always had the archetypal model of maiden, mother and crone. Instead of viewing these aspects of woman in sequential progression, we can live them simultaneously. I, for one, hope to go on for a long time still feeling the maiden and mother inside of me, while also acknowledging myself (or beginning to acknowledge myself) as a wise woman. I don't know of a similar mythic trilogy for men, but I certainly observe older men with younger women, still claiming the youth inside themselves. Unfortunately, we all know many men and women who seem old and set in their ways, with no zest for life, living out a one- dimensional view of how they think a person of a certain age should be.

Contributing to the multiplicity and confusion inside of ourselves, is a potent variable; the past that we carry with us. Even those of us who have consciously worked to grow and change ourselves and become more open and fluid, carry old voices inside of us, usually those of our parents and the culture we grew up in, telling us how we should be, and how we should act, and how our relationships should be. These old voices may be powerful and at war with the selves we are and want to be.

So, since relationships are so important to us — because they are, and because they help us to cope with the world, then what model for relationship do we want and need in the world of today? Here too, we carry inside models for relationship — the old cultural story that no longer fits — and we have no internalized models for the new demands of relationship today. The old ways do not work any more for three reasons: first, the world has changed, second, we're not the same people we were when we first engaged in our relationships, and third, to make matters more complex, neither are the people with whom we are in relationship — be they children or spouses or parents or whomever. So, we must ask, *'How do we create relationships that encompass the complexity and fluidity of self and other in a growth-enhancing way?'*

I suggest that we start with the concept of the 'we'. The relational entity is more than the sum of its parts. Picture the yin/yang symbol. The line that defines the yin and the yang doesn't belong to either of them. Since this is a difficult concept to describe in words, I'd like to suggest a clearer sense of what I mean by the 'we', by using imagery. Close your eyes for a minute. Take a deep breath in and out. And as you breathe in again, think of a relationship that is or was important to you, past or present. Think of a quality that describes the relationship. What color would you pick to describe it? What sound? If the relationship were an animal, what animal would it be? If it were a flower, which one? Open your eyes. Take a minute, to reflect on what you experienced.

Did that give you a sense of the 'we'? Were you able to think of 'we' instead of 'I' and 'him' or 'her'? When in relationship with another, the sum of the relationship is more than the constitutional parts, like water in which the hydrogen and the oxygen retain their particularity but merge into something new — as water. What we're talking about here is a relationship based on *mutuality* in which *both* parties are honored and *both* participate and grow. While honoring difference, there is still equality in this new model. In the past, mutuality has not been a typical characteristic of most of our relationships, particularly with primary partners. In order to create primary relationships based on mutuality, men and women need to see themselves, each other and their relationship in a different way.

Here's a concrete example: a few years ago I went to Hawaii with a man whom I didn't know very well. We'd met and spent time together at a conference in Greece, corresponded, spent a week together in California, before leaving for Hawaii. When we arrived we discovered that my insurance included rental cars and his did not, so we agreed that I would do the driving so he wouldn't have to pay an extra fee. A few minutes after I started driving, he started giving me directions, 'slow down', 'don't get so close to that car', etc. I pulled over to the side of the road, turned to him and said, 'I've been driving since I'm 18 years old and I've never had an accident. I feel totally capable of driving without your help. If you're not comfortable with that, I'll be happy to go back to the car rental place with you and you can buy your insurance so you can drive.' He stopped giving me commands. But, a few days later he made a nasty, critical remark, 'You walk too fast, you drive too fast, you eat too fast.' He really meant it as a critical judgement. Instead of getting hurt or angry and retaliating with a criticism, I said, 'We really do have a problem in our relationship — we each have very different paces, we need to figure out what to do about it.' I was really pleased with my response. All my years of studying relational psychology paid off in that moment! I saw it as a relational problem that we had a shared responsibility for fixing in the service of our relationship. I didn't get hurt and I didn't just accommodate and give up my own pace to please him which would have been my old pattern. For myself, I only want to be in relationships now with people who want to work at creating a mutually empathic and mutually authentic relationship. Traditionally, it has usually been the woman's job to facilitate the growth of others without reciprocity. That model of relationship is exploitive, not empowering.

The example I gave you of looking at the 'we' was in a couples relationship, albeit a brief one, but we also want to consider other relationships, so I'll give you an example from my relationship with one of my daughters. This spring, I took a trip to Bali with my youngest daughter, who had the time and money to pay her own way. I realized before we left that I was having concerns about her as a travelling companion, wondering if she was going to get up early in the morning and be active and zestful. And then I realized that although this was supposed to be about mutuality, I was still thinking about it in terms of her conforming to my pattern and my pace. I also realized that it was going to be challenging for me to give up my old pattern of paying for everything when I'm out with my children. So, I told my daughter about these two realizations — that I wanted mutuality, but I was aware of my old non-mutual patterns and the power that went with them. Just putting the issues on the table was enough. I gave up some power, she took more responsibility, and I opened up to receiving. It felt mutual to both of us and we had a great time together. We pooled our money and she took care of paying for taxis, tips, etc., from our pot, so there was no illusion of me paying for things. Creating mutuality in relationships does take a new consciousness, but it is well worth the effort, even when it involves giving up some power.

Over the last 20 years, there has been an expanding body of work in relational psychology. Among the 'mothers' of this field, Dr Jean Baker Miller and her colleagues at the Stone Center of Wellsley College have been studying women's lives to elucidate the characteristics of growth-enhancing interactions. Miller started with the hypothesis that the old masculine concept of development of the self through a sequence of separations leading to the achievement of a sense of separated individuation and autonomy doesn't apply to women, whose lives are more about connection than separation. Then she discovered that this autonomous view of the adult self doesn't really apply to most men either. Rather, she notes, 'men are usually supported by wives, mistresses, mothers, daughters, secretaries, nurses and other women (as well as other men who are lower than they are on the socioeconomic hierarchy)'. The Stone Center researchers now note, first — that all growth occurs in connection, and second — for connection to be effective, it must involve *mutuality* Instead of women fostering the development of others and not receiving nurturance of their own development, the Stone Center relational work envisions both parties participating in mutually empathic and mutually enhancing relationships. I said before that developing mutuality in relationships requires work, but is worth the effort. Here are the outcomes they have found of mutually growth-enhancing relationships:

- 1st outcome of this kind of relationship is the release of *zest* — a sense of being alive, the opposite of deadness;
- 2nd is increased *empowerment* — not as autonomy as something you do outside of relationship, but in relationship where all thrive and grow;
- 3rd is *increased clarity* about self and others;
- 4th is *increased self-worth;*
- 5th, good connection creates *momentum for more connection* — the ability to create diverse and differential relationships.

These are certainly qualities that both women and men want. We are all in recovery from the legacy of pain and hurt that we carry and we can heal by working on building mutuality.

While the desire for connection is a primary motive for all of us, there is often a gender difference in style. Steve Bergman, a psychiatrist at The Stone Center, introduced me to the concept of 'male dread'. Of course I knew it, I just hadn't given it a label. In heterosexual relationships, it's what happens to most men when a woman says, 'What are you feeling?' The more she pushes, the more he withdraws and the outcome is the opposite of the five outcomes I just enumerated. Although the desire for interpersonal connection is a human need, maybe the most basic human need, our culture has devalued nurturing and caring for others, calling it feminine and making it suspect in the ideal adult person. Our childrearing practices have not served boys in developing their empathic relational skills. They have been encouraged to be strong and independent at a cost to their emotional selves.

These asymetrical life-tracks of boys and girls have created relational difficulties resulting in a 60% divorce rate in the U.S.

John Gray, a psychologist with whom I studied relationships 15 years ago, has made millions of dollars with a book on the New York Times bestseller list for 220 weeks entitled, *Men Are From Mars, Women Are From Venus* about the differences between men and women and how we can build relationships which honor both. It's too simple to say women and men are from different planets. We all inhabit the same universe. While most women have spent a lifetime talking to their women friends, most men have nowhere to go with their feelings except to their women partners. Even when they do, they have not learned how to articulate what they are feeling so they end up feeling inadequate. We are all trying to learn the language of the 'we' instead of the language of the 'I'. Although defined as a feminine skill, not all women have an easy time of this. For most men, it's a new language and one rarely learns a second language with as much fluency as the first. When we run into difficulties in relationship, it's often the differences in our style and ability to communicate that creates the impasse and the frustration about the relationship. We need to develop a consciousness of the 'we' and work at developing a 'we' that encompasses differences — of gender, culture, and personality — and moves towards mutuality.

I started out talking about the cultural context and then moved into the relational. As we explore relational issues, our own or our clients', it's useful to ask is the problem- intra-personal, between who I am with these old tapes inside of me, and who I want to be; inter-personal — between me and someone else in the 'we' of our relationship; or is it cultural — created by social change, gender issues, etc.? Or is it some combination of all three? Our job as therapists and as human beings in relationships, is to transform these clashes and make them growth-enhancing.

A photograph of Suzanne Spector appears on page 161 at the end of Chapter 16.

The Language of Psychology as it Affects Women and Other Traditionally Disempowered Groups

20

Margaret S. Warner

The right to determine the meaning of one's own life situation is a crucial aspect of social power. In fact, some thinkers have suggested that control of the labeling of experience is a more fundamental form of social power than control over economic resources (Habermas, 1979). Typically within society, those in higher positions of authority define the reality of those in lesser positions. The rich define the reality of the poor, men define the reality of women, adults define the reality of children, English Americans define the reality of other American ethnic groups.

Psychological theories are, of course, intended to be personally empowering. However, in psychological speaking and writing, the structure of the language itself often implies that a single externally validated reality exists which is applicable to all groups. In this paper, I discuss ways in which a particular sort of 'compacted' language tends to suppress awareness that the author is presenting interpretations and values which may or may not be shared within various subcultural groups. Such language, by its very nature, tends to conceal and minimize power issues rather than opening them to multicultural dialogue.

The nature of compacted language

In compacted language, psychological phenomena are described as if they were objects with stable qualities rather than human experiences. (For an extended discussion of a number of similar issues related to the language of psychoanalysis, see Schafer (1976)). While I am pursuing a similar line of argument about language in general, I will not be using his full system for translating psychological terminology into action language.) For example, psychologists refer to 'weak ego strength', 'enmeshed relationships', 'inappropriate boundaries', 'stable introjects', and 'borderline personality'. In this paper, I focus on the concept of 'boundaries.' I am not intending to suggest that the concept of 'boundaries' is more problematic than other similar concepts, but only to use it as an example of difficulties which arise from this particular way of framing language.

Human experiences are differentiated from objects in the physical world by the fact that they occur for 'reasons' and the fact that such reasons are open to a range of sensible interpretations within various cultural and subcultural frameworks. A psychologist may say, for example, 'Susan's boundaries with her son are inappropriate.' In speaking this way, the psychologist is asserting that entities ('boundaries') exist which have particular qualities ('appropriate' or 'inappropriate'). And, this way of framing the sentence implies that such 'boundaries' exist as independent facts rather than resulting from interpretations being made by some person, or group of people, operating from a particular perspective.

Of course, when we speak in this way, we are not referring to a physical entity such as a wall. We are referring to some cluster of actions performed by Susan and her son for reasons.

Susan and her son may or may not agree with each other about what those actions were, why they were acting in those particular ways, or whether those actions were justified. An outsider may or may not feel that Susan and her son have a good understanding of the reasons for their behavior and may or may not agree as to whether the behavior is useful.

In discussing compacted language, I am not questioning whether the concepts themselves are valuable. Such concepts offer a shorthand way to identify clusters of experience and interaction, which may or may not be worth considering as a group. It is important to notice, however, that a great deal of subculturally relevant information is left out when psychologists use compacted language. In the above quote, for example, we do not yet know what sorts of actions are seen as showing 'poor boundaries'. Would it be seen as poor boundaries, for example, if Susan were hugging her son with great frequency? If she were questioning him about the details of his life and searching his room for evidence of gang activity? If she were feeling that he could stay home and take care of her heart condition rather than go away to college? Different subcultural groups may or may not agree about what is happening in these circumstances or whether these interactions can sensibly be seen as problematic. Sometimes psychologists clarify what sorts of actions are to be included within conceptual entities such as 'boundaries'. Often, however, such concepts are presented as if they were self-explanatory, or they are explained in other similarly compacted language. A psychologist, for example, might say that poor boundaries are part of 'enmeshed family systems' or that they are related to 'overgratifying child-rearing practices'. Yet, the sorts of actions which are seen as 'enmeshed' or 'overgratifying' are no more clear than those to be included within the concept of 'boundaries'.

Compacted language and the status of psychology as a science
For psychologists, part of the appeal of compacted language is due to the fact that it sounds so much like the language of the natural sciences. The natural sciences have gained explanatory power by isolating basic units, such as neutrons or chemical elements or bacteria, and empirically verifying stable relations among

them. (Of course, some of the more recent work in physics has raised the question of whether the physical world is as empirically observable and law-like as previously supposed.)

Psychology has had to struggle for recognition as a serious discipline, fighting allegations that psychological theories have more in common with art, literature or theology than with the 'hard' sciences. Descriptions of entities — such as 'boundaries' or 'ego states' — sound a great deal more scientific than descriptions of motivated action.

While there is some biologically based similarity among human beings, a great deal of the patterning of human life occurs in the context of cultural and subcultural meaning systems. Such meaning systems do induce a level of regularity into human affairs. However, these regularities do not occur in the same ways or for the same reasons as do those of the physical world. One of the most notable differences is that culturally and subculturally based patterns tend to shift over time and space. Many of the factors that make for a satisfying marriage will not be the same in the United States as in Japan. They will not be the same in the 1990s as in the 1950s. Even the cluster of relationships included as 'marriage' changes when we begin to consider same-sex unions, long-distance relationships, and blended families. As a result, while the natural sciences tend to resemble a house that is built with one brick placed on top of the other, the social sciences more closely resemble a complex fabric that is constantly woven, unraveled, and re-woven as cultural realities change.

The language of clinical psychology and the human science

Because of the differences between human and physical phenomena, the social sciences have a number of tasks not required of the natural sciences. One crucial task is the ongoing redefinition of conceptual categories as they relate to changing cultural and subcultural experience. This redefinition requires a multicultural perspective because such a large portion of human regularity is culturally and subculturally generated. While such phenomena can be studied by outsiders to some degree, crucial aspects can only be known or evaluated by persons who have been fully immersed in a particular cultural or subcultural niche. This ongoing re-examination of the units of dialogue is greatly hampered by the use of compacted language, since such language tends to be vague about what sorts of action or experience are included in any particular category.

As psychologists, we should be willing to demand that theoretical positions be explicated in understandable human action language. This is not to say that theories should be 'fully' explicated, since there is no real limit to the degree to which meaning could be unpacked and further explored. This explication is not the same as 'operationalizing' or putting propositions into 'behavioral' terms, since many culturally relevant terms (such as 'aggression' or 'privacy') cannot be reduced to a describable set of behaviors (Winch, 1958). We do need to aim for whatever level of explication is necessary for meaningful, multicultural dialogue about the issue at hand. Generally this requires language that is at least one level more descriptive and action-oriented than the kind of compacted language described above.

Take for example our question of what it means to have 'poor boundaries'. A discussion of the concept would sensibly include asking what sorts of actions might be included within the concept. A number of categories of action come to mind which the psychologist might include within the concept:

1. Entering or allowing others to frequently enter areas of body space that are private, without consent.
2. Expecting an amount of time in interaction that is greater than that expected within the culture.
3. Imposing one's own version of reality on others even when this version offers a poor understanding of the situation.

While these propositions are still quite general (and certainly incomplete), a number of issues become clearer when expressed in this way. It becomes possible to see the connection being proposed between a particular action and a cluster of actions. It is also easier to remain aware that such propositions contain culturally based expectations open to disagreement. For example, do we agree on what sort of bodily privacy can be sensibly expected by women? By children? By mental patients? A kind of touching or physical closeness that is seen as a violation of private space in one subcultural group may be quite ordinary in another. The kind of personal contact that is expected between clients and therapists in one school of psychotherapy may be entirely different than that expected in another.

Interpersonal power issues tend to be disguised when compacted language is used. When stated in compacted language, 'boundaries' sound like things that have a value-neutral existence independent of the person attributing them. When stated in action language, it becomes clear that 'boundaries' have to do with cultural expectations as to who should have what kinds of control over interpersonal space. To have 'poor boundaries' is to violate the power relations seen as appropriate by some authoritative group. The language itself makes it easy to make such an attribution without acknowledging that issues of interpersonal power are involved or offering any explanation as to why such power relations are seen as justified. A great deal of discussion is warranted as to what sorts of control can be reasonably expected in interpersonal situations — by women, by children, by clients, by welfare recipients, by patients in mental hospitals, to name just a few groups.

Compacted language and covert interpersonal power

When psychologists speak to clients in compacted language, they are exercising a covert form of social power. Consider, for example, statements such as 'Your behavior is inappropriate' and 'Your behavior shows a lack of boundaries'.

While sounding scientific and value-neutral, psychologists speaking in this way disguise the fact that they are presenting perspectives grounded in particular values and beliefs. By so doing, they implicitly claim the right to define the client's reality while obscuring the fact that such control is being exercised.

The use of compacted language can easily mimic the communication patterns of dysfunctional families. Certainly, many clients grow up with parents who claimed the right to name their experiences unilaterally while denying that they were doing so. This experience of disaffirmation tends to be very powerful for members of subcultural groups whose experiences are not acknowledged or prized by the society at large. Rather than recapitulating this pattern, I believe that psychologists should work to cultivate the opposite style of communication with clients — one in which separate sets of experiences can be openly expressed, fully heard, and respected.

For example, a compacted style of communication might take the following form: 'When you do X (such as staying in an abusive relationship or asking special favors of a therapist), you are showing Y entity or attribute' (such as poor boundaries, regressive behavior, weak ego strength). A more explicated version would offer an account of the speaker's interpretive rationale. It might take the form, for example, of: 'When you do X, I worry that Y might happen because of Z in my past experiences with you or because of my beliefs about this sort of experience.' Or, 'When you do X, I have Y feelings because of Z beliefs or circumstances in my life.'

A style of communication characterized by this sort of openness and respect would be similar in many ways to that which psychologists have advocated for communication among intimates (e.g., Guerney, 1977, and Rosenberg, 1999). Such communication would:

(a) be clear that the speaker is presenting a view rather than an objective truth of some sort,

(b) be clear about whose view is being represented,

(c) give as much information as possible about the reasons why this view is being held or advocated so that the person has grounds to make a personal judgement,

(d) show willingness to fully hear an alternate view and the reasons for that view,

(e) foster mutual agreement through communication and dialogue whenever possible, and

(f) be clear when power is being exercised and open about reasons why this is seen as justified by the speaker or the organization represented by the speaker.

Conclusion

Women have a long history of having others define their realities for them in various covert ways. We, then, have a particular interest in advocating that psychological language be clear and non-coercive. Before accepting psychological theories, we should require that they be explicated in descriptive, action-oriented language that opens the writers' positions to multicultural dialogue and critique.

We should expect psychologists to communicate with clients in ways that acknowledge that they have legitimate, separate personal and cultural realities.

Psychologists may advocate alternate views, but if they are communicating clearly, they need to present their views as opinions that they hold for some reasons rather than implying that they are describing value-neutral entities which have an independent existence in the world.

References
Austin, T. T. (1979) *Philosophical Papers*. Oxford: Oxford University Press.
Capra, F. (1975) *The Tao of Physics*. Berkeley: Shambhala.
Guerney, B. G. (1977) *Relationship Enhancement*. San Fransisco: Jossey Bass.
Habermas, J. (1979) *Communication and the Evolution of Society*. Boston: Beacon Press.
Harre, R. and Secord, P. F. (1972) *The Explanation of Social Behaviour*. Oxford: Blackwell.
Rosenberg, M. B. (1999) *Nonviolent Communication: A language of compassion*. Puddle Dancer Press.
Schafer, R. (1976) *A New Language for Psychoanalysis*. New Haven: Yale University Press.
Winch, P. (1958) *The Idea of a Social Science and Its Relation to Philosophy*. London: Routledge and Kegan Paul.

This photograph was 'editor's choice' from a selection Margaret sent. Irene chose it because it shows a different facet of Margaret from the one she has written about here — at her mother's side with whom, although not visible on the photograph, she had a close, loving relationship. Margaret's mother died recently.

THE POWER OF THE PREMISE: RECONSTRUCTING GENDER AND HUMAN DEVELOPMENT WITH ROGERS' THEORY

21

CAROL WOLTER-GUSTAFSON

This article explores fundamental epistemological and methodological themes in the visionary work of Carl Rogers and colleagues. These revolutionary themes contribute to the creation of an integrative, post-patriarchal, post-dualistic paradigm for psychology, human development, gender studies and other related fields. These themes hold significance far beyond the boundaries of personality and psychotherapy. Research on the perceptual and phenomenological approach to psychotherapy and personality development, generated by an amazing cohort of client-centered theory creators was prophetic and is still vibrant today. (Raskin, 1949; Seeman, 1949; Snygg and Combs, 1949; Rogers, 1951; Gendlin, 1962; Shlien, 1963; Shlien and Zimring, 1966; Patterson, 1966; Van der Veen, 1966). This extended reach into related fields is possible today because Rogers et al. redefined the domain in which they worked rather than revising the prevailing paradigms of psychoanalysis and behaviorism.

Rogers did not construct differential pathways for the development of females and males. Rogers consistently referred to others as persons and human beings. He did not posit some eternal essence or archetypes based on gender, or any fixed biological destiny or any reductionistic, partial and fixed explanation of our behavior. Instead, he insisted that the organism always operates as a whole and is always up to something. The fully-functioning person is increasingly in touch with her or his experiential flow (Rogers, 1959).

Jules Seeman, Director of Research at the Chicago Counseling Center during this fertile time of theory creation, reports that the revolutionary power of their work was not obvious to them at the time. Seeman (1999) explains, 'It was difficult for us to see far beyond the polar methods and orientations of the prevailing theories in which were we immersed'. With equal honesty Rogers writes:

> I didn't have the foggiest notion that it would spread beyond
> individual therapy. But there was one conviction I held that I now
> realize was very significant. It was this: I believed that if we could

discover even one significant truth about the relationships between
two people, it might turn out to be much more widely applicable
(Rogers, 1977, p.148).

The original premise of the person-centered approach stands in radical contrast to the dominant paradigms of this century which inherited, and perpetuated elements of Cartesian dualism. Instead, Rogers et al. offer a phenomenological description of the experiencing human and the relational universe into which we are born. The difference between working within this emerging wholistic theory and working within the more fragmentary theory which preceded it, is significant, and requires a major intellectual shift for each of us.

Redefining the domain of a field is necessary when assumptions no longer adequately explain phenomena and fresh data are brought to light. Thomas Kuhn calls this a paradigm shift. Early in this century, the model of Newtonian physics was critiqued and found to be lacking. It could no longer be revised into acceptability. A new, more encompassing model was required. Similarly in philosophy, European and Latin American existentialist and phenomenological philosophers uncovered the inadequacies and limitations inherent in the positivist philosophical model.

In the United States of America, Rogers was independently creating a method which mirrored the philosophical work in Europe. Since Rogers' model begins with valuing lived experience as the primary source of data, his way of constructing the new model grew organically. Thus, while European phenomenologists like Husserl were generative in creating the theoretical imperative for 'returning to the things themselves', that is, to lived-experience, Rogers and company were generative in *discovering the means* of *achieving* what was required in the new phenomenological model. Since their method began with valuing lived-experience, they were able to be faithfully descriptive of the process that enabled the principles to be lived out. Thus, my contention is that Rogers and colleagues found a way to *operationalize* phenomenological theory. They did so through the development of the core conditions of unconditional positive regard, empathy and congruence, deemed necessary and sufficient for effective psychotherapy, and they discovered an applicability far wider than first envisioned.

My thesis concerns the theoretical and methodological advantages of person-centered theory. Yet, these theories are not 'in the air', as Paulo Freire (1970) reminds us. Our psychological theories have evolved in the historical and cultural context of beliefs handed down from mythology, theology and philosophy in which differential and unequal realms of power and knowledge were taken for granted. Thus, gender often serves as a readily available and powerful illustration of habitual binary prejudices.

The work of Rogers and colleagues has direct, yet often unexplored, links to other post-positivist movements beyond phenomenology. For example, links can be found in selected feminist, postmodern and holistic and integrative scientific work. My intention is to suggest some areas of alignment. In order to do so, it is important to give some background to the enormous shift in perception caused by the phenomenological paradigm.

Understanding the phenomenological paradigm

Because philosophical world-views have infiltrated every field of knowledge, including the way the field is constructed, it is important to identify the defining characteristics of those views. According to scholars from physics to philosophy, dualism has been a fundamental feature of the western intellectual tradition. To understand why the person-centered approach is visionary, it is necessary to examine the wider philosophical context.

One characteristic pattern in intellectual history is that a prevailing paradigm is found to be flawed in some fundamental way. It is critiqued. A new more accurate schema is proposed. Conventional wisdom is found to be faulty in light of the new paradigm. Thus, the outmoded, but dominant paradigm is surpassed by some and defended by others. The certainty in philosophy that resonated with Newtonian physics has been corrected in light of physicist Werner Heisenberg's uncertainty principle (Bohm, 1980, p. 69) and the work in quantum theory. These major discoveries have, in turn, altered our certainty about epistemological and psychological theories. In philosophy, these themes have been taken up by the phenomenological philosophers. In psychology, Rogers and others, through rigorous application of the scientific method to clinical work, came to this appreciation for humility and non-judgmental 'letting be'.

There are two concepts central to phenomenological authors that describe my most profound experiencing in person-centered encounters. These encounters include moments in which deeply respectful listening, silence and speaking seem to bring me evermore present to myself and simultaneously to others. The fulfillment of the core conditions offers a language for describing how that environment is created. The concepts central to the phenomenological method are (1) 'bracketing the natural attitude' and (2) 'valuing lived-experience.' While these two concepts may be defined separately, they coexist experientially.

A central method for accurate understanding of the world, according to Husserl, is to put brackets around our natural attitude. This means putting into suspension our various beliefs, prejudices and commonly held knowledge. The idea is to see something as if for the first time, before the conventions of habitual perception automatically take over. Such automatic action causes us to foreclose upon our apprehension of reality. An illustration from photography may be useful. If a lens is not allowed to stay open to the light long enough, no accurate image will be made.

This need to put the 'natural attitude' aside matches Rogers' description of the ability in the fully functioning person, to be open to all data without the necessity to distort or dismiss. Another method in phenomenology is to look at the lived experience of phenomena, rather than a single feature of experience cut out and examined out of its context. This method matches the person-centered premise of starting with the person, accepted as being a process of experiencing that changes and flows. One can not 'bracket the natural attitude' with regard to a five-year-old boy and simultaneously believe that he is acting out of his Oedipal stage. In phenomenology, and in the person-centered approach, I have to relinquish my expert, pre-existing, knowledge about another, in favor of being freshly informed by the other.

The natural attitude and empathic understanding

Maurice Merleau-Ponty describes phenomenology as 'a philosophy which . . . does not expect to arrive at an understanding of man and the world from any starting point other than that of their "facticity" . . . which places in abeyance the assertions arising out of the natural attitude, the better to understand them'(Merleau-Ponty, 1962, p. 356). Spiegelberg (1969) defines the natural attitude as the common sense, everyday unreflective attitude of naive belief in the existence of the world.

To allow data to be perceived accurately, without distortion, one must be radically open to a phenomenon without first filtering it through the preconceived forms and prejudices that we habitually take as knowledge or truth. This goal was to be achieved through the method of a phenomenological reduction. Various theorists had their favorite ways of understanding that reduction and what it would yield. Spiegelberg describes Husserl's view of epistemological reduction as the new method of suspension of belief as the way to secure phenomena in their pure and indestructible form (Spiegelberg,1969, p.129).

With Merleau-Ponty, there are no claims being made to the truth as it exists in idealized essences as Husserl once attempted. Rogers consistently expressed his resistance to seeking an externally derived fixed essence. His cautious approach for what we claim to know as truth is evident in his paper, *Do We Need A Reality?* (Rogers, 1980). Instead of securing a pure indestructible form, Merleau-Ponty says that in Edietic Reduction, 'existence becomes a means rather than an end; a net to catch, like fish and palpitary algae, the living relations of experience. Immersed in this process, I am able to catch all the facts in their uniqueness prior to all linguistic formulations' (Spiegelberg, 1969, p. 535).

Rogers writes that empathy involved 'being sensitive, moment by moment, to the changing felt meanings which flow in this other person . . . sensing meanings of which he or she is scarcely aware' (Rogers, 1980, p.142). Rogers' brilliance in describing the nuances of empathic understanding come through in, 'Empathy: An Unappreciated Way of Being' in *A Way Of Being*. In a personal communication in April of this year Jules Seeman distilled what is essential in Rogers' life work, 'Carl would listen and go into the client's frame of reference **and stay there!**' Thus, Seeman (1999) affirms, 'His reflection of feeling was a prophetic phenomenological *tour de force*'.

My own direct experience of person-centered theory and practice leads me to concur with Merleau-Ponty that the great lesson of reduction is the impossibility of complete reduction (Spiegelberg, 1969, p. 534). When I reflect on instances of dialogue, where I have experienced high degrees of trust, care and precise, accurate empathic understanding, I have most certainly experienced myself as suspending the natural attitude and apprehending lived-experience. In an environment richly fulfilling Rogers' core conditions, I see the way to embody phenomenological methods for letting the things themselves emerge and am often surprised by what is unfolding.

In fact, Merleau-Ponty writes, '. . . since there is no thought that embraces all our thought . . . The philosopher . . . is a perpetual beginner'. (Merleau-Ponty, 1962, p. 365). It is Rogers' characteristic willingness to be the perpetual beginner that has led Adrian van Kaam, the Dutch existentialist psychologist to call Rogers' theory the 'most compatible' with the existentialist attitude and orientation (Van Kaam, 1981, p. 66).

Unconditional positive regard

To the degree I am able to offer unconditional positive regard, I find myself suspending my judgments. Thus, I meet the person in front of me fully, without the need to imprint my schemas on her/his experience. The rigors placed on the therapist or researcher to explore her biases and judgments are those of the philosopher attempting reduction, as expressed by Merleau-Ponty. He describes it as the device which permits us to discover the spontaneous surge of the life world (Spiegelberg, 1969, p. 534).

Physicist David Bohm, a protégé of Einstein, strikes the same theme writing about the underlying wholeness suggested in quantum physics. He maintains that fragmentation is continually being perpetuated by 'the almost universal habit of taking the content of our thought for a description of the world as it is' (Bohm, 1980, p. xi).

This way of bracketing the natural attitude, loosening our habitual ties with the world or alert letting-be; is also expressed in a saying by Lao-tse, which Rogers cites. 'It is as though he listened and such listening as his enfolds us in a silence in which at last we begin to hear what we are meant to be'(Rogers, 1980, p.41). All phenomena presenting themselves must be received and regarded unconditionally in Rogers' theory. Spiegelberg emphasizes this same feature of practice when he writes:

> What is all important in Phenomenology is that we consider all the data, real or unreal or doubtful, as having equal rights, and investigate them without fear or favor. This reduction will help us to do justice to all of them, especially to those which are under the handicap of initial suspicion as to their existential claim (Spieglberg, 1969. p. 692).

Since our culture has many taken-for-granted assumptions regarding what is natural for women, or women's essential nature or the natural inferiority of certain groups of humans, this feature of person-centered and phenomenological theory is significant. In light of these theories, any group or phenomena whose experience is under the handicap of initial suspicion as to their existential claims is the legitimate recipient of regard in its own voice. If the practitioner or researcher is to consider all data without fear or favor, then the ability to create and maintain a facilitative environment is critical. Rogers and colleagues have worked for decades on how to nurture the conditions of accurate empathic understanding, congruence, and unconditional positive regard so that what is true can emerge.

Ordering explicates and empowers

To the degree that women's knowledge has been pre-reflective, women have remained disempowered.

> The function of ordering pre-reflective material is meaning-making and in the process of explicating also empowers the meaning maker. When something previously left in the realm of pre-reflective consciousness is accurately symbolized in reflected consciousness, something new is brought into the world' (Wolter-Gustafson, 1984, p. 30).

According to Rogers, the need to know is concomitant, with the 'inward ordering of significant experiences' (Rogers, 1959, pp.186–7). The ordering process draws on what William Luijpen calls pre-reflective consciousness; 'an implicit, non-thematic, non-reflective (sic) consciousness, which consists of a simple presence to my existence' (William Luijpen, 1969, p.91).

Maurice Merleau-Ponty writes that in phenomenology, we 'concentrate upon reachieving a direct . . . contact with the world . . . and that contact has philosophical status'. We do not 'expect to arrive at an understanding of men and the world from any other starting point other than that of their "facticity"'(Merleau-Ponty, 1969, p.91). But it is the facticity of women's experience that is perpetually 'other' when it is differentiated from men's experience in human development theory at all.

Take for example this quote from the father of existentialism, Soren Kierkegaard, whom Rogers and others frequently quote with respect to being an authentic self. The quote admonishes us 'to be the self one truly is'. This 'self' is gender specific, that is a male self, as seen in the following quote. He writes,

> This being of woman (for the word existence is too rich in meaning, since woman does not persist in and through herself) is rightly described as charm, an expression which suggests plant life . . . and even the spiritual in her is present in a vegetative manner. She is wholly subject to nature, and hence only aesthetically free. In a deeper sense she first becomes free by her relation to man, and when man courts her properly, there can be no question of choice. Woman chooses, it is true, but if this choice is thought of as the result of a long deliberation, then this choice is unfeminine (Kiekegaard, 1959).

Clearly, the invisible bias in scholarship is only invisible when one does not look. The work of bracketing prejudgements is not easy in our most taken-for-granted categories of thought. The human condition comprises women's experience as well as men's experience and any attempt to gain knowledge, created from pre-reflective consciousness, needs a high degree of empathy to honor both the process and content. Rogers' theory does just this. In expressing the dynamic process and fluid quality of empathy Rogers writes:

> It means entering the private perceptual world of the other and becoming thoroughly at home in it. It involves being sensitive, moment by moment, to the changing felt meanings which flow in this other person, to the fear or rage or tenderness or confusion or whatever he or she is experiencing. It means temporarily living in the other's life moving about in it delicately without making judgments (Rogers, 1980, p.142).

It is this element of moving 'delicately without making judgments' that differentiates Rogers' stance from other human development theorists. It places him solidly with the phenomenologists, who seek to 'bracket the natural attitude' in order to come closest to knowledge of 'the things themselves'.

While phenomonlogists advocate bracketing, Rogers provides the means by which the suspension of judgment is achieved. When one begins with unconditional positive regard, one accepts 'the thing itself' as it is. When one begins with empathy, one's whole being is attuned to the apprehension of another in their process of meaning-making. When one begins with congruence, one is mindful of the separate thoughts, feelings and judgments that arise within, and acknowledge them to be one's own. These three core conditions make Rogers' theory a brilliant match for the process of hearing women's experiences directly. A highly empathic relationship provides a living context for receiving formerly pre-conceptual, pre-reflective knowledge.

Epistemology
Rogers holds that each person is the best source of knowledge on her/his own experience. This belief, taken into practice, requires respect for the person in such a way that it precludes the traditional expert-based, superior over inferior stance carried in the binary split in theory and in practice.

According to Rogers and colleagues, the person her/himself is in the best position to know their internal and intersubjective landscape. We are the experts on our own experience. This immediately sets a relation of radical respect in place. This deposes the expert other as the authority on my experience. His theory exposes the pervasive pattern of dominance and the imposition of another valuing system upon the organism as the origin of dysfunction, the distrust of the self and the erosion of our essential being in the world. Because of the essential importance of the relationship to the survival of the infant, and because of the need for positive regard by the infant, any infant will lose his/her voice when the powerful other makes their positive regard conditional.

Habitually, in the greater world culture, women's experience is represented as lacking equal authority in economic, political and social power, where women are not silenced altogether. Through his radical respect for women's and men's lived-experience, each person's own voice carries epistemological authority. Rogers' position is of significant import in the re-creation of psychology, and philosophy in post-patriarchal academia.

This movement to reclaim authority for the experiencing self has been evident in feminist and postmodern literature. The ferment in the field of knowledge construction is ongoing. There seems to be some agreement in the critique of the damage done by, (1) working within the confines of the Cartesian split and (2) the inattention to the unequal distribution of power. Both of these factors have a profound influence on what we know and how we know it. These movements have arisen independently and have sometimes been linked, but both are in constant flux themselves as they move beyond their critique and posit their own epistemological credos. For a thorough historical tour of the creation of philosophical and theological splitting of spirit/matter, mind/body, male/female etc., I recommend reading Genevieve Lloyd's important book, *The Man of Reason: 'Male' and 'Female' in Western Philosophy*.

As client-centered therapists, we are careful to hold an open attitude to the ever changing construction of self that emerges. We would not say to a client, 'But six months ago you said you hated your mother, you're really a mother-hater'. The same attitude is useful in understanding any theory under construction. It is unreasonable to fix a theory in time. For example, feminist theory is widely seen to have been through three waves in the modern era. The most current wave is represented by Linda Alcoff and Elizabeth Potter. In their introduction to *Feminist Epistemologies*, published in the Thinking Gender series for Routledge they write:

> Readers may be tempted to assume that because this anthology bears the word 'feminist' in its title, the issues treated in it are limited or reduced to gender issues. Not so. Growing awareness of the many ways in which political relationships (that is, disparate power relations) are implicated in theories of knowledge has led to the conclusion that gender hierarchies are not the only ones that influence the production of knowledge (Alcoff and Potter, 1993, p. 3).

They go on to note that cognitive authority is associated with a cluster of markings including race, class, sexuality, culture and age. Further, they state that development in feminist theory has demonstrated that 'gender as a category of analysis cannot be abstracted from a particular context while other factors are held stable. This reasoning replicated Heisenberg's uncertainty principle that it is impossible to measure both the position and momentum of a particle with precision. Rogers notes the limitation to the 'frozen moment' that such objective research yields as opposed to the 'understanding of the ongoing movement' research which he saw as preferable, albeit, more difficult to conduct (Rogers, 1961, p.127).

Alcoff and Potter report the strong consensus among feminists that the project of feminism be more inclusive. They write:

> The ontological status of women . . . has shifted for academic feminists in light of the influential arguments showing that women, per se, do not exist. There exist upper-caste Indian little girls; older,

heterosexual Latinas; and white, working-class lesbians (Alcoff and Potter, 1993, p.4).

The inherent good sense of Rogers' message is rediscovered. To understand humans, listen long and with care to the unique, irreducible, irreplaceable person. He writes:

> I believe that this way of knowing is limited only by the limits of our capacity for empathy, and to the degree of our ingenuity in getting at the internal frame of reference of the organism (Wann, 1964, p. 116).

The feminist effort to break free from the limitations of scholarship, which Linda Nicholson says, 'falsely universalized on the basis of limited perspectives', is characteristic of many forms of academic scholarship. She writes, 'It was the failure . . . to recognize the embeddedness of its own assumptions within a specific historical content. Like many other modern Western scholars, feminists were not used to acknowledging that the premises from which they were working possessed a specific location.' She goes on to describe the extension of this critique by the Postmodernists:

> Postmodernists have gone beyond earlier historicist claims about the inevitable 'situatedness' of human thought within culture to focus on the very criteria by which such claims to knowledge are legitimized. Postmodernists describe modern ideals of science, justice, and art, *as* merely modern ideals carrying with them specific political agendas and ultimately unable to legitimize themselves as universals (Nicholson, 1990, pp.4–5).

Maureen O'Hara , in writing about our 'turbulent Transmodern era' suggests that 'The post-modern discourse offers contemporary psychology the potential for reconciling and surpassing the limits of both objectivism and subjectivism' (O'Hara, 1997, pp.12–13).

The tendency to project our own meaning out beyond our own perception and call it Reality, is not compatible with the Rogers framework. In an interview with Richard Evans, Rogers says, 'The human organism immediately attaches a meaning to whatever is perceived. . . For me, perception is reality as far as the individual is concerned. I don't even know whether there is an objective reality. Probably there is, but none of us will really know that.' This causes Rogers to say again and again that he has no interest in labels, 'I'd rather [they] observe the phenomena themselves,' And again, we hear the need to suspend the natural attitude by an unconditional regard and empathic understanding of whatever presents itself as 'Reality' (Evans, 1975, pp. 6, 8).

Human development theory

Rogers (1959) grounded his theory of development in the relationship between infant and caregiver, the dynamics of power as evidenced by the absence or presence of definable nurturant qualities on the part of the caregiver. These conditions for optimal development include respect, empathy and authentic being with, rather than power over, and are not dictated by the caregiver's gender.

Human development is a daunting subject for study, yet that has never stopped parents and theory builders from constructing beliefs buttressed by all manner of evidence. Philosophy and theology as explanatory schemes held center court for centuries, but as the scientific revolution and the creation of psychology as a science gathered legitimacy, the competition for authority intensified. These competing theories seldom come labeled with their epistemological and ontological biases in large print. Rather they are often presented as evidence, based on research.

In turn, these research methods are not labeled with cautionary information on what they take under consideration and what they leave out. For example, most statistically based dissertations are not required to include a chapter on why this method is a reasonable and justifiable approach to studying the particular topic. Almost all dissertations based on qualitative research are so required. When studying human development we cannot responsibly evade basic epistemological questions. How do we know what we know? Who decides what constitutes knowledge?

Carl Rogers' theory offers a sophisticated and substantial approach to understanding human development primarily because of his insistence on starting with the schema as it is apprehended by the person, not with an explanatory schema devised externally to the person then applied to the person, for example, Freud's Electra theory or penis envy. Consistent with the phenomenological attitude, he sought to come into 'naive contact' with the life world of infant human beings suspending all labels.

The chapter by Peggy Natiello in this volume follows this phenomenological approach in exploring the meaning of gender. In *The Person-Centered Approach to Gender Splitting*, she faithfully describes her direct lived-experience of gender growing up in her particular family. She invites the reader into her experiential world, prior to the assignment of abstract theories. Natiello's writing brings us to 'the things themselves'.

How human development continues to split women and men

Women speaking our own voices, describing our own experience as authors and creators of knowledge, is typically missing in traditional academic scholarship. Instead, we study theories about women (their innate structures, what women really want) formulated primarily by male academics based on research methods deemed appropriate within the academic belief system of the day. These studies are predicated upon and generated from one of two academic meta-configurations. The first is psychoanalytic and its progression of stage-based developmental theories. The second is behaviorism in its original and evolutionary forms. Both came into prominence as theory-centered explanations of the way we are. Neither of these meta-configurations start with women's or mens' lived-experience as the legitimate source of knowledge.

Contributions from feminist theory

Current academic streams in gender development and study have drawn from the scholarship of Jean Baker Miller, Carol Gilligan, and many others. This work has exposed fundamental flaws in psychological and developmental theory. Their collective works critique the unexamined presumptions of patriarchal scholarship (Miller, 1976,1997). Their research documents the distortion and the suppression of girls' and women's voices (Gilligan 1982,1989,1992). They have brought the term women's voice to the attention, albeit reluctant and sometimes hostile attention, of mainstream academia.

What about boys and men? Carol Gilligan (1982, p.4) writes, 'My goal is to expand the understanding of human development by using the group left out in the construction of theory to call attention to what is missing in its account'. Seen in this light, the discrepant data on women's experience provide a basis upon which to generate new theory, potentially yielding a more encompassing view of the lives of both of the sexes.

Sadly, their vision of a more inclusive and accurate listening to our own voices is often erroneously misrepresented by those fueling dualistic discourse. Gilligan writes, 'the different voice I describe is characterized not by gender but theme'(Gilligan, 1982, p. 2). For those willing to listen non-defensively, their pioneering scholarship has a great deal to offer in enhancing our understanding of being human.

One prominent center of such research is based at Wellesley College. The Stone Center has generated dozens of research studies concluding that empathy and mutually enhancing relationships have been ignored in psychology. In a collection of their writings called, *Women's Growth in Connection*, Janet Surrey articulates a central tenet of their work, a mission statement. She writes, 'We have needed to create a different concept to suggest power with others, that is, power in connection or relational power' (Surrey, 1991, p.163). Their critique is valid in response to the dominant paradigm, but not if client-centered theory is considered. Their intent to create what has not yet been articulated does not take into account decades of existential, phenomenological and humanistic scholarship regarding the mutually empowering nature of empathy and alternate conceptualizations about shared power (Buber, 1965; May, 1972; Rogers, 1972, 1977; Friedman, 1983; Moustakas, 1981, 1995; Natiello, 1990, 1999).

As soon as claims of epistemological authority are redistributed from the expert to the person, the power balance begins to shift. Of course, acting from this shared power paradigm takes a great deal of awareness on several levels simultaneously. Peggy Natiello writes about the fundamental challenge to our habituated models of inequality that *collaborative power* requires. She also helps us envision what can be:

> We need to be constantly vigilant about our intentions — about the difference between what we say and really do. A subtle shift makes all the difference between a true experience of using our own power and a manipulation of others. The person-centered approach cannot

work if the sharing of power is not genuine (Natiello, 1990, p. 280).

Rogers' developmental theory of personality

The person-centered approach is in a unique and ideal position to illuminate the study of women and men and the creation of a knowing self. He sets the development of self in relation in such a way that the nature of empathic understanding is given paramount importance. The healthy development of the new human depends on a relationship with caretakers in which particular qualities in relation are essential. These qualities include understanding, respecting and trusting the phenomenological frame of reference of that new human.

The primary source of Rogers' theory from which I draw these forces or themes comes from 'A Theory of Therapy, Personality, and Interpersonal Relationships: As Developed in the Client-Centered Framework', from *Psychology: A Study of Science, Vol. III* edited by Sigmond Koch in 1959. It represents the most scientific articulation of Rogers' theory of personality. It is interesting to note that while Rogers used the prevailing language of personality development, his description of the process of development explicitly posits that the person always operates as an integrated whole, that is, acts as a unified organism. This theme has been carefully developed throughout the work of Jules Seeman and arrives in its fullness in his *Human Systems Model Of Psychotherapy* (Seeman, in press) Some forty years later after Rogers' first formulations about the organism operating as a whole, leading-edge neurochemistry researcher Dr Candace Pert (1997) provides evidence of the biochemical basis for awareness and consciousness. Her discovery of important neurotransmitters helps us to understand how this whole person integration is enacted within the human organism.

Carl Rogers' theory (1959) about the development of personality, and of the dynamics of behavior includes ten theoretical propositions, thirty-one theoretical process statements, and fourteen additional steps elaborating previous statements. Understanding this theory requires focused attention and rewards that attention with a richly textured appreciation of human development. For the purposes of this paper, I will lift out some central themes from this work.

Starting with his postulated characteristics of the human infant, Rogers writes that the organism:

1. perceives its own experience as reality
2. has an inherent tendency toward actualizing its organism
3. interacts with reality to satisfy the experienced needs for actualizing in the reality as perceived
4. behaves as an integrated whole
5. engages in an organismic valuing process, with reference to the actualizing tendency and behaves in accordance with the positive and negative valuing.
6. as awareness of the self emerges, develops a need for positive regard which is based on inferences by others
7. as the need for self-regard develops, the satisfactions or frustrations come to be seen as one's own self-regard complex, and

8. when self-experiences are sought out or avoided because they are seen as more or less worthy by significant others, acquires a condition of worth.

Thus, negotiating our maintenance of positive regard from significant and powerful others necessarily brings us up against our own organismic valuing experience.

Without receiving unconditional positive regard, we learn to keep positive regard by losing our voice in deference to others. We hone our ability to read the other for signals of worth. We cultivate and fine tune our capacity to abdicate our internal locus of evaluation and control. This attentiveness to the application of conditions of worth for obtaining positive regard is particularly burdensome for women, whose ultimate worth and essential nature has historically been pronounced as being-for-another (Simone de Beauvoir, 1952).

In short, the organism, that is each of us, perpetually seeks to actualize ourself and acts from our perceptual field as we perceive it. Each of us is born into relationship, thus, our valuing process is perpetually in contact with others whose perception of our immediate reality is often different than our own. It is only in the autonomy-based, separate-self, Western culture that we can entertain the following phrase, 'We are born alone'. Never. How ludicrous. The relationship may be one of abandonment or neglect, yet the relationship is a fact.

Our need for relationship continues. When we are tender infants and children, our inherent need for positive regard forces us to come up against this difference in relationships of unequal power. Where unequal power relations are perpetuated, whether by law or custom, the development of external locus of control is institutionalized. When the individual is unrecognized and disrespected in their biological family and the cultural family replicates the abuse, self is lost. Third World peoples and all in oppression share the same fight for life against devastating forces (Fanon, 1968; Rogers, 1977; Freire, 1970; Lorde, 1984; Bartke,1 990).

Our eighteen-month-old organismic valuing process is functioning with accuracy as quiet play perchance leading to sleep matches our internal state, but our caretakers lift us up and out into the car. We remain true to our knowledge of self from our internal frame of reference. We may fuss and vigorously protest and through our cries we hear the sweet sounding strains of, 'Oh, you've had enough sleep, you're going to love to go to the market. That's a good girl. You shouldn't fuss anymore'. This is the training ground for listening to someone who really knows what's good for you. The adult in charge has the power to move you physically, feed you and withhold food at their discretion and tell you who you really are. They teach you about the respect you deserve, the power you get to experience and the efficacy of your own power. The real world surely requires us to relinquish notions that our needs are the only needs in the universe, but the absence of regard for the sovereignty of the person is as surely characteristic of abusers and tyrants. Respect and acknowledgment of our needs does not mean their satisfaction.

This claim to epistemological certainty reflects the schematic world of those caretakers, their beliefs about every aspect of reality including gender, one of life's most fundamental cornerstones of identity. The moment we are born and proclaimed healthy, the first truth about us is our sex; 'It's a boy!' or, 'It's a girl!' In each case, that data carries proscriptive information meant to inform every aspect of our lives. To value something out of the set of expectations, the conditions of worth, for our gendered label is to court adversity. Our own organismic valuing system is vulnerable to being manipulated or crushed by others who know what a girl really is or what a boy really wants. No need to consult the person.

Conclusion

In this context it is easy to see why Rogers' theory is so radically liberating. In the person-centered system, the person herself and himself is recognized to be the expert on her/his experience. This never changes. We make sense of our world and act in ways we perceive as enhancing our actualizing selves. My intent here has been to pull out some substantial strands of Rogers' theory and place them in the context of the current dialogue on human development and its implications for gender study.

I see several potential areas for collaboration and theoretical alignment with colleagues committed to phenomenological, feminist, integrative, scientific, and postmodern ways of thinking. In collaboration we could move toward creating a more fully functioning paradigm of research, study and practice that truly honors all human beings.

As is often true with visionaries, their work is often far out ahead of the cultural milieu into which it is born. Rogers and his colleagues have suggested a framework for the proper study of human development in our stunningly original incarnations on this earth. Any theory that does not start with that uniqueness and complexity cannot begin to approach whatever knowledge we may construct. A theory for understanding humans that rests with our powerful empathic intent to understand offers us our best option.

References

Alcoff, L. and Potter, E. (1993) *Feminist Epistemologies*. New York: Routledge.

Bartke, S. L. (1990) *Femininity and Domination: Studies in the Phenomenology of Oppression*. New York: Routledge.

de Beavoir, S. (1952) *The Second Sex*. New York: Alfred Knopf.

Bohm, D. (1980) *Wholeness and the Implicate Order*. London: Routedege & Kegan Paul.

Buber, M. (1965) *Between Man and Man*. New York: Harper & Row.

Evans, R. (1975) *Carl Rogers, The Man and His Ideas*. New York: Dutton & Co.

Fanon, F. (1963) *Wretched of the Earth*. New York: Grove Press.

Freire, P. (1970) *Pedagogy of the Oppressed*. New York: Herder and Herder.

Friedman, M. (1983) *The Confirmation of Otherness*. New York: Dell Publishing.

Gendlin, E. (1962) *Experiencing and the Creation of Meaning*. New York: Free Press of Glen Cove.

Gilligan, C. (1982) *In a Different Voice*. Cambridge: Harvard University Press.

Gilligan, C. (1989) *Making Connections.* Troy, N.Y.: The Emma Willard School.

Gilligan, C. and Brown, L. (1992) *Meeting at the Crossroads: Women's Psychology and Girl's Development.* Cambridge Mass.: Harvard University Press.

Kierkegaard, S. (1959) *Either/Or, Vol. 1,* trans, Swenson & Swenson, Princeton: Princeton University Press.

Kuhn, T. (1962) *The Structure of Scientific Revolutions.* Chicago: University of Chicago Press.

Levant, R. F. and Shlien, J M., (1984) *Client-Centered Therapy and the Person-Centered Approach: New Directions in Theory, Research and Practice.* New York: Praeger.

Lloyd, G. (1984) *The Man of Reason: 'Male' & 'Female' in Western Philosophy.* Minneapolis: University of Minnesota Press.

Lorde, Audre, (1984) *Sister Outsider.* Trumansburg, New York: The Crossing Press.

Luijpen, W. (1969) *Existential Phenomenology* Pittsburgh: Duquesne University Press.

May, R. (1972) *Power and Innocence.* New York: Dell Publishing .

Merleau-Ponty, M. (1962) What is Phenomenology? In: Kochelmans, J, (Ed) *Phenomenology* New York:Doubleday & Company.

Miller, J. B. (1976) *Toward a New Psychology of Women.* Boston: Beacon Press.

Miller, J. B. (1997) *The Healing Connection.* Boston: Beacon Press.

Moustakas, C. (1981) *Rhythms, Rituals and Relationships.* Detroit: Harlo Press.

Moustakas, C. (1995) *Being-In, Being-For, Being-With.* Northvale, New Jersey: Jason Aronson Inc.

Natiello, P. (1990) The Person-Centered Approach, Collaborative Power, and Cultural Transformation. *The Person-Centered Review,* (5), 3.

Natiello, P. (1999) 'Sexism, Gender Dynamics and the Person-Centered Approach', In C. Lago and M. MacMillan (eds) *Experiences in Relatedness: Groupwork and the Person-Centered Approach.* Ross-on-Wye: PCCS Books.

Nicholson, L. (Ed) (1990) *Feminism/Postmodernism,* New York: Routeledge.

O'Hara, M. (1997) Emancipatory Therapeutic Practice in a Turbulent Transmodern Era: A Work of Retrieval. *Journal of Humanistic Psychology,* (37), 3.

Patterson, C.H. (1966) *Theories of Counseling and Psychotherapy,* New York: Harper & Row

Pert, C. (1997) *Molecules of Emotion,* New York: Scribner.

Raskin, N.J. (1949) *An Objective Study of the Locus of Evaluation Factor in Psychotherapy.* Ph.D. Thesis, University of Chicago.

Rogers, C. R. (1951) *Client-Centered Therapy.* Cambridge: The Riverside Press.

Rogers, C. R. (1959) A Theory of Therapy, Personality, and Interpersonal Relationships, as Developed in the Client-Centered Framework, in S. Koch (ed) *Psychology: A Study of Science. Vol. 3.* New York: McGraw Hill.

Rogers, C.R . (1968) 'Some Thoughts Regarding the Behavioral Sciences' In Rogers and Coulson (eds) *Man and the Science of Man,* Ohio: Charles Merrill Publishing Co.

Rogers, C. R. (1972) *Becoming Partners: Marriage and its Alternatives.* New York: Delacorte Press.

Rogers, C.R. (1977) *On Personal Power.* New York: Dell Publishing.

Rogers, C. R, (1980) *A Way of Being.* Boston: Houghton Mifflin.

Seeman, J. (1949) 'A Study of the Process of Non-Directive Therapy.' *Journal of Consulting Psychology.* 13, pp. 157–168.

Seeman, J. (In Press) 'Looking Back, Looking Ahead' in *Handbook of Research and Practice in Humanistic Psychotherapy.*

Seeman, J. (April 1, 1999) Personal Communication.

Shlien, J. and Zimring, F. (1966) Research Directives in Client-Centered Therapy. In J. Hart and T. Tomlinson, (Eds) *New Directions in Client-Centered Therapy.* Boston: Houghton Mifflin.

Shlien, J. (1963) Phenomenology of Personality. In J. Hart and T. Tomlinson, (Eds) *New Directions in Client-Centered Therapy.* Boston: Houghton Mifflin.

Snygg, D. and Combs, A. (1949) *Individual Behavior: a New Frame of Reference for Psychology,* New York: Harper and Bros.

Spiegelberg, H. (1969) *The Phenomenological Movement: An Historical Introduction.* The Hague:Martinus Nijoff.

Surrey, J. (1991) *Women's Growth in Connection.* New York: Guilford Press,

Van Kaam, A. (1981) in T. Weckowicz. *Humanistic Psychology: Concepts and Criticisms,* Joseph R. Royce (ed) New York: Plenum Press.

Wann, T. W. (1964) *Behaviorism and Phenomenology.* New York: University of Chicago Press.

Wolter Gustafson, C. (1984) Women's Lived-Experience of Wholeness. Unpublished Dissertation, 1984

Wolter-Gustafson, C. (1990) How Person-Centered Theory Informed my Qualitative Research on Women's Lived-Experience of Wholeness. *Person-Centered Review*, 5, (2), 221–232.

For a change I handed-off the camera — I'm always the one taking the picture, waiting to capture that special moment. It was hard to find a photo of me alone. This one is special. Betsy captured me smiling from an inner change manifested by an outer change.

CONTRIBUTORS

Jane Bingham: I'm 54 years old and live on the edge of the New Forest in Hampshire. I took early retirement from a career in teaching and lecturing in 1994 and have just completed my training on the Advanced Diploma in Person-Centred Counselling at Southampton City College. I am committed to the practice of Client-Centred Therapy and my experience, so far, has been as a counsellor in a General Practice surgery and, currently, in a secondary school.

Barbara Temaner Brodley received her doctorate in human development and clinical psychology from the University of Chicago. She started practicing client-centered counseling in 1955, employing the approach in many different settings over the years including seven years at the psychotherapy research center founded at the university by Carl Rogers. She has maintained a private practice with individuals, couples and families for 32 years as well as teaching client-centered therapy to graduate students and trainees at the Counseling Center and in programs in Europe. She is married and has two grown children.

Rose Cameron was born in Conan Bridge, near Inverness, and grew up in Edinburgh. While studying in Washington D.C. in the early eighties she began working with homeless people and was astonished to find that she felt not drained, but immensely energised after nightshifts that were often distressing and sometimes frightening, After training and working as a healer, and later as a person-centred counsellor, she began to understand more about the exchange of energy that happens in our encounters with each other. Her work as a therapist and as a trainer seeks to extend and clarify this understanding.

Irene Fairhurst is co-founder and past President of the British Association for the Person-Centred Approach. Born in 1941, she left her seaside home at the age of 17 to live in a community in East London where she became a volunteer youth worker and later a full-time youth and community worker. It was through her work with young people that she became aware of the person-centred approach as a way of being. Her further involvement in the work includes co-founding the Institute for Person-Centred Learning and working with Carl Rogers in Europe and the UK.

Jo Cohen Hamilton studied person-centered therapy at the University of Georgia from 1984–1987. She has applied person-centered principles to her work in various settings, including an inpatient hospital, a transitional day treatment program, a community mental health agency, a jail, college counseling centers, and graduate counseling training programs. She has been active in supporting several person-centred initiatives and is currently the editor of the Person-Centred Journal, published by the Association for the Development of the Person-Centred Approach.

Meg Hill: I came across the Person-Centred Approach at a crossroads in my life, having trained and worked in a psychodynamic mode for years. I had a sense of homecoming when I read *On Becoming a Person*. The approach gave me permission at last to integrate my personal philosophy of hopefulness, and the power of being fully present in the therapeutic process, with a way working.

Sarah Ingle: I live in Kent and have a grown up daughter and son. I write part-time and work part-time as a Systems Manager in a college of higher education. Person-centred therapy brought me to life some ten years ago, and I now accept myself with much greater awareness and love and have discovered I have something to say for myself.

Mary C. Kilborn: My first degree is in foreign languages. My interest in counselling started with my training as a marriage counsellor in the 1970s. Over the years I began to be drawn more to the Person-Centred Approach and my diploma training with PCT Britain was a profound experience for me. Since the early 1990s, I have been in private practice. I work as a supervisor and I am now involved with training — at the University of Strathclyde (Jordanhill) Glasgow and also in France. I have retain a keen interest in European languages and I love travelling.

Mhairi MacMillan: The Person-Centred Approach or, more poignantly, many 'persons' associated with it, has informed my life since 1976. In that year, I took part in my first FDI residential workshop and found a door opening on a new and brighter world. I have been 'leaving' the Approach at least since 1985, when I made my first farewell speech at the Cross-Cultural Communication workshop in Dublin. In fact, it's not a matter of 'leaving' but rather of finding myself on a path which both overlaps and parallels the PCA and of currently experiencing many endings and the taste of some new beginnings.

Peggy Natiello: In the past three years, my life has undergone change — a remarkable change that includes more personal freedom, professional experimenting, and a lot less income. I love it! What hasn't changed is my strong commitment to, and passion for, the person-centered way of living, loving and working in the world. I try to fine-tune my person-centered values in my roles as parent, partner, graduate faculty advisor, psychotherapist, writer and consultant.

Anne Newell: After working in both adult and child psychiatry, I worked as a student counsellor at the University of East Anglia from 1967–1982, and it was during this period that I became involved in the Person-Centred Approach. It transformed my life. In 1982, I went to work for Social Services, developing services in the community for the mentally ill and introducing PCA to those working with mentally ill people through interdisciplinary training courses in 'Listening and Responding'. From 1988–1996 I was Team Manager of mental health services and continued to develop and run services from a PC base. Since retiring in 1996, I have been particularly interested in the development of community and in living 'beyond the labels'.

Maureen O'Hara is acting President of Saybrook Graduate School and Research Center in San Francisco, is a Fellow of the American Psychological Association and the World Academy of Arts and Science, and is a Distinguished Clinical Member of the California Association of Marriage and Family Therapists. In 1974 she joined Carl Rogers in La Jolla, California and was one of the core team members who developed the Person-Centered Approach workshops from 1974–1982. She has published numerous book chapters and journal articles, and she is the producer of the video programs *Conversations with Carl Rogers* and *Myths that Maim*. Her work on feminism, social-constructivism and cultural contexts for self-development has made her both a vigorous critic and principal theory builder of the Person-Centered Approach. Maureen was born in Yorkshire and now resides with her husband Bob in California.

Lesley Rose was born in the 40s and brought up in Birmingham in an Orthodox Jewish environment. She studied classical languages at London University and is now a client-centred psychotherapist in private practice which includes working with a number of Employee Assistance Programme providers and a fertility clinic. She also composes and arranges music for the synagogue and plays the piano for a local synagogue choir which she finds therapeutic and relaxing. A mother of two adult children, she lives in Essex with her one-eyed cat and is currently developing her knowledge and skills as a gardener.

Ruth Sanford: My years in PCA began in 1972 with my retirement from public school education as teacher, counselor, administrator and researcher. They have been the richest years of my life. From 1975 I facilitated workshops with Carl Rogers in the US, Mexico, Europe, South Africa and the Soviet Union. I continue to write and facilitate workshops. I gratefully acknowledge the continued editorial and technical assistance of Ed Bodfish.

Suzanne Spector conducts workshops, groups and training programmes nationally and internationally in women's development, gender studies, and the Person-Centred Approach. She practises psychotherapy in Cardiff-by-the-Sea, California. From 1987–1997, she was Director of the Center for Studies of the Person, in La Jolla, C.A. and remains on the faculty of The La Jolla Programme. In her doctoral dissertation she studied single women in their fifties and researched in Russia, Uzbekistan, Japan, Great Britain, Italy and Turkey, as well as the United States. She was formerly a pioneer in humanistic education as the founder and Director of the Center for Open Education in Bergen County, New Jersey.

Sue Wilders: I live in Hackney, East London, with my 8 year old son. I am a woman in love, having found my soul-mate at last. I desire true freedom for society and of the soul. The Person-Centred Approach feels to me like a subversive step in that direction.

Maria Villas-Boas Bowen was born in Bahiz, Brazil in 1934 and died in Del Mar, CA., in 1994. She was a friend and colleage of Carl Rogers at the Western Behavioral Sciences Institute in La Jolla and was involved with him in the development of the Person-Centred Approach and later in the creation of the Center for Studies of The Person in La Jolla. As well as running a private psychotherapy practice in Solana Beach for 25 years, she was a world-renowned trainer in psychology and other health professions. She was a prolific writer and her work includes papers on sprituality, intuition, group therapy and training in the Person-Centred Approach. She lived in Del Mar, C.A. with her husband Jack, who died shortly after her, and son Andy.

Margaret S. Warner is a Training Staff member of the Chicago Counseling Center, an offshoot of Rogers' original counseling center at the University of Chicago. She is a professor at the Illinois School of Professional Psychology where her teaching focuses on empathic listening, work with difficult client process, and with client-centered groups. She is currently working with other facilitators to organize a client-centered group called 'Face to Face with Diversity', and she is busy organizing for the Chicago 2000 International Conference on Client-Centered and Experiential Psychotherapy. In the last three years she has been living collectively with two friends in a Victorian brownstone that they purchased together in the Hyde Park neighborhood of Chicago.

Carol Wolter-Gustafson: As professor, psychotherapist, parent, partner and person, the theme of cogruence is constant throughout my work. As a young girl, I was likely to say, 'It's not fair to say one thing and do another!' Now I say, 'My concern is integrating theory and practice.' This fundamental passion is at the heart of my work in the Person-Centered Approach in a variety of settings. It guides my work with my graduate school classes creating authentic democratic community with attention to issues of equity and human rights. It leads me to write about the inherent and revolutionary implications of the PCA in research methods, and the issues of gender, power and human development.

Also in this series

Person-Centred Approach
& Client-Centred Therapy
Essential Readers
Series editor Tony Merry

Person-Centred Therapy: *A Revolutionary Paradigm*

Jerold D. Bozarth 1998 ISBN 1 898059 22 5 234 x 156 pp 204 + vi £15.00

Jerold D. Bozarth is Professor Emeritus of the University of Georgia, where his tenure included Chair of the Department of Counseling and Human Development, Director of the Rehabilitation Counseling Program and Director of the Person-Centered Studies Project.

In this book Jerold Bozarth presents a collection of twenty revised papers and new writings on Person-Centred therapy representing over 40 years' work as an innovator and theoretician.

Divided into five sections,
- Theory and Philosophy
- Applications of Practice
- Implications
- The Basics of Practice
- Research

this important book reflects upon Carl Rogers' theoretical foundations, emphasises the revolutionary nature of these foundations and offers extended frames for understanding this radical approach to therapy. This book will be essential reading for all with an interest in Client-Centred Therapy and the Person-Centred Approach.

• • •

Experiences in Relatedness:
Groupwork and the Person-Centred Approach
edited by **Colin Lago** and **Mhairi MacMillan**
1999 ISBN 1 898059 23 3 234 x 156 pp 182+iv £15.00 pb.

Edited by two of the UK's principal practitioners of the Person-Centred Approach, this book is an international collection of specially commissioned papers. Contributors include Ruth Sandford (USA); Peggy Natiello (USA); John K. Wood (Brazil); Peter Figge (Germany); Irene Fairhurst, Tony Merry, John Barkham, Alan Coulson and Jane Hoffman (UK). This is the first substantial book within the person-centred tradition on group work since Carl Rogers' *Encounter Groups*. Topics include the history of the development of small and large group work within the PCA, theoretical principles of person-centred groupwork, working with issues of sexuality and sexism, the use of the group in training and groups, organisations, and the Person-Centred Approach.

The authors have uniquely caught the spirit of the person-centred approach in their various writing styles, which combine personal expression with disciplined reflections on experience. References to research studies sit comfortably alongside personal testimonies, philosophical reflections are underpinned by a wide range of references from other disciplines.